JOHN DEE
THE WORLD OF AN ELIZABETHAN MAGUS

John Dee
Ashmolean Museum, Oxford.

PETER FRENCH
JOHN DEE
THE WORLD OF AN ELIZABETHAN MAGUS

DORSET PRESS

New York

This edition published by Dorset Press
a division of Marboro Books Corporation,
by arrangement with Routledge
1989 Dorset Press

ISBN 0-88029-445-0

Printed in the United States of America
M 9 8 7 6 5 4 3 2 1

For Claire and Wellington French

Contents

	Acknowledgments	xi
	Abbreviations	xii
	Introduction	1
1	John Dee's Reputation	4
2	The Development of an English Magus	20
3	Elizabethan England's Greatest Library	40
4	John Dee and the Hermetic Philosophy	62
5	Magic, Science and Religion	89
6	John Dee and the Sidney Circle	126
7	John Dee and the Mechanicians: Applied Science in Elizabethan England	160
8	John Dee as an Antiquarian	188
	Conclusion	208
	Bibliography	210
	Index	251

Plates

Frontispiece: John Dee

between pages 116 and 117

1 Letter from Dee to Queen Elizabeth

2 Frontispiece to Meric Casaubon's *A True & Faithful Relation of What Passed for many Yeers Between Dr: John Dee . . . and Some Spirits*

3 Figures illustrating the Lullian art. Raymundus Lullus, *Opera*

4 The divine *mens* descending into the human body. Robert Fludd, *Utriusque cosmi . . . historia*

5 Correspondencies between the microcosm and the macrocosm. Robert Fludd, *Utriusque cosmi . . . historia*

6 Title page of John Dee's *Monas Hieroglyphica*

7 The structure of the universe. Robert Fludd, *Utriusque cosmi . . . historia*

8 The functioning of the senses, imagination and intellect in the mind. Robert Fludd, *Utriusque cosmi . . . historia*

9 The Copernican universe. Thomas Digges, *A Perfit Description of the Caelestiall Orbes*

10 Dee's minutes of the first angelic conference at which Edward Kelley acted as medium

11 Design for John Dee's great seal

Plates

12 Correlation of the *monochordum mundi* with the elemental, planetary and angelic spheres. Robert Fludd, *Utriusque cosmi . . . historia*

13 John Dee's 'Groundplat' for the English *Euclide*

14 John Dee's original title page for the *General and Rare Memorials*

15 A page from John Dee's 'Of Famous and Rich Discoveries'

16 Letter from John Dee to John Stow

Acknowledgments

My interest in John Dee began about five years ago. French R. Fogle first brought that extraordinary man to my attention: he urged me to take Dee as the subject of my doctoral thesis. As my adviser, he was unfailingly helpful and encouraging, even when things seemed most bleak. Albert Friedman read my thesis on Dee and offered trenchant criticisms. D. P. Walker and T. Julian Brown have prevented me from making some unpardonable errors in this book; they also have made valuable suggestions that I have incorporated into it. I warmly thank these scholars for giving unstintingly of their time and knowledge. But most of all, I wish to express my deep gratitude to Frances A. Yates. If she had not taken an abiding interest in my researches, this book might never have been completed. Working with her has been a privilege and a pleasure. Leanne Lachman, my friend and former colleague, kindly read a version of the typescript of this book and offered perceptive editorial advice.

Dartmouth College provided a fellowship that allowed me to undertake the initial research on this book in England. I have generously been given permission to reproduce material from the collections of the following institutions: the Ashmolean Museum, the Bodleian Library, the British Museum, and the University of London Library.

Abbreviations

AMBIX	Journal of the Society for the Study of Alchemy and Early Chemistry
HLB	Huntington Library Bulletin
HLQ	Huntington Library Quarterly
JHI	Journal of the History of Ideas
JWCI	Journal of the Warburg and Courtauld Institutes
MLQ	Modern Language Quarterly
N&Q	Notes and Queries
PMLA	Publications of the Modern Language Association
TLS	Times Literary Supplement

Introduction

John Dee, who lived from 1527 until 1608, was one of the most celebrated and remarkable men of the Elizabethan age. Philosopher, mathematician, technologist, antiquarian, teacher and friend of powerful people, Dee was at the centre of some of the major developments of the English Renaissance; in fact, he inspired several of these developments through his writings and his teaching. But Dee was also a magician deeply immersed in the most extreme forms of occultism: he was Elizabethan England's great magus. Perhaps the disproportionate emphasis on the sensational side of Dee's activities explains why neither a full biography, nor a comprehensive study of his work, has been published to date.[1] Few readers will know very much about John Dee, and fewer still will be fully aware of the vital role which he played in the evolution of English Renaissance thought.

A magus, Dee's world view was thoroughly of the Renaissance, though it was one which is unfamiliar today. He was one of a line of philosopher-magicians that stemmed from Ficino and Pico della Mirandola and included, among others, Trithemius, Abbot of Sponheim; Henry Cornelius Agrippa; Paracelsus; Giordano Bruno; Tommaso Campanella; and Dee's successor in England, Robert Fludd. Like Dee, these philosophers lived in a world that was half magical, half scientific. Astronomy and astrology were not yet completely separated, and Tycho Brahe still cast horoscopes, as did

[1] I. R. F. Calder's unpublished University of London dissertation, 'John Dee studied as an English Neo-Platonist' (1952), is probably the first attempt to study Dee's life and thought in detail. Although it has become dated because of subsequent research, it contains a large amount of valuable information and has been very useful in the preparation of this book.

Kepler. Chemistry was not fully differentiated from alchemy and was as much an occult cosmic philosophy as a form of science. Astrological amulets and talismans were regularly used by practitioners of medicine. Science was gradually emerging from magic, however, and the scientific attitude that we know today was developing in the midst of this group of philosopher-magicians. To John Dee everything was a form of science and everything was worth exploring. He was deeply interested in utilitarian mathematics, geography, navigation, mechanics and the fine arts – especially music, architecture, painting and drama. Even greater, though, was his interest in mathesis, or mathematical magic, and theurgy, the influence of supernatural powers. Dee considered these various studies inseparable, and it is this attitude that makes a study of his thought so useful in understanding the English Renaissance.

Although the attention being paid to Dee is increasing, much basic research remains to be done before a definitive assessment of this immensely complex figure can be made. A catalogue is needed of the printed books in his library – the greatest library in sixteenth-century England – and an attempt should be made to trace the books that belonged to Dee because he made copious marginal notes. An evaluation of the sources and the influence of his widely admired 'Mathematicall Preface' to the English *Euclide* of 1570 would certainly further the attempt to define Dee's place in the Renaissance.[1] Most importantly, though, a careful biography setting forth the details of his extraordinary life is yet to be written. The want of such basic aids to research hampers anyone presently studying Dee. For example, the absence of an adequate biography has made it necessary to include in this study facts about Dee's life which might otherwise have been omitted. In spite of the scholarship that must still be done, I believe that a fair evaluation can now be made of John Dee and his work, principally because of the recent studies prepared by scholars in Italy, England and America on the influence of Hermetic thought in the Renaissance.[2] Hermeticism, the gnostic philosophy based

[1] John Dee, 'Mathematicall Preface' to *The Elements of Geometrie of the most auncient Philosopher Euclide of Megara*, tr. Sir Henry Billingsley (London, 1570).
[2] Among them are: P. O. Kristeller, *Supplementum Ficinianum*, 2 vols (Florence, 1937); E. Garin *et al.*, *Testi umanistici su l'ermetismo* (Rome, 1955);

on the rediscovered texts of the legendary Hermes Trismegistus, is basic to Dee's thought. By building upon the contributions of modern scholars, I have tried to present the seemingly contradictory activities of John Dee as a coherent and understandable whole. This study does not attempt to close any doors; rather, I hope that I will open doors by outlining the role Dee played in Renaissance England.

P. O. Kristeller, *Studies in Renaissance Thought and Letters* (Rome, 1956); D. P. Walker, *Spiritual and Demonic Magic from Ficino to Campanella* (London, 1958); Frances A. Yates, *Giordano Bruno and the Hermetic Tradition* (London and Chicago, 1964); Frances A. Yates, 'The Hermetic Tradition in Renaissance Science', in *Art, Science, and History in the Renaissance*, ed. Charles S. Singleton (Baltimore, 1968), pp. 255-74.

John Dee's Reputation

John Aubrey's brief estimation of John Dee as 'one of the ornaments of his Age' may be as fair as any that has so far been made. Although Dee was a major intellectual force in Elizabethan England, many of his contemporaries – the 'Ignorant' Aubrey termed them – branded him a conjurer.[1] Posterity has not been any kinder than his less learned contemporaries. Because of Dee's interest in occult philosophy and because of the controversy surrounding his rather remarkable life, many erroneous notions developed about him and his activities, and these have frequently been embellished to the point of absurdity in successive centuries.

Opinions about Dee varied during his own lifetime. Most erudite scholars on the Continent and in England respected him as a learned man and a dependable source of information. So, also, did the English mechanicians, those self-educated and middle-class craftsmen and technologists who flourished in Elizabethan London. In court circles Dee enjoyed almost universal esteem, though, as Aubrey suggests, the commonalty feared him as a sorcerer and a necromancer, a black magician left over from the medieval past.

Dee's fame among Continental circles spread from Louvain where he went to study in 1548; noblemen from the court of Charles V (then at Brussels) and scholars from as far away as Bohemia and Denmark came there to discuss philosophy and science with him. They arrived, he informs us, with 'strange and no vulgar opinion' of his skills in the various arts and

[1] John Aubrey, *The Natural History and Antiquities of the County of Surrey* (London, 1718), I, 82.

4

sciences.[1] In 1550, shortly after his stay at Louvain, Dee was prevailed upon to give lectures on Euclid at the University of Paris. These caused a sensation.[2] He had previously begun a fruitful intercourse with Ortelius, Mercator and other important Dutch scholars that was to last through much of his lifetime and was to exert a profound influence upon English navigation.[3] Only twenty-three years old in 1550, Dee was already respected on the Continent, and his reputation continued to grow.[4] The admiration for him throughout Europe eventually resulted in the Russian emperor offering him a large annuity to take up residence at his court, saying that he had 'certain knowledge of his great learning and wisdome'.[5] This was only one of many offers from foreign kings and emperors (including Charles V) that Dee received, and refused, during his lifetime.

Among scholars and mechanicians in England, Dee was known primarily as a mathematician (which, in the opinion of Dee and his colleagues, was synonymous with philosopher). Mathematics was still suspected of being one of the black arts, however, and to ordinary people it was a frightfully dangerous study. It had barely begun to develop into the science we know today; even ordinary symbols such as the plus, minus and equal signs were only beginning to be used.

Nevertheless, many of Dee's contemporaries fully recognized his solid and important contributions to the mathematical sciences. One, Richard Forster, claims that it was only through

---

[1] John Dee, *The Compendious Rehearsal*, in *Autobiographical Tracts of Dr. John Dee, Warden of the College of Manchester*, ed. James Crossley, *Chetham Society Publications*, XXIV (Manchester, 1851), pp. 6–7. Dee wrote this as a supplication to Elizabeth, and it is unlikely that he would falsify any facts, since she knew so much about him.

[2] *Ibid.*, p. 8. See below, pp. 29–31, for more on his Parisian lectures and on the persons with whom he conferred in France.

[3] See below, Chapter 7, for Dee's role in the development of English navigation.

[4] As late as 1590, long after Dee became deeply immersed in practical cabala, or angel-magic, the great astronomer Tycho Brahe mentions in a letter to Sir Thomas Savile that he is sending a copy of his latest book, *De mundi aetherei recentioribus phaenomenis*, to the 'most noble and illustrious John Dee' for his opinion (*A Collection of Letters Illustrative of the Progress of Science in England*, ed. J. O. Halliwell (London, 1841), p. 33).

[5] *Calendar of State Papers, Domestic, 1581–1590*, pp. 354–5.

Dee's efforts that the mathematical disciplines were reborn in England, and Forster also says, 'Unless he re-interposes his Atlas-like shoulders, all [the mathematical disciplines] with the heavens of Copernicus and Rheinholdt will fall to ruin.'[1] Edward Worsop, a self-educated mechanician, writes that Dee is 'accounted of the learned mathematicians throughout Europe ye prince of Mathematicians of this age: as Cicero named Cratippus ye prince of Philosophers in his age'.[2] These are only two of the numerous testaments made to Dee's immense learning by his countrymen. Although he was most widely known to his fellow scholars as a mathematician and philosopher, he was also respected as a geographer, antiquarian, mechanician, teacher and theologian. Dee was indeed, as George Gascoigne claims, 'a great learned man'.[3]

John Dee's generally favourable reputation in English court circles seems to have developed early, continued through change of monarchs, and prevailed regardless of court factions. Except for the brief period from June to August of 1555 when he was in prison under Mary after a false accusation of 'lewde vayne practices of caculing and conjuring' to enchant the Queen, Dee was welcome at court.[4] After Elizabeth's coronation in 1558, he was often there, and Richard Harvey writes that it was '*M. Dee*, whome hir majestie vouchsafeth the name of hyr philosopher'.[5] The courtiers also respected Dee. He could count among his friends and patrons Sir Francis Walsingham, the Earl of Leicester, Sir Christopher Hatton, and even the sober Lord Burghley. The list could be enlarged.

Dee's services at court were many and varied. As court astrologer, he selected the most propitious day for Elizabeth's coronation. And once, when an image of the Queen with a pin stuck in its heart was found in Lincoln's Inn fields, a thoroughly alarmed Privy-Council asked Dee to counteract

[1] Richard Forster, *Ephemerides Meteorographicae* (London, 1575), sig. G4ᵛ.
[2] Edward Worsop, *A Discoverie of sundrie errours and faults daily committed by Landemeaters* (London, 1582), sig. G3ᵛ.
[3] George Gascoigne, 'The Epistle to the Reader', in *A Discourse of Discoverie for a new passage to Cataia*, by Humphrey Gilbert (London, 1576), sig. qq. iiii.
[4] *Acts of the Privy Council*, n.s., V, 143.
[5] Richard Harvey, *An Astrological Discourse* (London, 1583), p. 5.

any harm intended against her.[1] It was not only his magic which the court used: John Dee was frequently consulted before voyages of exploration, about affairs of state (particularly those requiring antiquarian knowledge), and on scientific matters. In 1583, he was given the task of reforming the Julian calendar for Britain. His work was widely admired, and the Queen went so far as to approve the draft of a proclamation implementing Dee's suggested reforms; but the bishops objected for religious reasons, and the intended improvements were not made.[2]

Queen Elizabeth was fond of her philosopher. Time and again she exhorted him to attend court more frequently. She sent him gifts of money and promised him livings. It was not until 1596, however, that he was finally granted the Wardenship of Christ's College, Manchester.[3] Elizabeth undoubtedly procrastinated in giving Dee a living because she astutely realized that finding him a suitable position would be a delicate task in view of his reputation as a conjurer; and when he did take over at Christ's College, he encountered only hostility because of his notoriety.[4]

The most valuable gift the Queen bestowed on Dee came early in his career when, he writes, she 'promised unto me great security against any of her kingdome, that would by reason of any my rare studies and philosophicall exercises, unduly seeke my overthrow'.[5] This promise was especially important to Dee because he seemed odd and out of place in Reformation England. His Hermetic philosophy with its theological, magical and scientific ramifications ran counter to the officially sponsored humanist education provided at the universities. As we shall see, he would not have appeared so

---

[1] Dee, *Rehearsal*, p. 21.

[2] *Calendar of State Papers, Domestic, 1581–1590*, p. 107. Two holograph copies of Dee's treatise are in the Bodleian: Ashmole MS. 1789, art. 3; and, Corpus Christi MS. 254, art. 4. British Museum, Additional MS. 32092, arts. 9–10, concern the rejection of reform by the bishops. They feared that such a reform so soon after the Pope had ordered one on the Continent would appear to be weakness on the part of English Protestants in their determination to resist the papacy.

[3] *Calendar of State Papers, Domestic, 1595–1597*, p. 45.

[4] On John Dee's residence in Manchester, see Charlotte Fell Smith, *John Dee: 1527–1608* (London, 1909), pp. 258 ff.

[5] Dee, *Rehearsal*, p. 21.

strange in one of the mystical academies that flourished in Italy and France under the aegis of powerful patrons, but the academic movement had not developed in England and John Dee was therefore a lonely and a suspect figure.

It was fortunate that Elizabeth was so farsighted in granting her philosopher protection because common opinion deemed him a sorcerer. Although he poured out his learning freely in private conferences and correspondence, John Dee published few books. Consequently, the exact nature of his various studies was not public knowledge, and the details of his life, for which his considerable fame had created demand, were often provided by people with ill-informed and, not infrequently, malicious opinions. It is easy to understand why the public thought of Dee as a sorcerer. After all, he was a magus and mathematician and admittedly performed 'marveilous Actes and Feates' that popular opinion ascribed to diabolic powers, even though they were 'Naturally, Mathematically, and Mechanically, wrought and contrived'.[1] The ordinary man could hardly be expected to admire what he did not fully understand.

Among those who understood Dee's role as a magus were some who praised his art openly, and thus contributed to his fame as a conjurer. The philosopher was forced to ask these *'Fonde Frendes'* to stop their indiscreet praise; he passionately cries: 'Such *Frendes* and *Fondlinges*, I shake of, and renounce you.'[2] Dee knew well that it was wise to keep his reputation for 'forbidden' knowledge within a limited circle. Fame as a man who produced wonderful machines and who attempted to delve into the secrets of nature would not bring him the esteem of his neighbours. This was clearly demonstrated when a mob plundered his house at Mortlake after he left for the Continent in 1583.

John Foxe, in his early editions of the *Actes and Monuments*, probably did more than anyone else to brand Dee as a conjurer; among other uncomplimentary references in the 1563 edition is the phrase, 'Doctor Dee the great Conjurer'.[3] The intensely Protestant *Actes and Monuments* enjoyed extraordinary

---

[1] Dee, 'Mathematicall Preface', sig. A.iv.

[2] *Ibid.*, sig. A.iiv.

[3] John Foxe, *Actes and Monuments* (London, 1563), p. 1444.

8

popularity throughout the Elizabethan period; in 1571, Convocation ordered a copy placed in every cathedral church, and the book was also to be found within most ordinary parish churches throughout the kingdom.[1] Finally, Dee could stand Foxe's 'damnable sklaunder' no longer and, in 1576, he issued a plea that Foxe be refrained from describing him as a 'Caller of Divels', and the *'Arche Conjurer'* of England.[2] Dee's plea was successful, for all references to him by name were suppressed in the 1576 edition of the *Actes and Monuments*.[3]

The silencing of Foxe did not, however, end the vicious rumours about Dee's activities. And during the final decades of his life there was, in fact, good reason for the continuing suspicions: John Dee had spent from 21 September 1583 until 2 December 1589 on the Continent where he had quite openly practised cabalist angel-magic with the disreputable Edward Kelley acting as his skryer, or medium.[4] Even though it was Queen Elizabeth herself who had commanded Dee's return to England (see Plate 1), he afterwards suffered neglect, poverty, and the increasingly strident abuse of his countrymen.[5] He continued to have a few influential friends – but a very few. 'I know no one', he bitterly complains to Sir Edward Dyer, 'of her Majesties most honourable privy Cownsaile, who, willingly & cumfortably will listen unto my Cumplaynt & declaration, how this Colledge of Manchester, is all most

---

[1] See the *Dictionary of National Biography* article on Foxe.

[2] John Dee, 'A necessary Advertisement', to *General and Rare Memorial pertayning to the Perfect Arte of Navigation* (London, 1577), sig. Δ.iiiᵛ. This work, written in 1576, was apparently passed around in manuscript form.

[3] An example of Foxe's deletion of Dee's name from the *Actes and Monuments* can be seen by comparing pp. 1412 ff. (1563) with pp. 1702 ff. (1576).

[4] Charlotte Fell Smith's book, *John Dee*, contains an extensive biographical account of the Dee–Kelley relationship. See also below, Chapter 5, for more information on this relationship and on Dee's cabalist theurgy.

[5] In 1594–5, Dee found it necessary to send the Archbishop of Canterbury a letter intended to convince the 'godly unpartiall Christian hearer' that he was a devout, zealous and faithful Christian philosopher and not a vile necromancer; it was eventually published with the title: *A Letter, Containing a Most Briefe Discourse Apologeticall, with a Plaine Demonstration, and Fervent Protestation, for the Lawfull, Sincere, Very Faithfull and Christian Course, of the Philosophicall Studies and Exercises, of a Certaine Studious Gentleman* (London, 1599). The letter failed to achieve its purpose.

9

become No Colledge, in any respect.'[1] Those who had encouraged Dee – who had made his life in Elizabethan England
bearable – were very old, or dead. Leicester had died in 1588,
Walsingham in 1590, and Burghley died in 1598 shortly after
this letter was written. The last years of Elizabeth's reign were
consumed by the growing power struggle among the courtiers,
and no one had time for the old 'conjurer'.

When in 1603 that witchcraft-conscious monarch, James I,
succeeded Elizabeth, life did not improve for John Dee. On
4 June 1604, he petitioned the King to have him tried for
sorcery, hoping that this would at last clear his name and
confound those 'Brainsicke, Rashe, Spitefull, and Disdainfull
Countrey men' who made his life so miserable. Dee dramatic-
ally and poignantly offers 'himself willingly, to the punishment of Death: (yea, wyther to be stoned to death: or to be
buried quicke: or to be burned unmercifully) If by any due,
true, and just meanes, the said name of *Conjurer*, or *Caller*, or
Invocator of Divels, or damned Spirites, can be proved.'[2] The
crux of this plea, it should be noted, is the emphasis upon the
evil nature of the demons with which John Dee was thought
to be dealing. He believed that he was only invoking angels, for
which the Bible offered excellent precedents, though his contemporaries, not unnaturally, were less certain. The philosophically esoteric cabalist theurgy (a natural part of the
cosmology of a Renaissance magus), in which Dee became
absorbed, dealt exclusively with the angelic hierarchies, but
the differentiation between this and the widely feared con-
juration of devils appeared tenuous to laymen. Dee received
no satisfaction from the King, but considering the seriousness
of conjuring charges during the reign of James, it is perhaps
merciful that he was ignored and that his death in December
of 1608 was at least peaceful.[3]

[1] British Museum, Harleian MS. 249, art. 13, fol. 104ᵛ. This letter is
dated 8 September 1597.

[2] John Dee, *To the King's most excellent Majestie* (London, 1604). Dee also
sent a petition to Parliament on 8 June 1604; written in doggerel verse, it
requested an 'Act generall against Sclaunder, and a speciall penal Order for
John Dee his case'.

[3] The last glimpses of Dee's life are sad indeed. In 1605 he was forced
by the hatred of the Fellows to relinquish his post as Warden of Manchester
and he returned to Mortlake a broken man. His third wife, Jane Fromond,

We have seen how contemporaries thought of Dee; it now remains to examine the strange twists and turns that his reputation has undergone since his death. Dee's fame for learning persisted well into the seventeenth century. His 'Mathematicall Preface' was twice reprinted and continued to be widely admired as a scientific text, and John Selden, the renowned jurist, referred to him as an authority of 'very great knowledge in sea-affairs'.[1]

But the generally accepted posthumous picture of John Dee – that of a fanatic deluded by devils and Edward Kelley – was established by Meric Casaubon.[2] His publication in 1659 of excerpts from the diaries that Dee kept of his supposed conversations with angels revived all the old doubts about Dee's conjuring.[3] In his long and dire preface, Casaubon warns that the text might be 'deemed and termed *A Work of Darkness*'. Despite that, he continues, 'I may and must professe in the first place, in Truth and Sincerity, that the end that I propose to my self (so far as I have contributed to the Publishing of the Work) is not to satisfie curiosity, but to do good, and promote Religion.'[4] Although Casaubon charitably admits that Dee dealt with the spirits in all simplicity and sincerity and concedes that he was

by whom he had all eight of his children, had died of the plague shortly before. Always uxurious, her death must have been extremely painful for him, especially when he was suffering from constant illness and increasing censorship. In his last years he was attended by his daughter Katherine, but he was penurious: 'Dr. Dee died at Mortlake in Surrey, very poor, enforced many times to sell some book or other to buy his dinner with as Dr. Napier of Linford in Buckinghamshire oft related, who knew him very well' (William Lilly, *The History of His Life and Times* (London, 1774), pp. 148–9).

[1] See below, pp. 165 ff. on the *Euclide*; John Selden's reference is in *Of the Dominion, or, Ownership of the Sea*, tr. Marchemont Nedham (London, 1652), p. 357.

[2] Casaubon (1599–1671) was the son of the distinguished philological scholar Isaac Casaubon, who had moved from Geneva to England, and who eventually proved that the Hermetic writings upon which the Renaissance magus based his philosophy were post-Christian. Meric was also a recognized classical scholar and a staunch supporter of the Anglican Church throughout the Civil Wars and Commonwealth, though Cromwell tried to enlist his services.

[3] John Dee, *A True & Faithful Relation of what passed for many Yeers Between Dr: John Dee . . . and Some Spirits*, ed. Meric Casaubon (London, 1659).

[4] Casaubon, 'Preface' to *A True & Faithful Relation*, p. 1.

one of the magicians who dealt with them by command rather than through a compact, the scandalized editor feels 'that these Spirits had as great hopes of Dr. *Dee*, as ever they had of *Bacchus* or *Mohamet*'.[1]

A contemporary witness provides some pertinent information about the reception of *A True & Faithful Relation*.[2] Apparently, most members of the government considered it subversive: they suspected that it had been produced by men loyal to the Church of England who wished to discredit those pretending 'so much to Inspiration'. Though it wished to do so, it was beyond the government's power to suppress the book because 'it was so quickly published & spread & so eagerly bought up as being a great & curious Novelty'. The council's suspicions were well founded. Casaubon was no friend of the government, which had deprived him in 1644 of his prebend at Canterbury and other livings, and he admits in a letter that the

> maine designe of this worke [the publishing of this *Relation*] was to set out to view of all men: the condition of those . . . under pretended colour of inspiration, & speciall guidance of the Spirit: & it is probable, that many were really deluded[3] (see Plate 2).

In 1677, John Webster attacked Casaubon for purposely slandering Dee. He suggests that Dee was the 'greatest and ablest Philosopher, Mathematician, and Chymist' of his age, and he wonders how 'Christian-like' it was for Casaubon to publish, almost fifty years after Dee's death, a folio of his 'conversing for many years with Spirits (wicked ones he meaneth)' and to 'register him among the damned'.[4] *A True & Faithful Relation*, Webster explains, was obviously not published as a simple relation of the facts that would allow readers to come to their own decisions; instead, Casaubon laboured to represent Dee as an 'infamous and wicked person'. Webster offers a

---

[1] Casaubon, 'Preface' to *A True & Faithful Relation*, pp. 29, 51.

[2] British Museum copy of *A True & Faithful Relation* (shelf mark 719. m. 12), contemporary notes preceding the printed text, fol. 5ᵛ.

[3] Bodleian, Ashmole MS. 1788, art. 3, fol. 65ᵛ.

[4] John Webster, *The Displaying of Supposed Witchcraft* (London, 1677), p. 7.

perfectly logical reason for his charge. Casaubon had previously tried to prove that all divine inspiration (a doctrine held by members of the government) was really nothing 'else but imposture or melancholy and depraved phantasie, arising from natural causes'. This position elicited charges of atheism and Webster contends that it was in order to clear himself of those charges that Casaubon decided to 'leap into the other end of the balance' and publish some notorious text that would make the existence of good and bad spirits manifest, thus disproving the imputation that he had contracted.[1]

By publishing the book, Casaubon felt that he could achieve two things. First, he could refute charges of atheism; and second, he could show that supposedly divine inspiration, at least in Dee's case, was diabolic deception.[2] It seems, then, that Dee's reputation became a pawn in the religious conflicts of the Commonwealth, and acquired a taint that has not yet been completely removed.[3] Any claim that Casaubon slandered Dee out of personal prejudice is not justifiable, but he was apparently quite willing to sacrifice Dee's credit in order to achieve his own objectives.

During the same period of time, a group was developing that believed John Dee had been the possessor of secret wisdom and angelically revealed knowledge. For instance, Elias Ashmole, the respected seventeenth-century scholar, was a great admirer of Dee, and he seems to have studied the 'Spiritual Diaries' seriously as a means of contacting angels. Ashmole's biographer, C. H. Josten, conjectures that he may even have attempted to repeat the angelic experiments.[4]

---

[1] *Ibid.*, p. 8.

[2] On the controversy surrounding the connections made between magic and the doctrine of divine illumination during the Commonwealth, see P. M. Rattansi, 'Paracelsus and the Puritan Revolution', *AMBIX*, XI (1963), 24–32.

[3] Samuel Butler adopted and further popularized Casaubon's view of Dee. Sidrophel, the conjurer in *Hudibras*, is strongly reminiscent of Dee, if not completely modelled on him, and is reported to have '. . . read Dee's prefaces before/The *Dev'l* and *Euclide* o'er and o'er./And all th'Intregues, 'twixt him and *Kelly*,/Lascus, and th'Emperor, [would] tell ye'. Butler's biting satire on the doctrine of divine inspiration is, of course, very much in line with Casaubon's views on the subject.

[4] Elias Ashmole, *His Autobiographical and Historical Notes, his Correspondence, and Other Contemporary Sources Relating to his Life and Work*, ed. C. H. Josten

Although Ashmole himself was not a Rosicrucian and does not seem to have associated Dee with that group, some members of the Rosicrucian fraternity adopted Dee as one of their own. Sometime after the publication in 1652 of Ashmole's *Theatrum Chemicum Britannicum*, which included a brief life of Dee, a Mr Townesend wrote to Ashmole that John Dee 'is acknowledged for one of yᵉ Brotherhood of yᵉ R. CR. by one of that Fraternity, who calleth himself Philip Zeiglerus, Francus'.[1] Dee can plausibly be identified with the Rosicrucian mode of thinking, which tended toward secrecy and science mixed with magic, but only if Rosicrucian is used as a generic term. It is improbable that he was a Rosicrucian in the sense of belonging to a secret fraternity with formal rules, secret ceremonies, and so forth. Actually, there is still question about whether or not the group even existed in Dee's lifetime.[2] Though it seems that he was not a Rosicrucian, claims that Dee was a member of that scorned society certainly did not encourage people to remember his solid achievements.

It is hardly surprising that John Dee's first biographer, Dr

(Oxford, 1966), II, 184–8; III, 1272–4; IV, 1335–6, 1756–8. Bodleian, Ashmole MS. 1790, art. 3, is Ashmole's epitome of Dee's magical system.

[1] Elias Ashmole, *Theatrum Chemicum Britannicum* (London, 1652), pp. 478–84; Bodleian, Ashmole MS. 1446, fol. 237ᵛ.

[2] For a valuable discussion of the relationship of Dee's thought to Rosicrucianism, see Frances A. Yates, 'The Hermetic Tradition in Renaissance Science', pp. 255–74; a summary of the problems surrounding the origins of the Rosicrucian brotherhood is found in her *Giordano Bruno*, pp. 407–16.

The only concrete evidence that could be used to support claims that Dee was a Rosicrucian is the existence of a manuscript (British Museum, Harleian MS. 6485) entitled 'Treatise of the Rosie Crucian Secrets', which is wrongly attributed to him. The treatise is not in Dee's handwriting, having been transcribed by Peter Smart in the eighteenth century. Also, Dee never listed this particular item among his works, published or in manuscript. It is quite possible that it was composed by Arthur Dee, John's eldest son, who lived at Norwich (where he was a close friend of Sir Thomas Browne's) and followed his father in the study of occult philosophy. His fame as a Hermetic philosopher, like his father's, reached the court of Russia, where he eventually went to serve. Little is known of this son of Dee's; one cannot help but wonder, however, how much he may have influenced Browne, who was one of seventeenth-century England's greatest literary exponents of the type of occult philosophy in which both the Dees were immersed.

Thomas Smith, accepted Meric Casaubon's jaundiced por-
trayal of Dee; it was rapidly becoming the orthodox interpretation in spite of scattered efforts to disprove it.[1] Few writers
subsequent to Casaubon have been as reserved as Bishop
Kennet, who found Dee 'very sober' though 'addicted to some
over curious and uncertain arts'.[2] Smith gathered facts from
Dee's papers, and he displays a certain appreciation of his
intellectual achievements; none the less, he emphasizes the
apparent madness of Dee's attempts at cabalist angel-magic:

> When he was unwilling to be wise according to the dictates
> of right reason and the sacred Scriptures, but had eagerly
> sought by an unlawful and impious ambition to surpass the
> powers of the human mind, by the just judgment of God
> being left to himself and given over to the arbitrament of
> his own will, he became the sport, the laughing-stock and
> the prey of daemons.[3]

The angelic conferences are deplored as an 'execrable insanity'.
Smith's *Life* was particularly important since it remained the
standard biography for 200 years; it also made Casaubon's
interpretation of Dee's attempts at practical cabala, or angel-
summoning, widely known on the Continent.[4] As a result,
during the eighteenth and nineteenth centuries, Dee came to
be regarded almost exclusively as a necromancer and a
deluded enthusiast of the most horrific kind.

[1] Thomas Smith, *Vita Joannis Dee*, in *Vitae quorundam eruditissimorum et illustrium virorum* (London, 1707).
Robert Hooke, for example, argued in an address to the Royal Society that Dee's 'Spiritual Diaries' – a 'Rapsody of incoherent and unintelligible Whimsies' – were a cryptographical history of 'Nature and Art' (*The Posthumous Works* (London, 1705), pp. 205–7). This seems unlikely; see below, pp. 110 ff.
[2] British Museum, Lansdowne MS. 983, art. 47, fol. 73. Bishop Kennet collected material for Anthony Wood.
[3] Thomas Smith, *The Life of John Dee*, tr. William A. Ayton (London, 1908), p. 44.
[4] In 1707, shortly after their publication, the *Vitae* were reviewed at some length in *Acta Eruditorum* (pp. 145–9). Due to the wide distribution of this review, scholars like Jean Nicéron accepted Smith's and Casaubon's conclusions and decided that Dee 'became the sport of demons' (*Mémoires pour servir à l'histoire des Hommes Illustres* (Paris, 1729), I, 351).

Nineteenth-century critics veered from the traditional thesis, however, when they subjected Dee's personal integrity to severe condemnation. It was righteously proclaimed that he had been 'dead to all moral distinctions, and all sense of honour and self-respect'.[1] More than one scholar seriously contended that Dee had desecrated graves in his attempts to have 'conversations and intercourse with the spiritual essences and departed beings': he had been more degenerate than the 'vampires and ghouls of Eastern story'.[2] What a far cry this nineteenth-century creation is from John Dee the respected philosopher and scientist!

Pejorative views of Dee began to be revised early in this century. Whatever its faults, and there are many, Charlotte Fell Smith's biography of him that appeared in 1909 must be given some credit for the re-adjustment of opinion in his favour. At the expense of properly treating Dee's significant and permanent contributions to knowledge, she continues to concentrate on the popular stories about him and Edward Kelley and on their attempts at angelic communication, but she has presented the facts of his life sensibly. Though she appears to be unaware of the philosophical ramifications of Renaissance angel-magic, her biography remains the standard published account of Dee's life.[3] She concludes her study by saying that people 'may see in him a vain, presumptuous and much deluded person, but at any rate they must acknowledge

[1] William Godwin, *Lives of the Necromancers* (London, 1834), p. 390.

[2] F. R. Raines, *The Rectors of Manchester, and the Wardens of the Collegiate Church of that Town, Chetham Society Publications*, VI (Manchester, 1885), p. 104.
Raines is probably basing his conclusions on William Harrison Ainsworth's popular romantic novel, *Guy Fawkes*, first published in 1841. The author pretended to historical accuracy and his fantastic, horror-drenched and lengthy descriptions of Dee's alleged necromantic experiments were accepted as fact by many people – even by some who should have had more sense.

[3] Richard Deacon's book, *John Dee: Scientist, Geographer, Astrologer and Secret Agent to Elizabeth I* (London, 1968), does regrettably little to establish Dee's true importance. In a rather sensational way, Deacon portrays Dee as 'a roving James Bond of Tudor times', the master of a massive espionage system. He considers the 'Spiritual Diaries' a form of enciphering used for spying purposes. Deacon's argument is tenuous at best, and his book is riddled with factual inaccuracies.

his sincere and good intentions; his personal piety; his uncommon purity of mind'.[1] Dee is essentially a romantic figure in this biography; and although the assessment of him is far less harsh than previous ones, Mrs Smith has not entirely escaped the influence of Meric Casaubon's presentation of 250 years before.

The first modern attempt to study Dee's considerable influence in his own social milieu was made by E. G. R. Taylor, who clearly demonstrated that his teaching and his work on scientific instruments were vitally important to the English navigators.[2] 'His unceasing efforts', she writes, 'for the instruction of mariners, and for the unveiling of the hidden corners of the earth, entitle John Dee to an honoured place in the History of Geography.'[3] Until he departed for the Continent in 1583, Dee was one of the prime forces behind Elizabethan expansion, and Miss Taylor's acknowledgment of his function was a major step in restoring his reputation as a noteworthy and serious scholar.

Shortly after Miss Taylor's study of John Dee as a geographer, F. R. Johnson similarly delineated his prominent role in the development of mathematics and astronomy in Renaissance England.[4] Johnson probably has done as much as any other scholar to re-establish Dee's position as a major figure in English Renaissance thought. After Robert Recorde's death in 1558, Dee became the most influential teacher and adviser on scientific subjects in England, and he retained this position for at least twenty-five years. Johnson suggests that Dee's contributions to the scientific thought of the period were far more valuable than Francis Bacon's because 'Dee actually was a scientist', and thus his 'Mathematicall Preface' was scientifically more valuable than Bacon's *De augmentis scientiarum*.[5]

[1] Fell Smith, *John Dee*, p. 305.
[2] E. G. R. Taylor, *Tudor Geography: 1485–1583* (London, 1930), pp. 76–139.
[3] *Ibid.*, p. 139; D. W. Waters (*The Art of Navigation in England in Elizabethan and Early Stuart Times* (London, 1958), *passim*) has followed Miss Taylor's lead in assigning Dee a major role in the saga of English geographical expansion. On Dee's interest in navigation, see below, pp. 177 ff.
[4] Francis R. Johnson, *Astronomical Thought in Renaissance England* (Baltimore, 1937), pp. 134–8, *et passim*.
[5] *Ibid.*, pp. 135, 152; Hiram Haydn (*The Counter-Renaissance* (New York, 1950), pp. 193–5) disagrees with certain of Johnson's claims about Dee.

More recently, Frances A. Yates has described John Dee as 'one of the most influential figures in the thought of Elizabethan England'.[1] She has been drawing attention to him for some years and has suggested that, among other achievements, he exerted considerable influence on the contemporary theatre through his introduction of Vitruvian architectural principles to England as early as 1570.[2] In her latest book, she explores this possibility and presents a new and exciting approach to the history of the English theatre in the Renaissance – an approach that uses Dee's Vitruvianism as a base.[3] This is a field that has, of course, been intensively studied for years, and yet a careful examination of Dee's work has shed new and valuable light on the subject. One is inclined to agree with Miss Yates's conclusion that

> to solve Dee would go far towards solving, not only the Elizabethan age itself but also its place in the History of thought. Its 'world picture' was not medieval but Renaissance; it was the world picture of John Dee, the half magical world which is moving, not backwards into the Middle Ages, but onwards towards the seventeenth century.[4]

Thus, certain scholars have shown that John Dee was a major intellectual force; they have tried to dispose of the misconceptions that have prevailed about him and that have sullied his name for centuries. Dee, nevertheless, is still frequently approached in the most condescending way. There are always those angels lurking in the background to make people uncomfortable. Because of them, as perceptive a scholar as Lynn Thorndike airily dismissed Dee's early advocacy of Copernicanism: 'he believed in so many things that were wrong that we could not give him personally any high credit, even if in this one instance he believed in something that happened to be

---

[1] Frances A. Yates, 'The Art of Ramon Lull: An Approach to it through Lull's Theory of Elements', *JWCI*, XVII (1954), 166.

[2] Frances A. Yates, *The Art of Memory* (London and Chicago, 1966), pp. 360–4; for other works in which Miss Yates considers Dee, see the bibliography attached to my study.

[3] Frances A. Yates, *Theatre of the World* (London, 1969).

[4] *Ibid.*, p. 19.

right.'[1] Clearly much work remains to be done before so complex a polymath as John Dee can be fully understood and properly appreciated.

John Dee presents a perfect example of the *de casibus* pattern that inspired so much Renaissance tragedy: in the eyes of many, he had pursued knowledge too adamantly and too far. But he was Prospero, not Faustus. In a broader sense, Dee and the diverse contemporary attitudes toward him epitomize the English Renaissance, which was both extremely esoteric and excessively practical. The courtiers protecting Dee obviously encouraged his magical studies and his Hermetic philosophy, in spite of popular disapproval of these studies. Within Dee's own circle, strange, magical areas of thought were being explored, but the circle also included those hard-headed Elizabethan mechanicians. Dee differed from the great Continental magi like Ficino, Pico, Agrippa and Bruno because, unlike them, he wrote tracts in English specifically for the benefit of the rising middle class of technologists and artisans. The 'Mathematicall Preface' to the English *Euclide* of 1570 is the prime example. Dee's apparently dual approach to knowledge was not so much a dichotomy, however, as a form of that heavily over-used term, 'the English compromise'. He always used magic to gain practical results. Although his experiments in theurgy are regarded as pointless endeavours today, he saw them as a means of pursuing science to a higher level, a way of gaining knowledge to help his fellow creatures. Dee's angel-magic produced no fruitful results, but his other magical studies led to important advances in the arts and sciences. In his thought, Dee bridged the worlds of the past and the future. The more overtly scientific attitudes of men like Francis Bacon and William Harvey evolved from the approach of Dee and his colleagues. The magical and the practical experiments did not represent two parallel movements; rather, they were inextricably tied together in a thought process that was evolutionary.

[1] Lynn Thorndike, *A History of Magic and Experimental Science* (New York), VI, 26.

The Development of an English Magus

At the time of John Dee's birth in London on 13 July 1527, England was on the verge of religious convulsions that were to be accompanied by sweeping alterations in the fabric of society.[1] Even if Henry VIII had not been provoked to drastic action by the divorce issue, he would have had a difficult time maintaining the status quo of the Roman Church in England. Henry simply unleashed forces that had been dormant in the social structure – the divorce alone created neither Protestantism nor anti-papal and anti-clerical feeling.

Many men, among them John Colet and Thomas More, had embraced the idea of reformation early in the century. It was Colet, in fact, who inspired Erasmus to apply humanist methods to Scripture. There is much validity in the thesis that, in combination with his great critical edition of the New Testament, Erasmus's ridicule of monks, of pilgrimages, and of the cult of saints – in a broader sense, of the medieval world – laid the groundwork for the Protestant Reformation. Later reformers gleaned from him the idea of applying the concept of anachronism to the entire history of the Roman Catholic Church. Erasmus wanted reform, of course, but without schism, intolerance or violence. Then Luther appeared and eventually, due to political pressure, Erasmus was forced to denounce him.[2] But it was too late.

[1] He was the son of Rowland Dee, a gentleman server to Henry VIII, and Johanna Wild. In the pedigree that Dee drew up for himself, his family was of the greatest antiquity and highest respectability and was traceable to Roderick the Great, the ancient Prince of all Wales (British Museum, Cotton Charter XIV, 1). Dee claimed a distant relationship with Queen Elizabeth herself. His family apparently joined the horde of Welshmen who entered England after the accession of Henry VII.

[2] On Erasmus, see Roland H. Bainton, *Erasmus of Christendom* (New York, 1969).

Henry VIII broke with Rome, and a narrow and extreme form of secular and religious humanism succeeded the liberal tradition of Erasmus, Colet and More in England. Triumphing during the reign of Edward VI, it was Erasmian in its critical attitude toward the past, but lacked the Erasmian spirit of tolerance and conciliation. Monasteries were suppressed; images were destroyed; books were burned. And all of this was supposed to be replaced by a new and enlightened humanism that would sever links with medievalism and popery.

Renaissance humanism had started with Petrarch in fourteenth-century Italy. His discovery of Cicero's letters to Atticus was the prelude to similar discoveries by other humanists of hitherto unknown Latin texts. Cicero became the great figure of classical culture, and his splendid Latin style came to represent the essence of the golden age of Roman civilization. As a result, rhetoric was central to all humanist studies, and it shaped the humanists' attitude towards man's intellectual and moral life. Though humanism embraces much more than the cultivation of oratory, the humanists did consciously limit their studies to grammar, rhetoric, poetry, history and moral philosophy. It was as teachers of these disciplines, as men who could hold a university chair of *humanitas* or *umanità*, that they were recognized by their contemporaries. They did not claim to be preparing a new encyclopedia of knowledge, and they had little, if any, interest in science and philosophy, especially that of their medieval predecessors.[1] From Petrarch onward, the humanists increasingly subordinated philosophy to rhetoric.[2]

[1] See Paul O. Kristeller, *Renaissance Thought* (New York, 1961), pp. 92 ff. Kristeller stresses that the term *humanista*, which seems to have developed out of university slang, was restricted in its contemporary application and by no means represented a new philosophical movement. In an excellent discussion of the term, Augusto Campana comes to essentially the same conclusions as Kristeller ('The Origin of the word "Humanist"', *JWCI*, IX (1946), 60–73). By narrowing the meaning of humanism value is added to it as a term. It has been used to represent so many movements that it has become, at best, ambiguous. Therefore, I use the word in the same sense as Kristeller and Campana have shown it was used during the Renaissance.

[2] On the relationship between rhetoric and philosophy among the humanists, see Jerrold E. Seigel, *Rhetoric and Philosophy in Renaissance Humanism* (Princeton, 1968).

With the advent of the Reformation in England the humanist tradition became ever more dryly rhetorical. The new humanism was by no means hospitable to John Dee, who was decidedly out of place in sixteenth-century England. He questioned the accepted values of his time. Moreover, his Hermetic Platonism, with its magic and mysticism, seemed subversive. Dee was in the tradition stemming from Ficino rather than in the one stemming from Petrarch. When rhetorical humanism had become highly developed in the fifteenth century, the next great discovery of the Renaissance occurred: the recovery of Greek texts with their philosophical and scientific revelations. In what might be termed the Hellenic movement, Ficino and followers like Pico della Mirandola believed they were restoring philosophy as part of a broad return to the classical world. Placing rather strict limits on the value of earlier rhetorical humanism, they emphasized philosophy, theology and science and perceived the universe in a new way with ancient wisdom as a guide. When dealing with Renaissance thought, therefore, it must be clearly recognized that humanism appealed to one type of mind, and Ficinian neo-Platonism appealed to another type.[1]

John Dee was well aware that the way to curry general favour in Renaissance England was to be proficient in ancient languages and humanistic studies, but he ignored this and sought to discover the deepest secrets of philosophy so as to understand the universe and its laws in order to help his fellow men. Just as scholastic theologians and humanists would have none of Ficino, Pico and Agrippa, so pedants at the English universities came to disapprove of Dee. Since he hardly seems to have been a product of sixteenth-century Cambridge, where and under what circumstances did Dee gain his immense knowledge of occult philosophy and science, which were subjects largely scorned by the new generation of humanists?

Dee was sent to Cambridge by his father in 1542, 'there to begin with logick, and so to proceede in the learning of good artes and sciences (for I had before, in London, and at Chelms-

---

[1] On the differences between the two traditions see Yates, *Giordano Bruno*, pp. 153–63. Of course traces of both attitudes sometimes appear in the same figure, but the two movements diverged increasingly during the sixteenth century.

ford been metely well furnished with understanding of the Latine tongue)'.[1] At St John's, in accordance with the curriculum of the time, his formal education would have centred on the trivium (grammar, logic, rhetoric) and, to a lesser extent, the quadrivium (arithmetic, geometry, astronomy, music), as well as the three philosophies (moral, natural, divine).[2]

Early in the sixteenth century, a new distribution of emphasis had been introduced within the trivium. Educational reformers like Erasmus, Vives and Elyot had instigated the abandonment of the one-sided emphasis on logic as a propaedeutic for metaphysics that had prevailed in the medieval curriculum. Grammar and rhetoric were stressed more, though Aristotelian dialectic remained highly significant in the universities. John Dee studied with a prominent group of scholars who promoted the new learning for which St John's became famous in the second quarter of the sixteenth century. Along with the new stress on grammar and Ciceronian rhetoric, Dee was exposed to Greek and Hebrew at the college.[3]

Though humanism dominated the educational apparatus of St John's, Dee's lifelong interest in fundamentally non-humanistic studies, which were closely involved with mathematicism, probably began at the college.[4] It was at this centre of English learning that Sir John Cheke, who did so much to foster humanistic studies, encouraged the students 'as well to the greeke toungue, as he did to the *mathematikes*'.[5] Nevertheless, deep study of mathematics would have taken place in

[1] Dee, *Rehearsal*, pp. 4–5.

[2] Mark H. Curtis, *Oxford and Cambridge in Transition, 1558–1642* (Oxford, 1959), pp. 86–7; Ernst Robert Curtius, *European Literature and the Latin Middle Ages*, tr. Willard R. Trask (New York, 1953), pp. 39–42. The structure of the Renaissance liberal-arts curriculum had been established in the later phase of the Roman Empire with such compendious collections of classical knowledge as Martianus Capella's *The Nuptials of Philology and Mercury* and Cassiodorus' *Arts and Disciplines of Liberal Letters*.

[3] Curtis, *Oxford and Cambridge*, pp. 94–6; Lawrence V. Ryan, *Roger Ascham* (Stanford, 1963), pp. 16–22.

[4] Chairs of mathematics were not established in either Oxford or Cambridge until the seventeenth century. In 1619, Sir Henry Savile founded chairs of geometry and astronomy at Oxford, but Cambridge had to wait until 1663 for a chair of mathematics.

[5] Richard Mulcaster, *Positions* (London, 1581), p. 244.

private circles rather than within the approved college curriculum. Despite his farsighted efforts to promote mathematics, Cheke was tolerated at Cambridge only as a teacher of Greek.[1]

Of his experience at St John's, Dee says:

> In the years 1543, 1544, 1545, I was so vehemently bent to studie, that for those yeares I did inviolably keepe this order; only to sleepe four houres every night; to allow to meate and drink (and some refreshing after) two houres every day; and of the other eighteen houres all (except the tyme of going to and being at divine service) was spent in my studies and learning.[2]

Trinity College was founded in December of 1546 by Henry VIII; and Dee's ability was recognized and rewarded with a fellowship as an under-reader of Greek at the new college. It was probably Cheke's recognition of Dee's mathematical knowledge, rather than his expertise in Greek, that procured this distinction.

John Dee was certainly immersed in the sciences, especially mechanics, by this time. At Trinity he produced Aristophanes' *Pax*, which included 'the performance of the *Scarabeus* his flying up to Jupiter's pallace, with a man and his basket of victualls on his back; whereat was great wondring, and many vaine reportes spread abroad of the meanes how that was effected'.[3] This was probably the first time such a spectacular machine had appeared on an English stage, and it was clearly an attempt to imitate classical theatrical effects.[4] The machine's construction undoubtedly required considerable mechanical skill, which Dee had not acquired as part of his curricular studies at Cambridge.

Apparently not satisfied with the scientific education available in England, Dee made the first of many trips abroad in May of 1547; his purpose was to 'speake and conferr with

---

[1] W. P. D. Wightman, *Science and the Renaissance* (London, 1962), I, 146.

[2] Dee, *Rehearsal*, p. 5. Thomas Smith, Dee's early biographer, writes that Dee gave himself to study 'quasi sacra voto obligatus' (*Vita*, p. 3).

[3] Dee, *Rehearsal*, pp. 5–6.

[4] Lily B. Campbell, *Scenes and Machines on the English Stage during the Renaissance* (Cambridge, 1923), p. 87.

some learned men, and chiefly mathematicians'. He went to
the Low Countries where he studied navigation with Gemma
Frisius, one of the most prominent geographers of the age, and
made the acquaintance of the renowned cartographer, Gerard
Mercator. After some months, Dee returned to Trinity College,
bringing with him some navigational instruments never before
seen in England.[1]

In 1548, after a brief residence, Dee received his Master of
Arts from Cambridge and by midsummer of that year he had
enrolled in Louvain. He writes that 'never after that was I any
more studient in Cambridge'; nor did he go to Oxford except
for an occasional brief visit.[2] He even refused a yearly stipend
to lecture on the mathematical sciences when it was offered by
several faculty members at Oxford in 1554.[3] Just why Dee
declined to associate himself with either of the English universities is not certain, but he did find both the atmosphere and the
type of humanist education available at Oxford and Cambridge uncongenial to his studies. As he later wrote to Cecil in
1563:

> Albeit that oʳ universities, both, in them have Men in
> sundrye knowledges right excellent, as, in Diuinitie, the
> hebrue, greke and Latin tung, &c. Yet foreasmuche as, the
> Wisdome Infinite of oʳ Creator, is braunched into Manifold
> mo sorts of wunderfull Sciences, greatly ayding Dyuine
> Sights to the better vew of his Powre and Goodnes, wherein
> oʳ cuntry hath no man (that I ever yet could hereof) hable
> to set furth his fote, or shew his hand; as in the Science *De
> Numeris formalibus*, the Science *De Ponderibus mysticis*, and the
> Science *De Mensuris Diuinis*; (by which three, the huge frame
> of this world is fashioned compact, rered, stablished and
> preserved) and in other Sciences, eyther wᵗʰ these Collaterall,
> or from them derived, or to themwords, greatly us fordering.[4]

[1] Taylor, *Tudor Geography*, pp. 78–83. They were an astronomer's staff
and ring of brass, both made by Frisius, and two Mercator globes. On Dee's
contribution to Elizabethan navigation, see below, pp. 177 ff.

[2] Dee, *Rehearsal*, p. 6; John Venn and J. A. Venn, *Alumni Cantabrigiensis*,
Pt. 1 (Cambridge, 1922), II, 28.

[3] Dee, *Rehearsal*, p. 10.

[4] As reprinted by John E. Bailey, 'Dee and Trithemius's "Steganography"', *N&Q*, 5th ser., XI (1879), 401–2, 422–3.

Cheke had left Cambridge, and the episode of the scarabeus indicates that the level of scientific sophistication there was far below what Dee was demanding. Mathematics and science were no more popular at Oxford than at Cambridge.[1]

Following the lead of Petrarch, Valla and Erasmus, many humanists at Oxford and Cambridge deprecated medieval philosophical culture, partly because of the 'barbarism' of medieval Latin style and partly because they wished to break with scholasticism, but largely because they did not fully appreciate the value of philosophy and science in everyday affairs. In effect, this movement dismissed Oxford's world-famous philosophical and scientific tradition; until this time and unlike many of the Continental universities, Oxford had continued to nourish an Augustinian Platonism that encouraged the study of Arabic discoveries in natural science and mathematics and avoided the ossification of the sciences at the level to which Aristotle had brought them. Since the new attitude of the Schoolmen was detrimental to the evolution of science, Robert Grosseteste, Bishop of Lincoln, and Roger Bacon, who resisted the enthronement of Aristotelianism at Oxford, went their own ways and fought the Schoolmen of Paris.[2] Their work was never entirely forgotten by their Oxford successors, and the devotion to mathematics, as well as to the scientific spirit implicit in the Platonism that continued to receive support, was passed on to a long line of scholars: it included the scientists (as distinguished as any in Europe) who flourished at Merton College during the fourteenth and fifteenth centuries; and later, Sir Thomas More and his circle.[3]

[1] E. G. R. Taylor, *The Mathematical Practitioners of Tudor and Stuart England* (Cambridge, 1967), p. 18; Christopher Hill, *Intellectual Origins of the English Revolution* (London, 1966), esp. pp. 301–14.

[2] Curtius, *European Literature*, pp. 56–7.

[3] Among the celebrated scientists of the Merton school were Thomas Bradwardine, whose *De proportionibus* was the first work to announce a general law of physics based on more than the most elementary calculations, and Richard Swineshead, whose *Calculationes* was widely admired in the Middle Ages and Renaissance. On Bradwardine, see the introduction to *Tractatus de proportionibus*, ed. H. Lamar Crosby, Jr. (Madison, Wisconsin, 1955), pp. 3–35. On Swineshead, see Thorndike, *History of Magic*, III, 370–85. R. T. Gunther (*Early Science in Oxford* (Oxford, 1923), II, 42 ff.) provides a basic history of the Merton school.

Others in the More circle who showed an interest in science were Thomas

The Development of an English Magus

During the Edwardian reforms, the old philosophical and scientific tradition came to be regarded as papistical and therefore evil, and the king's commissioners actually destroyed large numbers of books and manuscripts at the universities in 1550. Anthony Wood indignantly records that the libraries at Oxford were pillaged of works 'that treated of School divinity, or of Geometry, or Astronomy'; books that contained any type of 'Mathematical Diagrams' were particularly suspect and they were burned as 'Popish, or diabolical, or both'. In this atmosphere, it is hardly surprising that manuscripts by 'the learned Fellows' of medieval Merton were removed from the college library in cartloads and hauled to destruction.[1]

Thus, Oxford and Cambridge, rejecting their heritage, turned to Ciceronianism, which ultimately degenerated into grammatical pedantry. Later in the century, Philip Sidney deplored Ciceronianism as the 'chiefe abuse of Oxford' – wisdom had been rejected in favour of mere words.[2]

But the philosophical and scientific tradition that stemmed from the Oxford of Roger Bacon was not completely forgotten even though it had been forced underground because of its magical and papistical associations. John Dee embraced it. His library contained more manuscripts of Roger Bacon than of any other author, and the works of Robert Grosseteste, as well as those of other astronomers and mathematicians of medieval Oxford, were well represented.[3] Dee chose to dissociate himself from the developments taking place at the English universities when he found them inimical to his interests, and he eventually established a circle at Mortlake to carry on the medieval tradition scorned at Oxford and Cambridge and to absorb the new Platonism emanating from Florence.[4]

Linacre and Cuthbert Tunstall; both men produced scientific works (see Johnson, *Astronomical Thought*, pp. 76 ff.).

[1] Anthony Wood, *The History and Antiquities of the Colleges and Halls in the University of Oxford*, ed. John Gutch (Oxford, 1786), I, 89; II, 107.

[2] Philip Sidney, *Correspondence*, in *The Complete Works*, ed. Albert Feuillerat (Cambridge, 1926), III, 132. The letter is dated 18 October 1580.

[3] M. R. James, *Manuscripts formerly owned by Dr. John Dee with Preface and Identifications*, in *Supplement to the Bibliographical Society's Transactions* (London, 1921), pp. 10, *et passim*.

[4] Johnson, *Astronomical Thought*, pp. 137–9; Frances A. Yates, 'Giordano Bruno's Conflict with Oxford', *JWCI*, II (1938–9), 234–6.

By the time Dee left Cambridge for Louvain, he had already been studying alchemy, Hermeticism, and probably the cabala (magical subjects) for several years.[1] All of these subjects were closely connected with mathematics, which actually became a tainted discipline because of its association with them. Henry Cornelius Agrippa, the archmagician who was an important influence on Dee, states: 'The Doctrines of Mathematicks are so necessary to, and have such an affinity with Magick, that they that do profess it without them, are quite out of the way, and labour in vain, and shall in no wise obtain their desired effect.'[2]

Dee spent two years (until 15 July 1550) at Louvain where Agrippa had been a generation before. 'For recreation' he studied 'the method of the civile law', and he received a testimony from the university confirming his expertise in legal matters.[3] More to the point, Dee was also indulging his penchant for occult studies. During this period, he wrote a work in twenty-four books entitled 'Mercurius coelestis'; though it

---

[1] C. H. Josten, 'Introduction' to a translation of the *Monas Hieroglyphica* by John Dee, *AMBIX*, XII (1964), 86. The cabala was known in England early in the sixteenth century (see Joseph L. Blau, *The Christian Interpretation of the Cabala in the Renaissance* (New York, 1944), pp. 34–5, 79), for John Colet had read, though he claimed not to have understood, John Reuchlin's influential *De arte Cabalistica*. Also, Henry Cornelius Agrippa was in England for a time, staying at the home of Colet.

[2] The *De occulta philosophia* was first published in its complete form at Cologne in 1533. I have used the translation by J[ames] F[rench], *Three Books of Occult Philosophy* (London, 1651), II, 167.

[3] Dee, *Rehearsal*, p. 7. To account for the title of doctor that is so frequently associated with his name, it has sometimes been assumed that Dee earned a degree at Louvain; but according to Charlotte Fell Smith (*John Dee*, p. 9), this is not possible. Walter I. Trattner suggests that the title is purely honorary since Dee was '*doctus*, or learned' ('God and Expansion in Elizabethan England: John Dee, 1527–1583', *JHI*, XXV (1964), 17, n. 2). C. H. Josten, with some new evidence to support his assumption, suggests that Dee was in fact a doctor of medicine ('An Unknown Chapter in the Life of John Dee', *JWCI*, XXVIII (1965), 229, 236, n. 22). That Dee was knowledgeable about medicine is certain. It seems likely that, as Josten believes, he was awarded the degree of doctor of medicine by the University of Prague sometime around 1585/6. One problem remains: John Foxe refers to Dee as a doctor long before the date of the degree awarded by Prague University (*Actes and Monuments* (1563), p. 1414). Whether Dee was any kind of doctor at the early date that Foxe suggests remains unknown: but at least the title was more than complimentary.

was never published and is now lost, it was probably Hermetic in content, if the title is any indication.[1] Dee's role as tutor of influential people also began at Louvain when he instructed Sir William Pickering in logic, arithmetic, rhetoric, and various geographically oriented subjects.[2]

Dee interrupted his stay at Louvain by making several short trips during this formative period. On 30 April 1550, he went to Antwerp, where he probably first encountered Abraham Ortelius, who was then selling maps in the city. Dee returned from Antwerp, left for Charles V's court at Brussels on 25 May, went back to Louvain and remained only long enough to prepare for a journey to Paris.[3]

When he arrived in Paris on 20 July, he found that his fame had preceded him. He was prevailed upon to 'read freely and publiquely Euclide's Elements Geometricall, *Mathematicè*, *Physicè*, *et Pythagoricè*; a thing never done publiquely in any University in Christendome'.[4] He claims that the reading was given for the honour of his country; though very young, John Dee must already have been acutely aware that England had produced no magus comparable with those on the Continent. He says that his exposition was original and that the elicited response was extraordinary. 'My auditory at Rhemes College was so great', he later writes, 'and the most part elder than my selfe, that the mathematicall schooles could not hold them.' Many of the eager students were forced to listen at the windows. Dee dictated 'upon every proposition, beside the first exposition', and the audience was so astounded by his explanations that even the rising scarabeus at Trinity several years before had not, Dee thought, caused such wonder.[5]

What was so exciting about John Dee's lectures? What was his new approach? One can only theorize, but with an understanding of how his mind functioned, one can do so with some conviction. I believe John Dee was presenting himself to the

[1] Dee, *Rehearsal*, p. 26.

[2] *Ibid.*, p. 7; on Pickering, see John Strype, *Annals of the Reformation*, Pt. 1 (Oxford, 1824), II, 529. Pickering was one of the most accomplished knights of the period and was at one time a serious suitor for Elizabeth's hand.

[3] Bodleian, Ashmole MS. 423, fols. 294^{r-v}.

[4] Dee, *Rehearsal*, p. 7.

[5] *Ibid.*, pp. 7–8.

Parisians as an Agrippan magus. He expounded a theory of
numbers operating in the three worlds, a theory based at least
in part on Agrippa's *De occulta philosophia*, a work Dee knew
well.[1] He says as much when he points out that he explained
Euclid according to physical (elemental world), mathematical
(celestial, or middle world), and Pythagorean (supercelestial,
or religious world) concepts. Agrippa cites Pythagoras as a
religious magus, and Renaissance magi generally thought that
the Greek philosopher's mystical numerology operated on the
supercelestial level. Agrippa's widely read handbook on magic,
which was based on a synthesis of Hermetic Platonism and the
cabala as expounded by Pico della Mirandola, divided the
universe into the same three worlds that Dee chose to lecture
upon. The key to operations within these worlds is mathematics. That this tripartite and magically oriented exposition
of Euclid is what Dee explained to the Parisians is further suggested by his 'Mathematicall Preface' to the English *Euclide*
of 1570. The preface opens with a Platonically inspired discussion of number in the three worlds, but Dee concentrates
on the operation of number in the middle world, the world of
mathematical science, because the preface is primarily meant
to help mechanicians, not magi. He stresses the fact, however,
that mathematics also provides a means of operating in the
divine (supercelestial, alternatively intellectual) world, as well
as in the elemental (natural) world.[2] It is emphasized that

[1] For a summary of the *De occulta philosophia*, see Yates, *Giordano Bruno*,
pp. 130–43. The most reecnt full-length study of Agrippa is by Charles
Nauert, Jr., *Agrippa and the Crisis of Renaissance Thought* (Urbana, Ill., 1965).
Paolo Zambelli, in an important study ('Cornelio Agrippa di Nettesheim',
in *Testi umanistici su l'ermetismo*, ed. E. Garin *et al.* (Rome, 1955), pp. 105–62),
discusses the influence of Hermeticism on Agrippa. See also Walker, *Magic*,
pp. 90 ff. Chapter 5, below, contains a more detailed comparison of Dee's
and Agrippa's magic.

[2] Dee, 'Mathematicall Preface', sigs.* ff. Depending upon the particular
philosopher and the purpose for which he was writing, the purely intellectual world was used as an alternative to the supercelestial realm. In the
preface Dee equates the two. It should be remembered that the pure
intellect was thought by him and by others to be the divine essence within
man. Galileo, who apparently repudiated the Pythagorean occultism of
Dee's type of mathematics, nevertheless writes: 'I say that as concerns the
truth, of which mathematical demonstrations give us the knowledge, it is
the same as that which the Divine wisdom knows' (*Dialogue of the Great*

mathematics is the only discipline that participates in all three worlds.

As early as 1550, then, John Dee was expounding magical theory that was revived by Ficino in Florence and transformed by Pico and Agrippa.[1] All three of these Continental magi were censured, even Ficino, who was timid about the presentation of his magic and refused to operate at any time on the super-celestial level. It is no wonder that John Dee caused such excitement when he publicly expounded Agrippan magical theory, especially in France where the magical implications of Hermetic Platonism had been carefully avoided.[2]

Dee's Parisian lectures prompted many important scholars to seek his acquaintance. They included Orontius, who was a renowned geographer and Regius Professor of mathematics at the Collège de France. Ranconetus, the famous lawyer and a distinguished philosopher, mathematician, antiquarian and sometime President of the Parliament of Paris, also conferred with him. Both Turnebus, the highly respected classicist and Hermeticist, and Peter Ramus, his opponent and an important anti-Aristotelian and educational reformer, were anxious to hear about Dee's mathematical philosophy. Dee also met Gulielmus Postellus, who was for a time a professor of mathematics and philosophy at Paris and later taught at Vienna. He was a famous Orientalist, cabalist and eirenicist who dreamed of establishing a world religion and government; Dee had similar ideals. These are only a few of the famous men Dee actually mentions.[3] He was only twenty-three in 1550, but he was already acquainting himself with the ideas of the best minds on the Continent.

World Systems, tr. Salusbury, revised and annotated by Giorgio de Santillana (Chicago, 1953), p. 115). Kepler also believed in the divine essence of mathematical archetypes (see D. P. Walker, 'Kepler's Celestial Music', *JWCI*, XXX (1967), 228–50). For Galileo and Kepler, as for Dee, pure mathematics as a completely intellectual study was a means of participating in the divine *mens*.

[1] See Walker, *Magic*, pp. 3 ff.; Yates, *Giordano Bruno*, pp. 62 ff.
[2] D. P. Walker, 'The *Prisca Theologia* in France', *JWCI*, XVII (1954), 234–40.
[3] Dee, *Rehearsal*, p. 8. Others whom Dee lists are: Mizaldus, Petrus Montaureus, Danesius, Jacobus Sylvius, Jacobus Goupylus, Straselius, Vicomercatus, Paschasius Hamelius, Fernelius, Jo. Magnionus, Johannes à Pena.

Not long after his success in Paris, Dee returned to England replete with ideas from philosophical circles in France and the Low Countries. Geography and navigation, Hermeticism and the cabala, mechanics and Vitruvian ideas on symmetry and proportion were all subjects that were fairly advanced on the Continent by this time but had not yet taken deep root in England. John Dee was vitally interested in each of these subjects.

After Dee's return to England in 1551, Sir John Cheke brought him to the notice of William Cecil, who, in turn, introduced him to Edward VI. Dee presented the King with two treatises, and for his efforts on these compositions received a pension of 100 crowns.[1] Dee seems to have been closely associated with the proponents of religious reform at court. He entered the service of the Earl of Pembroke at the end of February in 1552.[2] More significantly, Dee was attached at some point to the household of the Lord Protector, the Duke of Northumberland. In his 'Mathematicall Preface', Dee lauds Northumberland's eldest son, 'the Noble, the Couragious, the loyall, and Curteous *John*, late Erle of Warwicke'. Dee stresses his former closeness to Warwick by suggesting, 'No twayne, (I thinke) beside my selfe, can so perfectly, and truely report' of his great virtue. Dee especially praises the earl for disclosing 'his harty love to vertuous Sciences' and for using arithmetic to excel in 'Martiall prowesse'.[3] At the request of the Duchess of Northumberland, Dee also wrote two treatises in 1553: 'The Philosophicall and Poeticall Originall occasions of the Configurations, and names of the heavenly Asterismes', and 'The true

---

[1] He exchanged the annuity in March of 1553 for the rectory of Upton-upon-Severn; Long Leadenham was added later in the year. These livings produced £80 per annum, and Dee continued to receive the proceeds for about thirty years; thus, while he depended on patrons for extra support, he did have a steady income for some time. See Fell Smith, *John Dee*, pp. 13–14; *Calendar of Patent Rolls, Edward VI, 1553*, V, 199.

[2] W. R. B. Prideaux, 'Books from John Dee's Library', *N&Q*, 9th ser., VIII (1901), 137. This member of the Herbert family, who with the Earl of Leicester recommended Dee to Elizabeth upon her accession, received the dissolved Abbey of Wilton from Henry VIII; his puritanical treatment of the nuns was notorious (John Aubrey, *Brief Lives*, ed. Oliver Lawson Dick (London, 1958), pp. 141–2).

[3] Dee, 'Mathematicall Preface', sigs.*.iiiiᵛ–a.i.

cause, and account (not vulgar) of Floods and Ebbs'.[1] Dee's function in Pembroke's household is not known, but he apparently acted as a tutor in the sciences to the Dudley family. His lifelong task of trying to reinstate the indigenous English scientific tradition and of attempting to free mathematics from its diabolical associations apparently met with some success among members of the influential Northumberland household.

The Duke of Northumberland wanted his children to have the best scientific education available, and he was particularly interested in English navigation.[2] The importance of John Dee's role as tutor to the Duke's children can be realized only if one remembers that one of the children was Robert Dudley, later the Earl of Leicester, who became one of the greatest patrons of learning in Elizabethan England. Not surprisingly, Leicester was reputed to be a champion of the sciences; this, as Miss Rosenberg points out, can be ascribed to the influence of his father's interests.[3] But Dee's tutoring must also have encouraged Robert Dudley's special concern with mathematics and, pre-eminently, with geometry; Anthony Wood assures us that no one knew the Earl better than Dee.[4]

Leicester made use of Dee's scientific knowledge, as did Elizabeth and others, but as we have seen a deep interest in philosophy and science was not to everyone's taste. The great humanist, Roger Ascham, wrote to Leicester in 1564 and chided him for deserting the study of the trivium in favour of the sciences: 'I think you did yourself injury in changing TULLY'S wisdome with EUCLID'S pricks and lines.'[5] How different was John Dee's attitude! One imagines that his response to Ascham would have been something like Pico della Mirandola's famous answer to a similar charge by Ermolao Barbo. Pico seemed to hear the great philosophers say:

> We live celebrated, O Hermolao, and we will live with those who come after us, not in the schools of grammar and pedagogy but in the circles of philosophers, in the assemblies

[1] Charles Henry Cooper and Thompson Cooper, *Athenae Cantabrigiensis* (Cambridge, 1861), II, 505–6.

[2] Eleanor Rosenberg, *Leicester, Patron of Letters* (New York, 1955), p. 21.

[3] *Ibid.*, pp. 19, 31, 41.

[4] Anthony Wood, *Athenae Oxoniensis* (London, 1815), II, 542.

[5] Roger Ascham, *The Whole Works*, ed. J. A. Giles (London, 1864), II, 103.

of the learned, where neither who Andromache's mother was, nor the number of Niobe's sons, nor other such trifling foolishness is considered, but where reasons for human and divine affairs are discussed and debated.[1]

It is an attitude like Pico's that Dee was trying to foster in England.

When Ascham wrote the aforementioned letter to Leicester, Elizabeth had been on the throne for six years and was protecting Dee. Before her accession, however, he underwent a terrifying ordeal that was related to his philosophic and scientific pursuits. Some time after the succession of Mary Tudor, Dee was invited to calculate her nativity, as well as that of her husband, Philip II. He apparently did so and then performed the same service for the Princess Elizabeth, who was at Woodstock. On 28 May 1555, the Privy Council directed that a letter be sent to the Master of the Rolls, Sir Francis Englefelde, 'to make searche for oone John Dye, dwelling in London, and tapprehend him and send him hither, and make searche for suche papers and bookes as he maye thinke maye towche the same Dye or Benger'.[2] A private letter from one Thomas Martyn written on 8 June asserts that Dee was imprisoned following an accusation by a certain George Ferrys that Dee was attempting to enchant the Queen, by calculating the nativities of the King, the Queen and the Princess Elizabeth.[3] Some years later (when reminding Elizabeth that he was a prisoner at Hampton Court the week before she was), Dee mentions that a man named Prideaux also falsely informed against him in the case. The political implications of the incident become apparent when one realizes that Benger was Elizabeth's 'Auditor' and that Prideaux was later pensioned by King Philip of Spain.[4]

---

[1] Giovanni Pico della Mirandola, *Opera Omnia* (Basel, 1572), II, 352. 'Viximus celebres Ô Hermolae & post hac vivemus non in scholis grammaticorum & paedagogiis, sed in philosophorum coronis, in conventibus sapientum, ubi non de matre Andromaches, non de Niobes filiis: atque id genus levibus nugis, sed de humanarum divinarumque rerum rationibus agitur & disputatur.'

[2] *Acts of the Privy Council, 1554–1556*, n.s., V, 137.

[3] *Calendar of State Papers, Domestic, 1547–1580*, p. 67, No. 34.

[4] Dee, *Rehearsal*, p. 20; on Prideaux's pension, see Strype, *Annals*, Pt. 2, II, 54.

Although John Dee managed to clear himself of the charge of treason, he was subsequently sent to the Star Chamber in the custody of the reactionary Catholic Bishop of London, Edmund Bonner, to be tried on ecclesiastical charges. Writing of the incident much later, Dee recalls that he was long a prisoner 'and bedfellow with Barthlet Grene, who was burnt'.[1] Although he was released without penalty on 29 August 1555, Dee feared for his life from this time on.[2]

The exact ecclesiastical charges against Dee are not clear, but under the reactionary reign of Mary, it is possible that Dee's intimacy with the reformers of the previous reign rendered him suspect. Yet, if his former associations aroused suspicion, one wonders why he was invited to cast horoscopes for the new monarchs in the first place. Miss Taylor suggests that Dee's early Copernicanism might have led to the inquisition into his religious beliefs and possibly to his continuing uncertainty about the safety of his life.[3] Although this would explain the religious examinations Dee underwent, I find the theory highly implausible. Dee's earliest published references to Copernicanism appeared in 1556, after he had been released from prison.[4] Also, he had the friendship, if not the protection, of his inquisitor, Bishop Bonner, after the trial; Dee may even have acted as his chaplain.[5] These facts suggest that Copernicanism had little to do with the investigation of Dee's religious beliefs. The whole incident remains something of a mystery. It is clear that Dee was able to acclimatize himself to the religious reaction that characterized Mary's brief reign, but being a magus in England could be dangerous indeed.

[1] Dee, *Rehearsal*, p. 20; John Dee, 'A necessary Advertisement', in *General and Rare Memorials*, sig. Δ. iiii.

[2] *Acts of the Privy Council, 1554–1556*, n.s., V, 176; Taylor, *Mathematical Practitioners*, p. 24. In a letter to Mercator shortly before Mary's death, Dee expresses the hope that Mercator, or Pedro Nuñez the celebrated Portuguese geographer, would carry on the work that he had started.

[3] Taylor, *Mathematical Practitioners*, p. 24. See below, pp. 97 ff., for a fuller exposition of Dee's Copernicanism.

[4] John Dee, 'Preface', to John Feild, *Ephemeris Anni 1557* (London, 1556), sigs. A^r-v.

[5] W. R. B. Prideaux, 'Books from John Dee's Library', p. 137. For the claim that Dee was Bonner's chaplain, see John Philpot, *The Examinations and Writings*, ed. Robert Eden (Cambridge, 1892), pp. 69, 80.

Dee returned to the Continent again before Christmas of 1562. He wrote to William Cecil on 16 February 1563 concerning the reasons for his journey, and he was then staying at Antwerp in the home of the prominent Dutch printer William Silvius, who later published his *Monas Hieroglyphica*. Dee's trip had already proven hugely successful, for he informs Cecil that 'by diligent serche and travaile (for so short a tyme) almost incredible', he had learned more about recondite philosophy than he had ever dared to hope possible.[1] Among other books, Dee was able to obtain a copy of Trithemius's *Steganographia*, 'for which a Thowsand Crownes have ben offred, and yet could not be obteyned'. His excitement about gaining access to this particular work is a clear indication that he had already become interested in angel-magic, though he did not attempt to practise it until 22 December 1581.[2]

The *Steganographia* was not published until 1606, but it had obviously been circulating in manuscript before then. It is concerned with cryptography and so would have been of interest to Cecil, who was understandably curious about such things. The angels in the first two books may be satisfactorily interpreted as a means of enciphering, but those in the third part seem to allow of no such interpretation; and it is therefore likely, as D. P. Walker suggests, that the sections purported to be about writing in code are really meant to conceal the true concern of the whole work: cabalist angel-magic, the summoning and employment of demons.[3] The first book gives the procedure for summoning the angels who govern the parts of the earth; the second section deals with those who govern time; and the last part of the work is primarily concerned with summoning a higher order of angels who rule the planets, and particularly Saturn.[4] As an example of the form the book takes, the head angel of Saturn is thought to be Orfiel, and under him are Sadael, Poniel (or Pomiel) and Morisiel, who supposedly govern in three-hour shifts; Trithemius presents extensive charts that outline their times of influence in exact

[1] As transcribed by Bailey in 'Dee and Trithemius's "Steganography"', pp. 401–2.

[2] The first recorded attempt to communicate with angels is described in British Museum, Sloane MS. 3188, fol. 8. See below, pp. 110 ff.

[3] See Walker, *Magic*, pp. 86–90.

[4] Johannes Trithemius, *Steganographia* (Frankfurt, 1606), pp. 160–80.

detail.[1] The whole operation involves fantastically complex calculations that are based on astrology and numerical equivalents assigned to the angels' names.

Trithemius's goal in this work is a form of telepathic communication that would be achieved by conveying the human spirit, with the imprint of the sender's thought, through the air to a recipient whose portrait the sender contemplates. The magic is implicitly a means of knowing all that is going on in the world, and the angel-magic underlying the *Steganographia* would have been far more significant to Dee than the treatise's outward concern with cryptography. Despite the modern view of such magical attempts, one is impressed by the practical benefit that Trithemius and Dee hoped to obtain from the use of angel-magic. If one substitutes the machines of our cosmological system for the angels of theirs, analogies with the wonders of modern electronics are not difficult to conceive. At any rate, Dee laments in his letter to Cecil that the type of knowledge found in the *Steganographia* is not available in England; therefore, he wishes to prolong his stay abroad.

After departing from Antwerp, Dee travelled to Zurich and, on 23 April 1563, visited Conrad Gesner, a well-known physician and scholar who, although he did not approve of Paracelsus personally, did advocate certain of his medical innovations.[2] By the summer, Dee was in Italy. He spent considerable time at the Duke of Urbino's court, which was renowned as a centre for the study of the exact sciences, especially in connection with military tactics and the fine arts: John Dee was an expert in these fields of knowledge.[3] He soon became friendly with Commandinus, the widely respected court mathematician, and they collaborated in the publication of a mathematical text, *De superficierum divisionibus*, that Dee had discovered.[4]

[1] Trithemius, *Steganographia*, pp. 166–7.

[2] Josten, 'Introduction', to Dee's *Monas Hieroglyphica*, p. 87; on Gesner, see Allen G. Debus, *The English Paracelsians* (New York, 1966), pp. 52–3.

[3] James Dennistoun, *Memoirs of the Dukes of Urbino*, ed. Edward Hutton (London, 1909), III, 259.

[4] This text was attributed to an Arabic scholar, Machomet Bagdedin∂; it is actually a work by Euclid translated into Arabic. See Raymond Clare Archibald, *Euclid's Book on Divisions of Figures* (Cambridge, 1915), pp. 1–9, *et passim*.

Dee went to Rome from Urbino, but did not remain there long; he was in Pressburg, Hungary, in September, and he may have attended the coronation of Maximilian of Habsburg as Hungary's king.[1] Dee returned to Antwerp to supervise the printing of his *Monas Hieroglyphica*, which was published on 31 March 1564. It had taken John Dee twelve days to write the *Monas*, a Hermetic treatise that he had been contemplating for seven years; and he took just seventeen days to complete the entire text of the book, which includes a very long and informative letter of dedication to Maximilian.[2] The *Monas Hieroglyphica* apparently reached England before Dee returned home. Writing in 1592 (long after the event took place), Dee thanks Elizabeth for her

> most gracious defending of my credit, in my absence beyond the seas, as concerning my booke, titled *Monas Hieroglyphica* (dedicated to the Emperour Maximilian, A. 1564) against such Universitie-Graduates of high degree, and other gentlemen, who therefore dispraised it, because they understood it not.[3]

Dee left Antwerp to accompany the Marchioness of Northampton back to England and to the court at Greenwich.[4] He and the Marchioness had arrived in England by 14 June 1564 because he refers to events that took place at court on that date, writing:

> After my retorne from the Emperor's court, her Majestie very graciously vouchsafed to account herselfe my schollar in my booke, written to the Emperor Maximilian, intituled, *Monas Hieroglyphica*; and said, whereas I had prefixed in the forefront of the book; *Qui non intelligit, aut taceat, aut discat*: if I would disclose unto her the secretes of that booke, she

---

[1] John Dee and Frederic Commandinus, eds., *Book of the Divisions of the Superficies*, tr. John Leeke and George Serle (London, 1661), p. 608; Josten, 'Introduction' to Dee's *Monas Hieroglyphica*, pp. 87.

[2] On the *Monas Hieroglyphica*, see below, pp. 64 ff.

[3] Dee, *Rehearsal*, p. 10.

[4] *Ibid.*, p. 10. She had gone to Flanders to consult physicians about a cure for cancer.

would *et discere et facere*; whereupon her Majestie had a little perusin of the same with me, and then in most heroicall and princely wise did comfort me and encourage me in my studies philosophicall and mathematicall, &c.[1]

Dee returned to England fully conscious of the dignity of the Renaissance magus; and despite the dangers attached, he attempted to fulfil that role in his homeland.

[1] Dee, *Rehearsal*, p. 19. It is possible, since Dee mentions returning to England after visiting the Emperor's court, that he went to Vienna to present a copy of his *Monas Hieroglyphica* to Maximilian in person.

Elizabethan England's Greatest Library

After John Dee returned from Antwerp in the party of the Marchioness of Northampton, he settled at Mortlake in a house belonging to his mother. He was established in the village before 1570. The Mortlake period, which lasted about two decades, was the time of his greatest influence in England.

In a survey of 1616, Dee's house – already called ancient – is described as a rambling place standing between the church and the river. Dee added rooms and buildings from time to time and also acquired adjacent properties.[1] The additional space was needed for his many collections. In connection with his antiquarian studies, for example, he gathered such things as Welsh and Irish records, genealogies and ancient seals.[2] He almost certainly used some of the extra buildings to house his many scientific instruments and laboratories. Also, his diary indicates that he frequently had students in residence, which is understandable since one contemporary recalls that there were four or five rooms in the house filled with books.[3]

There is no better framework for a study of Dee's philosophy than an examination of his library. This is absolutely basic to any attempt to understand his intellectual and cultural life; and since the library was available to many important sixteenth-century figures, it perhaps has something to tell us about the spirit of the Elizabethan age as a whole.[4] By examining the

---

[1] Fell Smith, *John Dee*, pp. 30–1.

[2] Dee, *Rehearsal*, pp. 27–31.

[3] Ashmole, *Autobiographical and Historical Notes*, IV, 1335.

[4] See Yates, *Theatre of the World*, pp. 1–19. Miss Yates's study of Dee's library has appeared since I first wrote this chapter. Her work has not prompted me to make any significant changes in my own evaluation of Dee's library because we have arrived at similar conclusions.

library, we find that Dee was a man of universal interests: the range of books on his shelves was extraordinary. This type of study also brings to light some relatively obscure sources containing modes of thought that were integral to Dee's philosophy, and this places the content of future chapters of this book in better perspective.

We must begin with 15 January 1556, the day on which Dee sent a supplication to Queen Mary imploring 'the Recovery and Preservation of Ancient Writers and Monuments'.[1] Wisely couching his request in terms of the desecration of the old religion, Dee probably hoped that Mary would be as willing to restore the old learning as she was to restore the old faith; she actually sent commissioners to the universities to ensure that no books prejudicial to the Catholic religion remained in their libraries.[2] Dee writes to her:

> Among the exceeding many most lamentable displeasures, that have of late happened unto this realm, through the subverting of religious houses, and the dissolution of other assemblies of godly and learned men, it has been, and for ever, among all learned students, shall be judged, not for the least calamity, the spoile and destruction of so many and so notable libraries, wherein lay the treasures of all Antiquity, and the everlasting seeds of continual excellency in this your Grace's realm.

He suggests that, if 'speedy diligence be shewed', a great deal could still be saved.[3] Dee felt that the preservation of the treasures of the realm would be facilitated by establishing a royal library, and he offered to travel and obtain copies of all the important manuscripts in such great Continental libraries as the Vatican and St Mark's, if only the Queen would bear the charges of the journey. Dee even dreamed that printed

---

[1] Dee's original *Supplication* is British Museum, Cotton MS. Vitellius. C. VII, art. 6; the *Supplication* has been printed in *Autobiographical Tracts of Dr. John Dee*, ed. Crossley, 46–7. I have used the printed edition.

[2] Sears Jayne, *Library Catalogues of the English Renaissance* (Berkeley and Los Angeles, 1956), p. 41.

[3] Dee, *Supplication*, p. 46.

books might be procured 'in wonderfull abundance'.[1] His plan was visionary, but Mary had more pressing problems at the time, and nothing came of Dee's supplication.

He was not the first Englishman to encourage the founding of a royal library. The antiquary John Leland wrote to Thomas Cromwell in 1536 and begged for his assistance in the task of preserving the books that were being dispersed and destroyed during the spoliation of the English monasteries; his idea was to bring them together to form a collection for Henry VIII. Leland had travelled through England in 1534 and the years immediately following on an alleged royal commission that he received during the twenty-fifth year of Henry's reign (1533/4), and he must have been well aware of the vast riches of the monastic libraries.[2] He was apparently able to persuade the government to preserve some of the displaced manuscripts in the royal library; but in other cases, Leland did the same thing that John Dee was to do later – he personally acquired many of the manuscripts.[3] Both men collected the unwanted manuscripts of the Middle Ages. When Dee wrote his petition to Queen Mary, he was already laying the foundations of his own immense library.

The time was ripe for the formation of a great collection. After the crippling dissolution of the monasteries, the havoc caused during the Edwardian reforms, and the visitations to the universities by Mary's commissioners, John Dee was not exaggerating when he wrote: 'No one student, nor any one college, hath half a dozen of those excellent jewells [manuscripts], but the whole stock and store thereof [is] drawing nigh to utter destruction and extinguishing.'[4] Dee's distraught testimony is not the only one of its kind. John Bale wrote several times of the national disgrace involved with the destruction of the English libraries. In a preface published with Leland's 'New Year's Gift' of 1546 in *The Laboryouse Journey* (1549), Bale complains:

[1] Dee, *Supplication*, p. 49.

[2] Francis Wormald and C. E. Wright, *The English Library before 1700* (London, 1958), pp. 152–3.

[3] F. J. Levy, *Tudor Historical Thought* (San Marino, Calif., 1967), pp. 126–7.

[4] Dee, *Supplication*, p. 47.

If there had been in euery shyre of Englande, but one solempne lybrary to the preseruacyon of these noble workes and preferrement of good lerynynges on oure posteryte, it had been yet sumwhat. But to destroye all without consyderacyon, is and wyll be vnto Englande for euer, a moste horryble infamy amonge the graue senyours of other nacyons. A great nombre of them whych purchased those superstycyous mansyons, reserued of those lybrarye bokes, some to serue theyr iakes, some to scoure theyr candelstyckes, and some to rubbe their bootes. Some they solde to grossers and sope-sellers, and some they sent ouersee to the bokebynders, and not in small nombre, but at tymes whole shyppes full, to the wonderynge of the foren nacyons. Yea, the unyuersytees of thys realme, are not all clere in this detestable fact.[1]

At that time, whole libraries could be bought for almost nothing. When Duke Humphrey's collection at Oxford and much of the university library were sold, some of the manuscripts were purchased by Dee.[2] He continued to buy books and manuscripts at home and abroad whenever his finances allowed; occasionally he was given them as presents.

On 6 September 1583, just before departing for the Continent, Dee compiled a catalogue of his library; he claims that it numbered 'in all neere 4,000: the fourth part of which were written bokes'.[3] In a recent study of Renaissance library

[1] As quoted by Wormald and Wright, *English Library*, p. 153.

[2] On the final leaf (fol. 197) of Bodleian, Corpus Christi MS. 143, the following notes appear: 'Cest livre est a moy Homfroy duc de gloucestre', and written beneath is, 'et a ceste heure voyre en l'an de notre signeur 1557 a moy, Jehan Dee, Angloys, quel je achetai par le poys payant pour chacune livre un gros'.

[3] Dee, *Rehearsal*, p. 27. Two copies of Dee's 1583 library catalogue in his own hand exist: British Museum, Harleian MS. 1879, arts. 5–6; Cambridge, Trinity College MS. O. 4. 20. A copy made by Elias Ashmole from the manuscript now at Cambridge is in the Bodleian, Ashmole MS. 1142, II; there is also a second seventeenth-century copy in the Bodleian, Additional MS. C. 194. I have used the Harleian manuscript in my study of Dee's library of printed books but have depended on M. R. James (*Manuscripts formerly owned by Dr. John Dee*, pp. 1–39) for my remarks on his manuscript collection. James has attempted to identify the whereabouts of manuscripts belonging to Dee, having based his *Lists* on the Trinity MS. Halliwell also provides a list of Dee's manuscripts, which is much shorter than James's, at the end of his edition of *The Private Diary*.

catalogues, Sears Jayne puts the content of Dee's library at about 170 manuscripts and 2,500 printed books.[1] Many of the volumes contained more than one work, so Dee's estimate is fairly accurate.[2]

According to the evidence available, no library in sixteenth-century England matched the French historian Jacques de Thou's vast collection of 8,000 printed books and 1,000 manuscripts, but John Dee's library probably rivalled the other private Continental collections. Grolier's famous library, for instance, contained about 3,000 volumes, which still is not as many as Dee's.[3] John Dee's immense achievement is placed in proper perspective when one observes that the largest collection in England other than his was that of Lord Lumley. The Lumley library boasted about 2,800 volumes and 3,000 separate works in 1609, though the essential collection was gathered by 1596.[4] This was about 1,000 works less than Dee's library contained twenty-five years earlier, and Dee's collection was more varied. Though the mob that sacked his house at Mortlake after Dee left for the Continent in 1583 apparently did considerable damage to his library, there is no reason to believe that he did not continue to add to his collection after his return to England.[5]

A collection like Lumley's, or Donne's 1,400 authors in addition to his own papers, or Burton's much later library of 2,000 volumes is exceptional for an English library of the time.[6] Any library of more than a few hundred volumes must be considered remarkably large for the sixteenth century. Neither of the English universities had anything to compare with Dee's collection: in 1582, the University Library at Cambridge only had about 451 books and manuscripts, and Corpus

[1] Jayne, *Library Catalogues*, p. 125.

[2] See, for instance, James, *Manuscripts formerly owned by Dr. John Dee*, p. 18, item T 24, which contains thirty-one separate works.

[3] Wormald and Wright, *English Library*, p. 8.

[4] Sears Jayne and Francis R. Johnson, *The Lumley Library: The Catalogue of 1609*, British Museum Bicentenary Publications (London, 1956), p. 10.

[5] Dee, *Rehearsal*, pp. 27–32. Dee estimates that he lost about 500 books. A later library catalogue in his hand exists (British Museum, Additional MS. 35213, art. 1), but it is extremely fragmentary.

[6] Raymond Irwin, *The Origins of the English Library* (London, 1958), p. 131.

Christi College at Oxford had about 379 volumes in 1589.[1]

It is not surprising, therefore, that John Dee's library was famous enough to draw a visit from Queen Elizabeth. On 10 March 1575, Dee writes: 'The Queens Majestie with her most honourable Privy Councell, and other her lordes and nobility, came purposely to have visited my library.'[2] He apparently had already gathered a considerable portion of his collection by this time.

If the essential requisite of a university is an excellent library, F. R. Johnson has pointed out that Dee's home at Mortlake might truly be considered the scientific academy of England during the first half of Elizabeth's reign. As Johnson has indicated, Dee's scientific library was undoubtedly the greatest in England and quite possibly was better than any on the Continent.[3] It has been assumed for too long, however, that Dee's collection was almost entirely a scientific one. M. R. James says, for example, 'Had it survived intact it would have been a first-class repository of mediaeval science books excluding medicine', and he erroneously adds that Dee's library contained 'very little theology, and no ancient poetry'.[4] The practical scientific works, which formed only a part of the library, have frequently been segregated from the collection as a whole for special attention by those who have attempted to rehabilitate Dee's reputation as a practical scientist. Miss Taylor understandably lists Dee's geographically oriented scientific works in an appendix to *Tudor Geography*, but because this is the only selection of printed books from his library readily available and because of testimonies like Johnson's and James's about the scientific superiority of Dee's collection, other significant assets have regularly been overlooked.

The most striking aspect of John Dee's library is that, along with his purely scientific holdings, there are so many non-scientific works. Indeed, if one were to remove the material

[1] Jayne, *Library Catalogues*, pp. 77, 67; other lists of institutional libraries of the Renaissance are found on pp. 63–92.

[2] Dee, *Rehearsal*, p. 17.

[3] Johnson, *Astronomical Thought*, pp. 138–9.

[4] James, *Manuscripts formerly owned by Dr. John Dee*, p. 10. James erred because he apparently did not consider the printed books in Dee's collection.

concerning practical science from the collection, there would still be a library extensive enough to vie with the largest in England at the time. His collection was one that serves admirably to define the interests of a Renaissance magus who took all knowledge for his province. Practical scientific works, and especially mathematical ones, certainly form a very large segment of Dee's library, but it is only when these works are placed within the context of his total collection that their function can be properly understood. If one segregates them from the rest of the collection, as usually has been done, one's view of Dee is distorted. He was a scientist who genuinely tried to apply his knowledge to utilitarian ends, but he was also a magician-philosopher who worked within a philosophic framework that was much broader than that of practical science alone.

Though Plato seems to have had a much greater influence on Dee's thought than Aristotle, the library contained more works by the latter. There were sets of the complete works of each, and many individual works by both Greek philosophers were scattered throughout the library. It is worth mentioning that Dee possessed at least four copies of Plato's *Timaeus* with Chalcidius' commentaries, a work that heavily influenced Renaissance philosophy because of Plato's almost Christian recounting of the creation and because of the dialogue's mathematicism.[1] Dee possessed many works of other important classical philosophers, including those of Lucretius (he had a copy of his *De rerum natura*), two sets of the works of Diogenes Laertius, the works of Isocrates, and many books by Pliny. There were copies of the *Orations* of Demosthenes and Quintilian and a large number of books by and about Cicero. It should be mentioned here that Dee was clearly not an enemy of classical rhetorical studies, but he despised the use made of them by the pedants at the English universities. The important Neoplatonists were, as one might expect, well represented and

[1] British Museum, Harleian MS. 1879, art. 5; for Aristotle's works, see fols. 20, 23ᵛ; for Plato's works, see fols. 20ʳ⁻ᵛ; for individual works of both philosophers, *passim*; for the *Timaeus*, see fols. 24, 29ᵛ; also, a manuscript of that dialogue owned by Dee is Bodleian, Corpus Christi MS. 243, and James, *Manuscripts formerly owned by Dr. John Dee*, p. 29, no. 143, identifies a second manuscript copy.

included Plotinus, Proclus and Synesius among others.[1]

Unlike many of the humanists who despised the philosophers of the Middle Ages because of their 'barbarous' Latin style, Dee revered them and had a large number of medieval works in manuscripts – which he was assiduously trying to preserve – as well as in printed editions. It is especially noteworthy that almost the largest number of manuscripts by any one author in Dee's library were those of Ramon Lull (1234–1316), though they were indiscriminately mixed with pseudo-Lullian works.[2] Dee's Lullist holdings are rivalled only by the works of Roger Bacon and his followers, and the collection of printed books by Lull is actually far more extensive.[3]

Modern study of Lullism is at a relatively early stage of development, but a brief description of this philosophy, which was so influential in the Renaissance and was intensively studied by Dee, is fundamental if we are to understand the various elements that formed his philosophical outlook.[4] Lullism is essentially a mystical philosophy that purports to be capable of demonstrating truth in all areas of knowledge. Lull, 'Doctor Illuminatus', was forming his ideas almost contemporaneously with the development of scholasticism, but he was basing his art on Augustinian Neoplatonism rather than on the rediscovered Aristotle.[5] Sometime about 1272, Lull had a vision on Mount Randa on Majorca in which he saw God's various attributes, or dignities as Lull terms them, infused through all of creation. These dignities – there are nine in the simplest form of the art – include such absolute traits as goodness, wisdom, virtue, power and eternity, which are considered

[1] British Museum, Harleian MS. 1879, art. 5; for Lucretius, see fols. 28, 53ᵛ, 57; for Diogenes, see fols. 32ᵛ, 47; for Isocrates, see fol. 21ᵛ; for Pliny, see fols. 25ᵛ, 39, *et passim*; for Demosthenes, see fols. 37, 54ᵛ; for Quintilian, see fol. 38; for Cicero, see fols. 21ᵛ, 35, 48, 58, 83, 84ᵛ, 85ᵛ; for Plotinus, see fol. 22ᵛ; for Porphyry, see fols. 76ᵛ, *et passim*; for Proclus, see fols. 31, *et passim*; for Synesius, see fols. 24, 39ᵛ.
[2] On Lull, see Edgar Allison Peers, *Ramon Lull: A Biography* (London, 1929).
[3] British Museum, Harleian MS. 1879, art. 4, esp. fols. 58–64, *et passim*.
[4] On Lull's art, see Yates, 'The Art of Ramon Lull', 115–73; 'Ramon Lull and John Scotus Erigena', *JWCI*, XXIII (1960), 1–44; *Memory*, pp. 173–98.
[5] Yates, 'Ramon Lull and John Scotus Erigena', pp. 3–50.

modes of God's creative activity and the causes of all created perfection. Connected to each of these dignities are nine relative predicates such as equality, minority, agreement, beginning and contrariety. According to Lull, these sets of absolute and relative principles, in their various combinations, form the basis of all arts and sciences. He applies these combinations to a hierarchy, or ladder, which consists of nine levels of creation and extends throughout the universe in a continuous scale, descending from God to angels, to stars, to man, to imagination, to animals, to plants, to elements and to instruments. In the Lullian art, one can move freely up and down the ladder of creation.

The most distinctive feature of Lullism, however, is the equation of the various absolute and relative qualities and the different levels of creation with letters of the alphabet; in the simplest form of the art, the letters B through K are used. The letters are placed, for instance, on a series of three wheels, one set within the other. (See Figure Four of Plate 3.) The two inner wheels revolve independently, and the combinations that result when the wheels stop reveal answers to a set of questions concerning the action of the different attributes within each level of creation.

Lull also incorporated in his art the theory of the four elements, the concept of man as microcosm, and the idea that reality is organized according to mathematical symbolism. The actual workings of the art are almost unbelievably complex, though the abbreviated form outlined above was developed by Lull himself in the *Ars brevis*. Lull claimed that the master of his art could know everything about the universe *and* retain this information in his memory.

There was a widespread revival of interest in Lull's art during the Renaissance. A chair of Lullism was established at the University of Paris, and King Philip II, one of the champions of Catholic orthodoxy, became adept at the Lullian art before his death; even the sceptical Montaigne was indebted to Lull.[1] The appeal of such an occult system to a man like John Dee is

[1] René Taylor, 'Architecture and Magic: Considerations on the *Idea* of the Escorial', in *Essays presented to Rudolf Wittkower on his sixty-fifth birthday*, Pt. 1, *Essays in the History of Architecture*, ed. Douglas Faber *et al.* (London, 1967), p. 106; Peers, *Lull*, pp. 382 ff.

obvious. With the acceptance of pseudo-Lullian alchemical and cabalist works as authentic, an image developed of Lull as a sort of early magus who cultivated Hermeticism and the cabala.

Although Lull was not an alchemist, the application of Lullist theories to the elemental level becomes a kind of alchemy – the quintessential Hermetic art – or so the Renaissance believed. Certain similarities between Lullism and magical operations become apparent if one recalls the desire of the Renaissance magus to operate with number in the three worlds (as John Dee explained in his early lectures to the Parisians) and if one considers that much of *magia* was based on the Platonic idea of a world soul, itself musically and mathematically constructed, that descended from God and infused the universe. Operation with symbolic numbers is not so very different from operation with symbolic letters, and letters were often transformed into numbers in the cabala of the Renaissance.[1] The world soul that infused the universe of magic and provided the base for the magus's operations is not unlike the dignities of God that infused the universe of Ramon Lull. Also, the nine levels within the Lullian ladder of creation can be combined into trinitarian structures corresponding to the three worlds of the cabalists; in fact, Pico della Mirandola, who introduced cabalist thought into Renaissance Platonism, identified the cabala with Lullism. In a later Renaissance transformation, the letters B through K used in the Lullian art became associated with the Hebrew letters that the cabalists contemplated and that supposedly signified angel names and the attributes of God.[2] These Hebrew letters, which were thought to have a summoning power over the angels, were the same ones used by practical cabalists like John Dee in operations to contact angels.

The revival of interest in Lullism during the Renaissance stemmed partly from the concern with finding the key to universal knowledge and finding a system of notation that

---

[1] See Blau, *Christian Interpretation of the Cabala*, pp. 41–64.

[2] On Lull and the cabala, see Blau, *Christian Interpretation of the Cabala*, pp. 117–18. John Dee possessed (British Museum, Harleian MS. 1879, art. 4, fol. 85ᵛ) a copy of the pseudo-Lullian work, *De auditu kabbalistico* (Venice, 1518), which the Renaissance believed was authentic and proved that Lull was a cabalist. See below, pp. 111 ff.

could express that knowledge, with the cabala and its attendant hieroglyphs, with a memory system that would allow knowledge to be retained, and with logic and method. Lull and his students certainly must have viewed the art as one of the most magnificent achievements of the human intellect, and it is hardly surprising that in the Renaissance, with its emphasis on man's intellectual powers, it was studied enthusiastically. The mystical aspects of this philosophy would, of course, attract Dee, but it should also be remembered that Lullism was a distant ancestor of symbolic logic and was in Leibniz's mind when he discovered the calculus.[1] It had its practical side.

In addition to the vast collection of Lullian and pseudo-Lullian works, Dee possessed many works by such early- and late-medieval thinkers as Boethius, Cassiodorus, Duns Scotus, Albertus Magnus and Aquinas, as well as the numerous works of Roger Bacon and his followers.[2] It is apparent, from the large number of medieval authors, that Dee was trying, almost alone and without the encouragement of mystical academies like those that flourished in Italy, to effect in England that same transformation of medieval thought that was a natural part of Italian Renaissance Platonism.

There is no doubt that John Dee was well acquainted with the philosophical currents of Renaissance Italy. He travelled in Italy, and his library included the works of practically all the major philosophers of the Italian Renaissance. One of the most copiously represented was Marsilio Ficino. Dee possessed a set of Ficino's complete works, as well as his translations and commentaries on Plato and Plotinus. In addition, copies of the *De religione Christiana*, the *De triplici vita, libri tres* (especially important for understanding Ficino's magic), the *Theologica Platonica* and the *Epistolae* were to be found on his shelves.[3] The

---

[1] Yates, *Memory*, pp. 381–7.

[2] British Museum, Harleian MS. 1879, art. 5; for Boethius, see fols. 22ᵛ, *et passim*; for Cassiodorus, see fol. 74ᵛ; for Duns Scotus, see fols. 24, 74ᵛ, *et passim*; for Albertus Magnus, see fols. 20ᵛ, 21, 24, *et passim*; for Aquinas, see fols. 22, *et passim*; on Roger Bacon and his followers, see above, pp. 26–7; also, works by all the above as well as other medieval writers are found in James, *Manuscripts formerly owned by Dr. John Dee, passim*.

[3] British Museum, Harleian MS. 1879, art. 5; for Ficino's works, see fol. 24ᵛ; for his translations and commentaries on Plato and Plotinus, see fols. 20ᵛ, 22ᵛ; for *De religione*, see fol. 35ᵛ; for *De vita*, see fols. 39ᵛ, 42ᵛ; for *Theologica Platonica*, see fol. 42ᵛ; for the *Epistolae*, see fol. 64ᵛ.

presence of this collection is hardly surprising because Dee's Hermetic Platonism is directly traceable to Ficino.

Dee also owned a set of Pico della Mirandola's works and a copy of his *Conclusiones*.[1] Though he did not have an exceptionally large collection of Pico's works, which he claimed were readily available, Dee saw a close connection between himself and Pico; the bond was both intellectual and personal because in the 'Mathematicall Preface' Dee compares 'the Raging slaunder of the Malicious Ignorant' against Pico to the persecution he had suffered himself in England. Dee also stresses the fact that he wishes the *Conclusiones*, which he had studied with care, 'were red diligently' by everyone.[2] Pico's attempt to fuse Aristotle and Plato reflects Dee's attitude towards those philosophers and clarifies why he had so many works by both.

John Dee, then, was well versed in the ideas of Ficino and Pico, the founders of reformed Renaissance magic. He also had the writings of many other important Italian Renaissance figures. The various works of Cardanus, the famous and profound magician whom Dee had met, were copiously represented.[3] Dee also possessed the works of Giorgio and Laurentius Valla, and he had a number of books by Patrizi, who followed the magical tradition of Ficino and Pico. The library contained Pomponazzi's works, as well as a separate copy of his *De incantationibus*, in which that Aristotelian asserts that there are three types of magic, all of which can be explained by natural causes and which in no way depend on demonic interference; Dee refused to accept this position.[4] The list could go on, and in later chapters I shall describe additional influential works of the Italian Renaissance that were on Dee's shelves, but other areas in which the library was rich must be considered.

[1] British Museum, Harleian MS. 1879, art. 5; for Pico's works, see fol. 24ᵛ; for the *Conclusiones*, see fol. 44ᵛ.

[2] Dee, 'Mathematicall Preface', sigs. A.iiᵛ, *.iᵛ.

[3] British Museum, Harleian MS. 1879, art. 5; for Cardanus, various titles, see fols. 21, 23, 23ᵛ, 30ᵛ, *et passim*. Cardanus was resident in John Cheke's house in 1552 and Dee met him then. See *N&Q*, 8th ser., I (1892), 126.

[4] British Museum, Harleian MS. 1879, art. 5; for Giorgio Valla, see fol. 25ᵛ; for Laurentius Valla, see fol. 54; for Patrizi, various titles, see fols. 32, 45ᵛ, 74ᵛ; for Pomponazzi's works, see fol. 46ᵛ; for *De incantationibus*, see fol. 49; on the *De incantationibus*, see Walker, *Magic*, pp. 107–11.

Works by Paracelsus, the revolutionary doctor who was profoundly influenced by alchemy and Hermeticism, were copious. In fact, Dee's collection of Paracelsian writings was probably the largest in England – over 100 items are listed in the library catalogue. When counted along with the works of Galen and such books as Vesalius's *Anatomy*, the number of books by Paracelsus indicates that John Dee had much more than a passing interest in medicine which adds strength to the probability that the title of doctor that is so often associated with his name is more than honorific.[1]

Dee was so excited about obtaining the cryptographical and magical *Steganographia* by the alchemist Trithemius, Abbot of Sponheim, that he spent ten straight days copying it. There were several copies of Trithemius's *Polygraphia* and *De septem secundadeis* (a work on cabalist angel-magic) in the library, and Henry Cornelius Agrippa, who was reputed to have been the student of Trithemius, was also well represented in the collection.[2] Agrippa's magic formed the framework in which a late-Renaissance magus like Dee operated, and the library contained several copies of his extremely influential *De occulta philosophia*, and one copy of the almost equally important *De incertitudine & vanitate scientiarum*.[3]

In the *De vanitate*, which was first published in 1530, Agrippa declares that all forms of rational knowledge are useless, though he studied the very subjects he so sweepingly condemns for most of his life. There are sections in the work on the futility of such subjects as grammar, poetry, 'Mathematickes in general', music, optics, painting, Lull's art, the 'Arte of Memorie', and so forth.[4] Agrippa ends by proclaiming:

---

[1] British Museum, Harleian MS. 1879, art. 5; for Paracelsus, various titles, see esp. fols. 60v–62v, 90v–91v; for Galen's works, see fols. 32v, 76; for Vesalius, see fol. 57v. On Dee's title, see above, p. 28, n. 3.

[2] On the *Steganographia*, see above, pp. 36–7. British Museum, Harleian MS. 1879, art. 5; for Trithemius, various titles, see fols. 25, 26, 27, 28v, 35v, *et passim*. On Trithemius and Agrippa, see Nauert, *Agrippa*, p. 30.

[3] British Museum, Harleian MS. 1879, art. 5; for *De occulta philosophia*, see fols. 39, 44v, 53v; for *De vanitate*, see fol. 48v; Dee also had a copy of Agrippa's commentaries on Lull's *Ars brevis*, fol. 59v.

[4] Henrie Cornelius Agrippa, *Of the Vanitie and Uncertaintie of Artes and Sciences*, tr. Ja[mes] San[ford] (London, 1569), *passim*.

Understande you therefore now, that there needeth not
muche labour in this place, but Faithe and Praier: not the
studie of longe time, but humblenes of Spirite and cleannesse
of Hart: not the sumptuous furniture of many bookes, but
a pure understanding, and made fitte for the truthe as the
keye is for the locke: for the great number of bookes chargeth
the learner, instructeth him not, and he that followeth many
authours erreth with many.[1]

As Walker has pointed out, this particular work of Agrippa's
is a *Declamatio invectiva* and was by no means intended to be
taken with complete seriousness.[2] Indeed, it was probably
meant to be a sort of safety device should Agrippa get into
trouble with the ecclesiastical authorities when the complete
edition of the *De occulta philosophia* (a full survey of Renaissance
magic written by 1510) was published in 1533; he could
always point to the earlier book and claim that he had re-
tracted his 'erroneous' views. As we shall see, Dee's own magic
was profoundly indebted to Agrippa's *De occulta philosophia*.[3]

Agrippa based his cabalist theurgy largely on the works of
the eminent Hebraicist, John Reuchlin; Dee lists a copy of
Reuchlin's *De verbo mirifico* in his library catalogue. And,
though it is not included in the catalogue, Dee was familiar
with his *De arte cabalistica* and probably possessed a copy of it
as well.[4] Thus, we see that Dee owned the current works on
Renaissance magic and the cabala. Mystico-magical works of
this type eventually consumed all of his interest and led him
to those seemingly amazing attempts to converse with supernatural beings; however, they also influenced his religious
views and shaped his entire philosophy.

---

[1] *Ibid.*, fol. 187ᵛ.

[2] Walker, *Magic*, pp. 90–1. On Agrippa's scepticism, see Nauert, *Agrippa*,
passim. Nauert takes Agrippa's *De vanitate* too much at face value, and his
interpretation must be read with this in mind.

[3] On Dee's indebtedness to Agrippa, see below, Chapter 5.

[4] British Museum, Harleian MS. 1879, art. 5; for *De verbo mirifico*, see
fol. 46ᵛ. Dee refers to specific passages in Reuchlin's *De arte cabalistica* in
British Museum, Sloane MS. 3188, fol. 12ᵛ. In the same marginal note,
Dee also refers to Agrippa's *De occulta philosophia*. On Reuchlin and the *De
arte cabalistica*, see F. Secret, *Les Kabbalistes Chrétiens de la Renaissance* (Paris,
1964), pp. 44–72.

Contrary to M. R. James's assertion, Dee had a large number of theological works, though they were not necessarily of the most orthodox kind. Naturally, he had numerous Bibles, and he even had a copy of the Koran. The patristic writers were well represented by such as Justin Martyr, Clement, Augustine, Cyprian, Lactantius and Eusebius, and the works of Josephus and Philo could also be found in the collection.[1] Although his library was comparatively deficient in Protestant theological writers, Dee possessed Luther's *Catechism* and *Chronica*, Thomas Rogers's *The Second Coming of Christ*, and Calvin's *Institutes* as well as his *Adversus astrologiam*.[2]

Clearly, Dee was not an ardent Protestant; nor, on the other hand, was he a reactionary Catholic. He was, I believe, a religious Hermeticist, and the number of *prisci theologi* in his library seems to substantiate this conclusion. The *prisci theologi*, who were pre-Christian but divinely inspired according to Renaissance philosophers, usually included Hermes Trismegistus (alternatively called Mercurius) and Zoroaster, Orpheus, Pythagoras and Plato, as well as Philolaus and other minor Greek philosophers. The elaborate chronology that was established for the propagation of knowledge among the *prisci theologi* was generally as follows: Plato and his predecessors, Orpheus and Pythagoras, travelled to Egypt where they learned the Mosaic oral and written philosophy and studied the secrets of Egyptian wisdom, which was assumed by some Renaissance figures to be even more ancient than that of Moses. They brought this combined knowledge back to Greece and profoundly influenced subsequent Greek philosophy, which was believed to point towards Christianity.[3] The figure of Zoroaster, who represents Chaldean wisdom, vied with Hermes, who represents Egyptian wisdom, for the significant role of being most ancient. Although Ficino, for example,

---

[1] British Museum, Harleian MS. 1879, art. 5; for the Bibles, see esp. fols. 48, *et passim*; for the Koran, see fol. 22; for Justin Martyr, see fol. 26ᵛ; for Clement, see fol. 43ᵛ; for Augustine, see fols. 47, *et passim*; for Cyprian, see fol. 65; for Lactantius, see fol. 39; for Eusebius, see fols. 39, *et passim*; for Josephus's works, see fol. 74ᵛ; for Philo's works, see fols. 22ᵛ, 28.

[2] British Museum, Harleian MS. 1879, art. 5; for Luther, see fols. 69, 89; for Rogers, see fol. 72; for Calvin, see fols. 38, 54.

[3] D. P. Walker, 'The *Prisca Theologia* in France', pp. 210–12.

alternately placed Zoroaster before and contemporary with Hermes, the latter was usually considered the most important. *priscus theologus* by Renaissance writers.[1]

Dee had copies of the Hermetic *Asclepius* and *Pimander*, as well as the edition of the *Corpus Hermeticum* produced at Paris in 1554 by the classical scholar and Hermeticist Turnebus (with whom Dee had exchanged ideas there in 1550). This important edition included the original Greek, Ficino's Latin translation, and Ludovico Lazzarelli's Latin translation of a tract unknown to Ficino.[2] Works by Zoroaster, Orpheus and Iamblichus were also to be found on Dee's shelves.[3] The large number of Plato's works has already been mentioned. Dee's virtually complete collection of *prisci theologi*, coupled with the fact that he had the works of Dionysius the Areopagite, the Christian magus, as well as a separate copy of his *De mystica theologia*, shows that John Dee was indeed deeply immersed in religious Hermeticism.[4] In addition, many of the patristic writers Dee favoured, such as Augustine, Cyprian and especially Lactantius, make frequent references to Hermes Trismegistus and the *Hermetica* in their writings.[5]

Religious Hermeticism – the whole cult of the *prisca theologia* – encouraged religious toleration and inspired a new and

---

[1] Frances A. Yates, *Giordano Bruno and the Hermetic Tradition*, p. 15. See also the next chapter of this book for additional details.

[2] British Museum, Harleian MS. 1879, art. 5; for the *Asclepius* and *Pimander*, see fol. 54; for the *Corpus Hermeticum*, see fol. 29ᵛ. On Turnebus's edition, see Walker, 'The *Prisca Theologia* in France', p. 209; also A. J. Festugière, *Hermétisme et Mystique Païenne* (Paris, 1967), p. 33. Festugière points out that the additional text inserted in the *Corpus Hermeticum* by Turnebus was in fact composed of three extracts from the Hermetic fragments of Strobeus.

[3] British Museum, Harleian MS. 1879, art. 5; for Zoroaster, see fols. 27ᵛ, 43ᵛ; for Orpheus, see fol. 46; for Iamblichus, see fol. 26.

[4] British Museum, Harleian MS. 1879, art. 5; for Dionysius, see fols. 26ᵛ, 44ᵛ; on Dionysius, see below, pp. 99 ff.

[5] On Augustine, see Walker, 'The *Prisca Theologia* in France', p. 208. On Augustine and Lactantius, see Yates, *Giordano Bruno*, pp. 6–12. Although Augustine disapproved of the *Asclepius* because of its magic, Miss Yates points out that Renaissance writers usually managed to find ways to ignore his condemnation. For the numerous references to the *Hermetica* found in the patristic writers, see *Corpus Hermeticum*, tr. A. J. Festugière with text established by A. D. Nock (Paris, 1954), IV, 104 ff.

liberal approach to religion in the sixteenth century.[1] Religious Hermeticists like Dee thought that a religion of the world, one of love and unity, could be developed through the rediscovered *prisca theologia*, and they envisioned a healing of the breach in Christendom. Religious Hermeticism did away with dogmatic theology, stressed the mystical unity of all religions and the oneness of God, and emphasized pristine Christianity and man's innate knowledge of the Divinity; the writings of the *prisci theologi* were used to support these ideas. This attitude was in striking contrast to the one taken by the Puritans in England, who spoke little of Hermeticism and toleration, but Dee none the less propounded them both and undoubtedly encouraged them among his circle.[2] His was certainly not the Puritan ethos.

John Dee's library was by no means restricted to scientific, philosophical and theological works, and the sides of his personality revealed by the wealth of books on disciplines other than those are no less relevant to understanding him as a whole. His extensive history collection reflects his passionate love of antiquarianism, as well as his obsessive concern with the establishment of an historical precedent for British empire.[3] He owned numerous manuscripts of medieval British historical works, and practically all the major productions of contemporary British antiquaries were in his library.[4] As we shall see later, Dee's nationalism was strong but, like his religion, was based on broad concepts. He had a mystical vision of Britain as the leader in reuniting Christian Europe and re-establishing the new golden age of civilization for the benefit of the entire world. Besides the British works, he had many classical historical writings, including the works of Livy, Plutarch's Greek and Roman *Lives*, and several sets each of Herodotus and Thucydides.[5]

[1] For a fuller exposition of Hermeticism, particularly John Dee's Hermeticism, see below, Chapters 4 and 5. On religious Hermeticism in the sixteenth century, see Walker, 'The *Prisca Theologia* in France'; also Yates, *Giordano Bruno*, pp. 169–89.

[2] See below, Chapter 6, for a more detailed discussion of this topic.

[3] See below, pp. 180 ff., and Chapter 8.

[4] See James, *Manuscripts formerly owned by Dr. John Dee*, p. 10, *et passim*; and British Museum, Harleian MS. 1879, art. 5, esp. fols. 71–2ᵛ.

[5] British Museum, Harleian MS. 1879, art. 5; for Livy, see fol. 25ᵛ; for Plutarch, see fols. 22ᵛ, 25ᵛ; for Herodotus, see fol. 26; for Thucydides, see fols. 26, 54ᵛ.

Dee's library was also surprisingly complete in ancient poetry. In fact, his collection of classical poets seems altogether exceptional for a man who has been represented as so scientifically oriented. Dee had three copies of Ovid's *Metamorphoses* and one of the *Ars amatoria,* three sets of the works of Homer, three of Hesiod, and two of Pindar. He also possessed the works of Theophrastus, Lucan, Statius, Vergil, Horace (including the *Ars poetica*), Theocritus and Prudentius, plus several anthologies of classical poetry.[1]

His collection of classical dramatists was also impressive. He had Seneca's works and two sets of his *Tragedies,* two sets of Euripides' *Tragedies,* and one set each of those of Aeschylus and Sophocles. Two sets of the *Comedies* of Plautus are listed in the catalogue.[2] The large amount of classical drama should arrest attention; when considered together with Dee's copies of Vitruvius's *Architectura* and Alberti's works, which were so important in the restoration of classical theatre in Europe, the collection leaves no doubt that Dee was interested in the revival of classical drama in England.[3]

John Dee was interested in the fine arts generally. He did, however, consider architecture the queen of arts and sciences. Paraphrasing Vitruvius, he writes in the 'Mathematicall Preface':

An Architect (sayeth he) *ought to understand Languages, to be skilfull of Painting, well instructed in Geometrie, not ignorant of Perspective, furnished with Arithmetike, have knowledge of many*

[1] British Museum, Harleian MS. 1879, art. 5; for Ovid, *Metamorphoses,* see fols. 20ᵛ, 38, 52ᵛ; for *Ars amatoria,* see fol. 38; for Homer, see fols. 21, 38ᵛ, 41ᵛ; for Hesiod, see fols. 33ᵛ, 41ᵛ, 43; for Pindar, see fol. 34ᵛ; for Theophrastus, see fol. 27; for Lucan, see fol. 41ᵛ; for Statius, see fol. 84; for Claudian, see fol. 57ᵛ; for Vergil, see fol. 26ᵛ; for Horace, see fol. 27 for Theocritus, see fol. 48ᵛ; for Prudentius, see fol. 49ᵛ; for the anthologies, see fols. 38ᵛ, 41ᵛ, 84ᵛ.

[2] British Museum, Harleian MS. 1879, art. 5; for Seneca, works, see fol. 26ᵛ; for Seneca, *Tragedies,* see fols. 48, 49; for Euripides, see fols. 47, 48ᵛ; for Aeschylus, see fol. 76ᵛ; for Sophocles, see fol. 48ᵛ; for Plautus, see fols. 48, 52.

[3] British Museum, Harleian MS. 1879, art. 5; for Vitruvius, see fols. 20ᵛ, 36, 41, 87; for Alberti, see fols. 35, 46, 87. On these architects and the revival of classical drama, see Campbell, *Scenes and Machines, passim;* but see especially Yates, *Theatre,* pp. 20–41, *et passim.*

histories, and diligently have heard Philosophers, have skill of
Musike, not ignorant of Physike, know the aunsweres of Lawyers,
and have Astronomie, and the courses Caelestiall, in good knowledge.

Why is so much learning necessary? Because the architect is a
universal scholar who must be able to teach, demonstrate,
describe and 'judge all workes wrought', whether it be a house,
a church, a city or the structure of the universe.[1] Dee conceived
of architecture (in this he follows Alberti) as an 'immaterial'
art whose basis is within the imagination, an art whose essence
is to be found in abstract principles of mathematical proportion and cosmic harmony. Moreover, for Dee, as for other
Renaissance Platonists, architecture had a magical dimension
because ideally structures were patterned after potent celestial
harmonies.[2] As early as 1570, Dee was making such theories –
the heart and soul of the neoclassical revival – available in
English to the rising class of Elizabethan artisans.[3]

Not unexpectedly, Dee owned works on music by Boethius
and Aristoxenus, Zarlino and Glareanus. He also possessed the
influential work by Francesco Giorgi, *De harmonia mundi*
(Venice, 1525), which develops and enriches the theory of
musica humana, mundana and *instrumentalis* descending from
Boethius. His catalogue lists the latest works on painting and
sculpture by Dürer and Gauricus, and he had Lucas Paciolus's
De divina proportione (Venice, 1509) with illustrations by
Leonardo da Vinci.[4] There were other books of a similar
nature.

Miss Yates has rightly claimed that 'the whole Renaissance

[1] John Dee, 'Mathematicall Preface', sigs. d.iii^r-^{v}.
[2] On the cosmic implications of Renaissance architecture, see Rudolf
Wittkower, *Architectural Principles in the Age of Humanism* (London, 1949);
see also Taylor, 'Architecture and Magic'. Miss Yates reprints Dee's comments on architecture in full in *Theatre*, pp. 190–7.
[3] In his introduction to Euclid's fifth book, which is on proportion, Dee
recommends: 'It ought of all other to be throughly and most perfectly and
readily knowne' (fol. 125^v).
[4] British Museum, Royal MS. 15. B. IX, contains a copy of Boethius's
De institutione musica that belonged to Dee. British Museum, Harleian MS.
1879, art. 5; for Aristoxenus, see fol. 31; for Zarlino, see fols. 21^v, 86; for
Glareanus, see fol. 22; for Giorgi, see fol. 25; for Durer, see fols. 20^v, 26^v,
75; for Gauricus, see fol. 31^v.

is in this library'.[1] But, as she suggests, it was the Renaissance of Pico and Ficino and was concerned more with philosophy, science and magic than with humanistic studies. It was a Renaissance with strong mystical leanings, one that lacked the 'doctrinal ferocity' of the Reformation and Counter-Reformation.

One could add a great many more authors and works from Dee's library to those already listed, and it should be stressed emphatically that I have not bothered to discuss the immense number of scientific works in his collection because it has been generally acknowledged that in this area Dee's library was of impressive quality and vast scope. My purpose has been to show the framework into which the scientific works should be set. None the less, one significant exception must be made. This discussion would not be complete without mention of John Dee's friend and fellow mathematician, Peter Ramus, whose works appear with notable frequency (almost a dozen items) on the library list.[2] Dee had the *Geometria, Arithmetica, Scholae in liberales artes, Dialecticae institutiones* and *De religione Christiana*, among other titles.

Ramus was a utilitarian mathematician and educational reformer who in no way appears to have been interested in the complex of metaphysical and mystical speculation that appealed so strongly to John Dee.[3] The fact that Dee was in contact with Ramus as early as 1550 and the fact that they corresponded about mathematical texts have not generally been realized; and when scholars have searched for ways in which Ramism may have entered England, Dee has never, to my knowledge, been considered.[4] Yet his close contact with the Sidney circle (which for so long has been closely associated with Ramism in England), with English mechanicians, and with other practical scientists of the time makes it possible that Dee may have linked the type of educational reform Ramus

[1] Yates, *Theatre*, p. 12.

[2] British Museum, Harleian MS. 1879, art. 5; for Ramus, various works, see fols. 28, 32, 33^v, 38, 40^v, 41^v, 43^v, 47^v, 74^v, 82^v, 84^v.

[3] R. Hookyaas, *Humanisme, Science et Réforme: Pierre de la Ramée (1515–1572)* (Leyden, 1958), p. 81, *et passim*.

[4] See, for example, Walter J. Ong, *Ramus, Method, and the Decay of Dialogue* (Cambridge, Mass., 1958), esp. pp. 351 ff.

was advocating in France with a parallel one in England. Although Dee's interest in Ramism was probably limited, the presence of so many works by the practical Ramus in Dee's library becomes intriguing when one recalls that these are mixed with much larger numbers of magical and mystical works by Ramon Lull, Trithemius, Ficino, Paracelsus and Agrippa.

Concerning Dee's library, one thing is certain: it was at the service of English scholars and mechanicians, and they frequently used it.[1] Dee had settled in Mortlake before 1570 and remained there until late in 1583. During that time, his home became a kind of academy that looked back to the earlier Platonic academies in Florence, emulated the More-Colet circle, and looked forward to the English Royal Society. At Mortlake, Dee carried on the old traditions almost undisturbed by the iconoclasm that marked the English Reformation.

How much did Dee's magnificent library influence those to whom it was readily available? This is a question I must leave unanswered at present, for though it will be broached to some extent in subsequent chapters, study of Dee and the type of thought he was trying to foster in sixteenth-century England remains at a fairly rudimentary stage.

After surveying Dee's library, one has a better idea of the books and ideas that were circulating in Elizabethan England, at least among Dee's circle. His catalogue reveals a library that was universal in scope, a collection in which antiquarians, geographers, practical scientists, architects, artists, theologians, even physicians, could find the most recent works on their subjects as well as relevant and hard-to-find pre-Reformation manuscripts. The outline I have provided in this chapter is necessarily schematic, but we have already seen that Miss Taylor has used the catalogue in her discussion of the development of English geography; F. R. Johnson has done the same in his history of English science during the period; and, more recently, Miss Yates has employed it for her researches on the evolution of architecture and drama in England. These are only three areas in which the catalogue has provided scholars

---

[1] Johnson, *Astronomical Thought*, p. 139. After Dee's death and subsequent to long litigation, his library was sold and dispersed (James, *Manuscripts formerly owned by Dr. John Dee*, pp. 5–10).

with vital information about Elizabethan England. Other significant aspects of the library that might contribute to our knowledge of the intellectual climate of the English Renaissance remain unexplored. After all, it was a Renaissance pervaded by mysticism and occultism as well as by rationality and practical science, and there was not as complete a break with the past as has often been suggested. We have seen, for instance, that vast numbers of Paracelsian and Lullist works were available in sixteenth-century England. Scholars of the time did not have trouble finding a storehouse of information about the past, nor did they have to travel to the Continent in order to keep up with the latest developments; Dee's library was readily accessible.

As his library reveals, Dee was catholic in the most fundamental sense of the word, willing to consider both sides of an argument and to synthesize when possible but unwilling to dismiss any point of view out of hand. He wished to embrace all knowledge that might be useful to man. In the vital area of religion, as well as in other areas, Dee's catalogue proves this. The works of Plato are balanced by those of Aristotle; Paracelsus' works are countered by those of Erastus (an anti-Paracelsian); opponents of astrology are represented along with its supporters; and the number of esoteric magical and mystical works is about equal to the very practical and scientific ones. The collection underlines the apparent dichotomy of John Dee's interests. Succeeding chapters will offer an explanation of this dichotomy as a coherent philosophy tied together by a pervading interest in Hermeticism and magic.

John Dee and the Hermetic Philosophy

Mortlake was ideally situated for John Dee because it was within easy access by water of London and the favourite residences of Elizabeth: Richmond, Hampton Court and Nonesuch. Barn Elms, the country seat of Secretary Walsingham, was nearby. It was also close to Syon House, home of Henry Percy, the 'Wizard Earl'. As Dee's Mortlake neighbour Goodwife Faldo told Elias Ashmole, Dee was 'wel-beloved & respected of all persons of quality thereabouts: who very often invited him to their houses, or came to his'.[1]

Apparently visitors descended on Dee's home in vast numbers. The Queen and her whole court rode out to visit her philosopher upon occasion.[2] Daniel Rogers, the diplomat and antiquary, came to see Dee at Mortlake; so did Abraham Ortelius, Rogers's famous uncle.[3] Adrian and Humphrey Gilbert, half-brothers to Sir Walter Ralegh, were frequently Dee's guests, and a visit from John Hawkins, 'who had byn with Sir Francis Drake', is noted in Dee's *Diary*.[4] Sir Francis Walsingham came to consult Dee about navigational matters with Sir Edward Dyer; both these men, and especially the latter, constantly visited Dee.[5] Sir Philip Sidney travelled to Mortlake several times, as did his uncle the Earl of Leicester;

---

[1] Ashmole, *Autobiographical and Historical Notes*, IV, 1335.

[2] John Dee, *The Private Diary*, ed. J. O. Halliwell, *Camden Society Publications*, XIX (London, 1842), 8–9, 20.

[3] Dee, *Diary*, p. 4. Ortelius's visit is not recorded in the printed *Diary* but is recorded in Bodleian, Ashmole MS. 487, next to the date 12 March 1577.

[4] Dee, *Diary*, pp. 3, 6, 8, 11, *et passim*.

[5] *Ibid.*, pp. 19, *et passim*.

and Mr Bacon 'from the court' – presumably Nicolas Bacon, father of Francis – is also recorded as a visitor.[1]

The crush of society eventually became too much for Dee. When he asked Elizabeth for the living of Saint Cross's in Hampshire in 1592, he explained:

> I would faine retyre my selfe for some yeares ensuing from the multitude and haunt of my common friends, and other, who visit me. Which thing without offense, and lose, or breach of some folkes friendship, cannot be conveniently performed, while I continually am at my house at Mortlake; the passage and way to my house there is so easy, neere, and of light cost from London or court.[2]

Though the living that Dee requested in order to pursue his philosophical studies was promised to him by the Queen through the influence of the Countess of Warwick, he never received it.[3] Perhaps he was too highly regarded to be allowed to leave. Elizabeth was shrewd.

It was during the busy years at Mortlake that much of Dee's important work was done. At last England had a resident magus and scientist equal to those who had evolved in Continental countries, and if we can deduce anything from his constant stream of visitors, Dee was exposing some of the most influential figures in Elizabethan England to his philosophy – at least in private conference.

John Dee personified the Renaissance magus in his fullest dignity (though in a rather extreme form since he came so late in time). Pico della Mirandola describes the powers of a magus in the *Oration on the Dignity of Man*:

> O supreme generosity of God the Father, O highest and most marvelous felicity of man! To him is granted to have whatever he chooses, to be whatever he wills. Beasts as soon

---

[1] Dee, *Diary*, pp. 2, 16, 20.

[2] Dee, *Rehearsal*, pp. 39–40.

[3] *Ibid.*, pp. 44–5. The Countess of Warwick was the wife of Ambrose Dudley and a favourite of Queen Elizabeth. The family of her husband, in which Dee had acted as tutor during the Duke of Northumberland's period of power, remained close to him.

as they are born (so says Lucilius) bring with them from
their mother's womb all they will ever possess. Spiritual
beings, either from the beginning or soon thereafter, become
what they are to be for ever and ever. On man when he
came into life the Father conferred the seeds of all kinds
and the germs of every way of life. Whatever seeds each man
cultivates will grow to maturity and bear in him their own
fruit. If they be vegetative, he will be like a plant. If sensi-
tive, he will become brutish. If rational, he will grow into a
heavenly being. If intellectual, he will be an angel and the
son of God. And if, happy in the lot of no created thing, he
withdraws into the centre of his own unity, his spirit, made
one with God, in the solitary darkness of God, who is set
above all things, shall surpass them all.[1]

This was the spirit of the Renaissance Hermetic tradition that
began with Ficino – to give man in his power, his intellectual
capacity, his beauty, a place beside God. The relationship
between God and man was defined in a new and revolutionary
way and was to have far-reaching results.

Dee was full of the awesome pride (as well as the abject
humility when dealing with divine things) that invested the
Renaissance magus. He bluntly proclaims, 'If in the foresaid
whole cours of his tyme, he had found a Constant & Assistant
CHRISTIAN ALEXANDER: BRYTAN, should not have bin, now,
destitute of a CHRISTIAN ARISTOTLE.'[2] In his long and informative dedicatory letter to King Maximilian that prefaces the

[1] Giovanni Pico della Mirandola, *Oration on the Dignity of Man*, tr.
Elizabeth Livermore Forbes, in *The Renaissance Philosophy of Man*, ed.
Ernst Cassirer *et al.* (Chicago and London, 1967), p. 225. Compare this
with the following quotation from the Hermetic *Asclepius* that inspired
Pico: 'And so, Asclepius, a great miracle is man, a being worthy of reverence
and honour because he enters into the nature of a god as if he himself were
a god; he is familiar with the race of demons, knowing that he issued from
the same origin; he despises that part of his nature that is only human, for
he has placed his hope in the divinity of the other part. Oh! The nature
of man is made of such a privileged mixture.' The quotation is taken from
Corpus Hermeticum, Nock and Festugière, II, 301–2. The French edition is
more accurate than any English edition of the *Corpus Hermeticum* and therefore it is used throughout this book. All translations into English are my
own.
[2] Dee, 'A necessary Advertisement', sig. Σ.*.iv.

Monas Hieroglyphica (1564), Dee stresses the rarity of the true philosopher, the complete magus. 'Of those,' he writes,

> who devote themselves wholeheartedly to philosophy you may hardly be able to name but one who has even had the first taste of the fundamental truths of natural science. Yet the republic of letters can muster only one man out of a thousand, even of those scholars who have entirely dedicated themselves to studies of wisdom, who has intimately and thoroughly explored the explanations of the celestial influences and events [as well as] the reasons of the rise, the condition, and the decline of other things.

Dee wonders, 'What, then, shall we say of him who, having surmounted all those difficulties, has aspired to an exploration and understanding of the supracelestial virtues and metaphysical influences?' Where in the whole world, he muses, might such a singular hero be found? Only one in a 'million of honest philosophers' could meet the criterion.[1] Not unexpectedly, John Dee represents himself as just the prodigy he describes, and he is perhaps justified since he had access to most of the knowledge that his age had to offer. He believed that he had embodied universal wisdom in his Hermetic treatise, *Monas Hieroglyphica*.

'All, and especially those who have a name in the more profound investigations of philosophy and wisdom,' Dee proclaims at the beginning of his dedication to Maxmilian,

> will be forced to acknowledge it [an] exceedingly rare [event] that (for the everlasting memory of men) this [work] be sealed with my London seal of Hermes, so that in it there may be not even one superfluous dot, and that not one dot may be wanting [in it] to signify those things which we have said (and things far greater yet).[2]

He predicts that grammarians will change their concepts. Arithmeticians will develop a new notion of number 'as something, as it were, concrete and corporeal' at man's service, and

[1] Dee, *Monas Hieroglyphica*, tr. Josten, pp. 117–19. Josten's translation is prefaced by a valuable introduction, and it contains numerous annotations. I shall use this edition throughout. All bracketed insertions are Josten's.

[2] *Ibid.*, p. 123.

geometers will find the principles of their art insufficiently established. Musicians, astronomers and opticians will discover that their sciences are revolutionized by Dee's work. After studying the treatise, the cabalists will recognize that their art is universal and not, as had been thought, confined to the Hebrew language; this new cabala, exemplified by the *Monas Hieroglyphica*, will reveal the secrets of the entire creation through new arts and methods.[1] But it will do even more. In order to discover the secret behind Dee's 'London seal of Hermes' and to understand what 'things far greater' than universal wisdom he thought his treatise would reveal to the *cognoscenti* – indeed, to comprehend the *Monas Hieroglyphica* and Dee's philosophy at all – we must turn to the vast and complicated topic of Renaissance Hermeticism.[2]

Marsilio Ficino, to whose academy in Florence the revival of Platonism in Renaissance Europe can be traced, translated the newly recovered *Corpus Hermeticum* at the insistence of Cosimo de Medici before he translated any of Plato's works; Plato had to wait his turn.[3] The earlier translation coloured Ficino's entire conception of Platonism, the core of which he came to view as a religious gnosis derived from Egyptian wisdom as revealed in the *Hermetica*.[4] Ficino and Cosimo both believed that the texts attributed to the legendary Hermes Trismegistus were far more ancient than the works of Plato.[5] In fact, as

[1] Dee, *Monas*, pp. 127–35.

[2] See above, p. 2, n. 2, for works on Hermeticism.

[3] It was in 1463 that Cosimo ordered the translation to be made. Ficino worked quickly and completed it before Cosimo died in 1464. He entitled the fourteen tracts that he translated – all that were known to him – *Pimander*. His contemporaries followed his lead and used the title *Pimander* to designate the *Corpus Hermeticum*, but in fact *Pimander* is the name of only the first treatise in the collection. This distinction should be kept in mind when contemporary references to the work are made. See Yates, *Giordano Bruno*, pp. 12–14. I am deeply indebted to this book by Miss Yates.

[4] Yates, *Giordano Bruno*, p. 17.

[5] Hermes is the same as the Egyptian divinity Toth, the god of learning and medicine. He was regarded as the scribe who registered the actions of the living and the dead, so they were judged by his records. He was also the revealer of the divine will to men. The Greeks took over the Egyptian divinity and fused him with their god Hermes. Sometime about the beginning of the Hellenist period the epithet Trismegistus, or Thrice-Greatest, was attached to his name. See A. J. Festugière, *La Révélation d'Hermès Trismégiste* (Paris, 1950), I, 67–88.

mentioned in the previous chapter, Ficino and a long line of philosophers succeeding him thought that Plato had imbibed the wisdom of Hermes during travels in Egypt and that this had shaped his thinking. Since the *Hermetica* supposedly preceded the writings of Plato, they were closer to the purest and earliest source of revealed wisdom and were contemporary with and perhaps even earlier than the writings of Moses. Many Renaissance figures therefore held the Hermetic writings in equal esteem with the Mosaic revelations.

A striking example of the reverence in which Hermes Trismegistus was held during the period appears in Siena's cathedral.[1] In the middle of the pavement one finds a representation of Hermes portrayed as a huge old man with a long beard, dressed in a flowing robe. Under his feet is found the inscription: 'HERMES MERCURIUS TRISMEGISTUS CONTEMPORANEUS MOYSI.' With his right hand, he extends to a deferential wise man an open book engraved with the words: 'SUSCIPITE O LICTERAS ET LEGES EGIPTII' – 'Support thy letters and laws, O Egyptians'. A man dressed in the garb of the Renaissance is standing behind the wise man in the role of spectator and witness to the ceremony. In his left hand, Hermes holds a table set on two crouching sphinxes that carries the quotation: 'DEUS OMNIUM CREATOR SECUM DEUM FECIT VISIBILEM ET HUNC FECIT PRIMUM ET SOLUM QUO OBLECTATUS EST VALDE AMAVIT PROPRIUM FILIUM QUI APPELLATUR SANCTUM VERBUM.'[2] This quotation is modified to stress the Christian implications of the Hermetic text; in the original, the second God is clearly the world rather than the Word Incarnate. The meaning of the composition is evident: Hermes Trismegistus, contemporary of Moses, was an inspired gentile prophet who foretold Christianity, the knowledge of which he had gained through his mystical association with the divine *mens*. This is how Hermes

---

[1] On the following, see Yates, *Giordano Bruno*, pp. 42–3; also Festugière, *Hermétisme et Mystique*, pp. 28–9. A reproduction of the pavement appears as a frontispiece in *Giordano Bruno*.

[2] This is a Latin abbreviation of a passage in the *Asclepius* (*Corpus Hermeticum*, Nock and Festugière, II, 304–5) conflated with one in *Pimander* (*Corpus Hermeticum*, Nock and Festugière, I, 8). 'God, the Creator of all things, made the second visible god and made him first and alone, [the second god], in whom He was well pleased, He loved deeply as [he was] His own son, who is called Holy Word.'

Trismegistus was assessed from the time of Tertullian and Lactantius until the seventeenth century. The Renaissance accepted the authenticity of the *Hermetica* on good authority, the authority of the fathers, and Dee subscribed to this traditional dating.[1]

The Hermetic texts were actually composed by various writers at the beginning of the Christian era (between A.D. 100 and 300).[2] They were probably all composed by Greek writers, and they contain a mixture of Platonism and Stoicism, some Jewish philosophy and probably some Persian.[3] It was not until 1614, however, that Isaac Casaubon, the learned philological scholar residing in England, accurately dated the *Hermetica*. The correct dating of the *Corpus Hermeticum* did much to shatter the foundation on which Renaissance magi structured their philosophy, but these texts continued to exert a considerable influence even after Casaubon's discovery.[4] During the period under consideration, however, it was not doubted that the Hermetic writings were authentic pristine revelation dating from hoary antiquity. With Hermeticism we encounter one of the mainstreams of Renaissance thought that inspired John Dee.

Before turning to the texts themselves, it should be emphasized that the *Hermetica* had an immense circulation that was not confined to esoteric circles. The *Asclepius* had been known throughout the Middle Ages, but it was Ficino's translation of the *Pimander* that instigated the full acceptance and rather astounding popularity of the Hermetic texts during the Renaissance.[5] Their impact might be compared with a modern discovery of Dead Sea scrolls that revealed revolutionary information about Christianity, but even this is not a valid comparison because religion is not the all-embracing concern today that it was during the Renaissance. At any rate, Ficino's *Pimander* was first published in 1471 and went through sixteen editions before

---

[1] Festugière, *Hermétisme et Mystique*, pp. 28–9; also below, p. 85.

[2] *Ibid.*, pp. 30–3.

[3] Festugière, *Révélation*, I, 84–7.

[4] Yates, *Giordano Bruno*, pp. 398–431; see also E. Garin's 'Note sull'ermetismo del Rinascimento', in *Testi umanistici su l'ermetismo*, pp. 9–19. It was Isaac Casaubon's son, Meric, who published Dee's 'Spiritual Diaries'.

[5] *Corpus Hermeticum*, Nock and Festugière, II, 167 ff.

the end of the sixteenth century; it also appeared with other works in many editions.[1] Despite their magical basis, even the orthodox Catholic King Philip II had almost 200 Hermetic works – among them Dee's *Monas Hieroglyphica* – in his library at the Escorial.[2] In his *History of the World*, Sir Walter Ralegh repeatedly refers with admiration to Hermes and the *Hermetica*, and a theologian like Philippe Du Plessis-Mornay also found much in the texts to include in his *A Woorke concerning the Trewnesse of the Christian Religion*.[3] These are merely a few examples chosen from literally hundreds that reflect the dispersion and influence of these writings.[4] Clearly, it was not only immensely learned magi like Ficino, Pico, Bruno, Dee and Fludd who studied the *Corpus Hermeticum* and accepted it as authentic revelation.

What did these writings that captured the Renaissance imagination contain? They are extremely diverse, but the differences were not particularly noticed, or perhaps were ignored, by most Renaissance scholars until Casaubon. Festugière has divided the Hermetic treatises into two types.[5] The earliest group, which was written during the first and second centuries, deals with astrology, magic, alchemy, and the occult sciences generally. Festugière terms the thought propounded in these 'popular Hermeticism', which differs radically from the Aristotelian conception of science and from preceding Greek rationalism as a whole.[6] A second group, written somewhat later, is concerned with philosophy and theology – essentially gnosticism. Festugière labels the content of these 'erudite Hermeticism', which revolves around a religious philosophy based on the tenet that man is able to discover the divine within himself through a mystical rapport with the world and mankind. Festugière rightly concludes that there is little in the tracts that unifies them completely; indeed,

---

[1] Kristeller, *Supplementum Ficinianum*, I, lvii–lviii, cxxix–cxxxi.

[2] Taylor, 'Architecture and Magic', pp. 102–6.

[3] Walter Ralegh, *History of the World* (London, 1687), esp. pp. 180 ff. On Du Plessis-Mornay, see below, pp. 157 ff.

[4] See above, p. 2, n. 2, for works in which their dispersion and influence is discussed in detail; also see below, Chapter 6, for further examples.

[5] Festugière, *Hermétisme et Mystique*, pp. 30–50.

[6] See below, pp. 160 ff.

they sometimes include contradictions and by no means represent a rationally coherent philosophical system.

As Festugière points out, however, there are areas of unity in the Hermetic texts, and it is the unifying elements that mattered to Ficino and his followers.[1] The most striking factor that unites the Hermetic writings is a pervasive and intense piety. They represent various individual attempts to gain salvation and intuition into the divine, though Hermes always appears as the central figure. To order phenomena as a means of approaching God, it is essential to depend on divine inspiration and direct revelation, and the divine essence embedded within man must be regenerated. These texts all support a philosophical and psychological shift from the realm of reason to the realm of belief, or faith, in scientific as well as religious matters.[2]

Invariably, the Hermetic treatises also assume, either explicitly or implicitly, an astrological cosmos wherein the lower world is ruled by the stars and the seven planets.[3] Each celestial body is in turn controlled by demons, and according to Hermetic doctrine, it is the 'governors' of the seven planets who are especially powerful. Time is also astrologized: the thirty-six decans, originally Egyptian sidereal gods, rule over the sections of the zodiac according to ten-degree divisions. Hermes explains to his pupil Tat:

> I have already hinted, my child, that there is a body that envelopes the entire world: represent this body to yourself as a circular figure, for it is the form of the All. . . . Picture now that, under the circle of this body, have been placed the 36 decans, in the middle between the universal circle and the circle of the zodiac, separating the circle of the All and circumscribing the zodiac, moving along the zodiac with the planets, and then, being at the heart of the revolution of the All, they have, alternatively, the same power as the Seven [governors].[4]

[1] Festugière, *Hermétisme et Mystique*, pp. 38–40.

[2] *Ibid.*, p. 40, and Festugière, *Révélation*, I, 1–18.

[3] Yates, *Giordano Bruno*, pp. 22, 45–6. Festugière provides an exhaustive study of Hermetic astrology in *Révélation*, I, 89–186.

[4] *Corpus Hermeticum*, tr. A. J. Festugière with text established by him (1954), III, 34–5. This astrological framework is reminiscent of Trithemius's *Steganographia*.

The religious experience of the gnostic, then, always takes place within an astrological framework, but the context is not fully deterministic since the treatises deal with ways to escape the celestial influences.

The texts actually outline two opposing ways of achieving gnosis.[1] 'Optimist' gnosticism accepts the universe as divine; God reveals himself in everything, and through his intellect, man can become like God in order to comprehend him. By a religious approach to the universe and by inscribing a representation of the universe within his own *mens*, man can ascend and unite with God. 'Pessimist' gnosticism, on the other hand, rejects the world as evil, and the material aspects of man and the universe are regarded as being a form of divine punishment. Man can escape the confines of the body (and, incidentally, any harmful celestial influences) through piety and asceticism; by elevating himself above matter, the evil nature of which is perceived through the *mens*, he can mount through the spheres to God. Though the two forms of gnostic experience are based on fundamentally different attitudes toward the material universe, both achieve their common end through the mind contemplating the universe. Since Renaissance philosophers accepted all the treatises as the revelation of Hermes Trismegistus and because several of the texts include a mixture of optimist and pessimist gnosis, the differences between the two types of gnosticism were considered only minimally.

Brief summaries of two of the treatises will convey the content and atmosphere of the Hermetic writings.[2] The tracts as a whole are in dialogue form, usually with Hermes acting as the teacher of divine mysteries, and they often culminate in a form of ecstatic illumination. My summaries will leave much out since the treatises are rather repetitive and I shall present their core as briefly as possible.

Pimander, or *Corpus Hermeticum* I, presents a story of creation in many ways resembling that found in Genesis.[3] Both accounts

[1] Festugière, *Révélation*, I, 83–4; Yates, *Giordano Bruno*, p. 22.

[2] These summaries are partly direct translation and partly paraphrase of Festugière's text. For summaries of these and other treatises, see Yates, *Giordano Bruno*, pp. 20–42.

[3] *Corpus Hermeticum*, Nock and Festugière, I, 7–19. This tract embodies a mixture of 'pessimist' and 'optimist' gnosis.

tell of an original darkness and the spirit of God brooding over primordial moisture, and both see the act of creation as being performed by the word of God (the Word, or *Logos*, being the Son of God). The *Pimander* states that man was created in the image of God and that he was given dominion over all other species, and Trismegistus and Moses use almost identical words in telling of God's command that the species should increase and multiply. In the *Pimander*, as in Genesis, a fall is recorded in which man descends from the purely intellectual sphere into the bodily sphere; and the God of the *Pimander*, like the Biblical God, grants man the ability to recapture the state from which he has fallen. Such similarities impressed Ficino and his contemporaries and were convincing proof to the Renaissance mind that Hermes had indeed been divinely inspired.

The Hermetic dialogue opens with Pimander – the *Nous*-God, or the divine *mens* – revealing himself to Hermes Trismegistus, whose corporeal senses have been suspended as though in a heavy sleep. Hermes informs Pimander that he wishes 'to be instructed about beings, to understand their nature, to know God'. Pimander's aspect then changes and Trismegistus sees a vision of limitless light, serene and joyous. Shortly afterwards, a darkness engulfs part of Pimander, and out of it, in an atmosphere of moisture, comes an indescribable fire from which issues an 'unarticulated' cry. From the light of Pimander, a 'sacred Word' emerges that covers 'Nature', and the fire then ascends from the moist region to the sublime. Pimander explains the vision: the light 'is I, *Nous*, your God, the one who existed before the humid nature that has appeared from the darkness. The luminous Word issuing from the *Nous* is the son of God.' Trismegistus, in turn, perceives in his own *mens* 'light consisting in an incalculable number of powers' and becoming a limitless world.[1] The world of luminous powers is the ideal world, the archetype of the known universe that was formed by an interior division of God's will, which received the Word and ordered the phenomenon of the universe.

The *Nous*-God subsequently creates a *Nous*-demiurge who is made of fire and air and, in turn, creates seven 'governors' who rule the sensible world. Their governance is labelled 'destiny'. After this, the *Nous*-Word unites with his brother, the

---

[1] The world in the Hermetic writings is the same as the universe.

Nous-demiurge, and the *Nous*-Word-demiurge controls the seven governors and thus the entire world.

In a pivotal section, Pimander reveals a story of man's creation that is significantly different from the account in Genesis:

> Then the *Nous*, father of all beings, being life and light, gave birth to a Man similar to himself, whom he loved as his own son. For man was beautiful, reflecting the image of his Father: for it was truly his own form with which God fell in love, and he delivered to him all his works. Then, because he had noted the creation that the demiurge had formed in the fire, Man also wanted to produce a work, and permission was granted to him by the Father. Having entered therefore into the demiurgic sphere, where he had to have full power, . . . the Governors were enamoured of him, and each gave him part of his own power.

Nature burned with love for man, since she recognized that he was imbued with the power of the seven governors and also had the form of God. Man returned her love and they coupled:

> Nature in effect, having united herself in love to Man, produced a completely astonishing offspring. . . . Incapable of waiting, [she] gave birth immediately to seven men corresponding to the nature of the Seven Governors, at the same time male and female, and mounting towards the sky.

According to the *Pimander*, then, man is of divine origin and is directly related to the star-demons. He is man as magus. How different an origin from the man created out of dust in Genesis!

Some time after man's creative act, in which he had assumed a body to consummate his love for nature, 'the bond that united all things was broken by the will of God'. From that point, Pimander explains, the man who cherishes 'the body issued from the sin of love, that one lives in darkness, erring, suffering in his senses the things of death'. But man can rejuvenate his divinity through intellect, since 'it is light and life that constitute the father of all things, and man was born of him'. 'If

73

therefore,' Pimander informs Trismegistus, 'you learn to know yourself as having been made of life and light and what the elements that constitute you are, you will return to life.' Only those men who are pious and good and pure have intellect, however; and Pimander warns that other men, evil ones, are filled with a 'vengeful demon'.

Thus, though there are striking similarities between the *Pimander* and Genesis, there is one fundamental difference: in the Hermetic treatise, man once was, and through his intellect can become again, like God. His original divine powers remain within him to be regenerated and used.

A second tract is *NOUS to Hermes*, or *Corpus Hermeticum* XI.[1] In it the divine *Nous* addresses Hermes and explains that the gnostic experience is achieved by reflecting the universe within the mind, by grasping the divine essence of the material universe and imprinting it within the psyche. This is achieved through man's divine intellect.[2]

'God is the All', begins *Nous*. He is eternity, the world, time, the future: 'God made Eternity, Eternity made the world, the world made time, time made the future.' God is therefore the source of all things. The essence of God is 'wisdom', his energy, 'intellect and soul'. 'Eternity is the power of God, and the work of Eternity is the world, which had no beginning, but which is continually becoming by the action of Eternity.' This, explains *Nous*, is why nothing in the world will ever perish or be destroyed; all is enveloped in eternity. 'God is in the intellect, the intellect is in the soul, the soul is in matter; and all things exist by means of Eternity.' The great body of the world, which contains all bodies, has a soul full of intellect and of God, who fills the interior and envelops the exterior, 'vivifying the All'.

Therefore, the treatise recommends, contemplate through me, *Nous*, 'the world which offers itself to your sight, and attentively consider its beauty'. See that the hierarchy of the skies was formed in order and follows an eternal course. Realize that all things are full of light. Look at the moon; perceive the earth

[1] *Corpus Hermeticum*, Nock and Festugière, I, 147–57. This tract embodies 'optimist' gnosis.

[2] Tract XII (*ibid.*, I, 174–83) expands on the divinity of man's intellect. For a summary of this tract, see Yates, *Giordano Bruno*, pp. 33–4.

situated at the middle of all. Consider the immense number of
mortals and immortals, and also those in between. *Nous* says
that everything is full of soul and everything is in movement.
The world is one; the moon is one; divine activity is one; and,
therefore, God must be one because he alone 'created all
things'. As all his senses prove, man cannot exist without
activity, and it is understandable that God needs to be far
more active, which is reflected constantly in his works. Things
come to life only through his activity, and 'life is the union of
intellect and soul'. Death is the rupture of this union, though
'nothing dies': material things do not dissolve in death as it
appears but instead are transformed and become invisible.

Nous admits that this view is hard to accept, but he contends
that it is absolutely true. He advises Hermes to judge this
doctrine for himself in the following manner:

> Command your soul to take itself to India, and there, sooner
> than your order, it will be. Command it to pass over the
> ocean, and in an instant it will be there, not as if it had to
> voyage from one place to another, but as if it had always
> been there. Command it to fly to heaven, it has no need of
> wings: nothing can obstruct it, neither the fire of the sun,
> nor the air, nor the revolution of the heavens, nor the other
> celestial bodies.

And if you wish, Hermes, 'to crack the vault of the universe
itself and contemplate that which is beyond (at least if there is
anything beyond the world), you can do so'. See what swiftness
and power man possesses.

> It is therefore in the same manner that you must conceive
> of God: all that is, he contains within himself like thoughts,
> the world, himself, the All. If in that event you do not make
> yourself equal to God, you cannot know God: because like is
> intelligible only to like.

For man nothing is impossible. Consider yourself immortal and
capable of understanding everything: all art, all science, the
character of every living being. Mount to the highest heights;
descend to the lowest depths. Assemble within yourself all the

sensations of creation, and be fire and water, dryness and moisture. Imagine that you are everywhere at once – on earth, in the sea, in the sky – that you are not yet born, that you are young and old, that you are dead and beyond death. 'If you embrace in thought all these things at once, time, place, substances, qualities, quantities, you will comprehend God.' What therefore, demands *Nous*, is more 'manifest than God'? He is not invisible, for it is in the miraculous power of God to reveal himself in all things. 'Intellect renders itself visible in the act of thinking, God in the act of creating.'

As *Pimander* and *NOUS to Hermes* show, the Hermetic texts glorify man as magus, and by virtue of his divine intellect (see Plates 4 and 5) they equate him with God.[1] Primordial Hermetic man was identical with astral man; the true man, in the eyes of Hermeticists like Paracelsus, Agrippa, Dee and his English follower Fludd, remained the star-demon within. On the surface, this notion seems rather innocent, but it implies a new and daring view of the universal structure, and it prepared the way for the most monumental intervention in the divine order that man had ever attempted. Through his intellect man could perform marvellous feats – it was no longer man *under* God, but God *and* man. Pico's previously quoted description of man's role in the universe fits perfectly into this Hermetic context, and so does John Dee's *Monas Hieroglyphica*. Much of the arrogant self-esteem that inspired Dee's claims about revealing universal knowledge, and strangely contrasts with his deep Christian humility, comes from this source.

The major concern of Dee's 'magic parable', the *Monas*

---

[1] Plates 4 and 5 come from Robert Fludd's massive *Utriusque cosmi maioris scilicet et minoris, metaphysica, physica atque technica historia*, which consists of two tomes with two sections each, plus an appendage (*De praeternaturali utriusque mundi historia* (Frankfurt, 1621)) to the second tome. The entire work was published in parts by Johann T. de Bry, and the main sections were issued at Oppenheim from 1617 to 1619. The technical history of its publication is confusing (see Yates, *Memory*, p. 322, n. 2). Fludd (1574–1637) succeeded Dee as England's most famous Hermetic philosopher. He may have studied many of Dee's now lost treatises, and he was profoundly influenced by Dee's 'Mathematicall Preface' to the English *Euclide*. (On Fludd's indebtedness to Dee, see Yates, *Theatre of the World*, pp. 42 ff.) We may take Fludd's illustrations as fully representative of traditional Hermetic philosophy.

Hieroglyphica, is, I believe, the gnostic ascent to the One, to God. Dee contends that, after some type of mystical

> advance has been made, he who fed [the monad] will first himself go away into a metamorphosis and will afterwards very rarely be held by mortal eye. This . . . is the true invisibility of the *magi* which has so often (and without sin) been spoken of, and which (as all future *magi* will own) has been granted to the theories of our monad.[1]

The process of man's spiritual transformation is therefore the deepest subject of this work, rather than the mundane alchemical quest for gold.[2] Anagogical understanding of Dee's work will supposedly enable man to release himself from his body and return to his original divine nature; this is the revelation 'far greater' than universal knowledge that Dee promised to the *cognoscenti*.

Dee was by no means certain whether he was introducing a new discipline or uncovering an old one. He thought that, through anamnesis, he had perhaps been able to discover within himself the secrets of the ancient magi and develop them exactly as his spiritual ancestors would have wished.[3] He also hints that, through intense inner contemplation leading to direct mystical contact with the divine *mens*, he may have learned the gnostic secrets, and his intention is to open this avenue to others who understand the *Monas Hieroglyphica*. Towards the end of the work, he explains:

> I know that, by these few [remarks], I am providing not only starting points, but conclusive proofs to those in whom inwardly there blazes fiery strength and a heavenly origin, so that they may indeed readily lend their ear to the great Democritus, announcing to those who wish to effect a healing

[1] Dee, *Monas*, pp. 135–7.

[2] For a knowledgeable alchemical interpretation of the *Monas Hieroglyphica*, see Josten's 'Introduction', esp. pp. 101 ff. On the relationship between alchemy and psychology, see Carl Jung, *Psychology and Alchemy*, tr. R. F. C. Hull (London, 1953). Though Jung's work provides some valuable insights into the psychic effects of alchemy, it is not always historically sound.

[3] Dee, *Monas*, p. 121.

of the soul and a deliverance from all distress that this doctrine is not mythical, but mystical and arcane; as also [they may listen] to that [author] who has asserted that the logos of the creative universe works by rules so that man, godly-minded and born of God, may learn by straight-forward work and by theological and mystical language.[1]

Obviously, this refers to the story of creation revealed in the *Pimander* and to man's divine origin – to man the star-demon.

Dee considered his hieroglyph (see Plate 6) – in other words, his 'London seal of Hermes' – a unified construction of signifi-cant astro-alchemical symbols that embodied the underlying unity, or *monas*, of the universe.[2] The work is meant to explain the symbol, though it does so in a purposely obscure manner.

Everything, Dee begins, is dependent upon the circle and the straight line, and these, in turn, are formed out of the point – 'hence, things first began to be by way of a point, and a monad'. He consequently places the point at the centre of all, adding that it is also meant to represent the earth. Around the earth revolve the sun (the circle), the moon (the interlocking crescent), and the other planets.[3] Though it 'appears here to be, as it were, above the solar circle', the moon always 'respects the Sun . . . as her master and King'. The sun and moon are

[1] Dee, *Monas*, pp. 199–201.

[2] Josten ('Introduction' to Dee's *Monas*, p. 106) suggests that Dee may have based his concept of *monas*, an 'essential oneness', on the *Smaragdine Table*, the bible of the alchemists that was attributed to Hermes Trisme-gistus. As a more immediate source, Josten points to Agrippa's *De occulta philosophia*, II, iii. Both of these are plausible, and indeed likely, sources. The idea of oneness, however, pervades the *Corpus Hermeticum*. Spiritual regeneration, which is the essential concern of Dee's *Monas Hieroglyphica*, is also a fundamental preoccupation of the then newly discovered *Hermetica*. Dee clearly believed he was moving away from the old alchemy and developing a new and more efficacious discipline that included the cabala and much more. Paracelsus was the chief exponent of the new alchemy with its cabalist and other accretions (see Walter Pagel, *Paracelsus* (Basel and New York, 1958)). Dee possessed a vast number of Paracelsian works and they must have been a major source for his *Monas Hieroglyphica*, but one should not underestimate Dee's originality in developing a new alchemy. After all he thought that no one, not even the ancient sages, had completely understood the arcana that invest his hieroglyph, and his work was popular among the *cognoscenti*.

[3] Dee, *Monas*, p. 155.

shown intersecting to suggest their conjunction and generative faculty. That this faculty exists is proven, 'surely', by the fact that 'one day was made out of evening and morning by joining the lunar half-circle to its solar complement'.[1]

Both the sun and the moon rest on a 'rectilinear cross' that represents the ternary and the quaternary. The ternary supposedly consists of 'two straight lines and one point which they have in common and which, as it were, connects them'. The quaternary, on the other hand, is composed of 'four straight lines including four right angles, each [line being] (for this purpose) twice repeated'.[2] Somewhat mystifyingly, the cross also signifies the 'octonary' in a 'most secret manner' that earlier magi never understood but that the initiated reader 'will especially note'; this reference is apparently to the eight linear edges of the cross. Dee carries his analogies even further. He sees the cross as a symbol of the 'septenary' too. Claiming that the 'magical ternary' of our earliest 'forefathers and wise men consisted of body, spirit, and soul', Dee thinks it manifest that 'a remarkable septenary, [consisting] to be sure of two straight lines and a point which they have in common, and of four straight lines separating themselves from one point', is contained in the cross. More than this, Dee suggests that the secret of the four elementary compounds (heat, cold, moisture, dryness) is 'intimated by the four straight lines going forth from one indivisible point and into opposite directions'.[3] From the numerous permutations of the cross, all of which Dee sees as symbolic, one gets a good idea of the extraordinary complexity of the hieroglyph.[4] At the bottom of the cross, appearing as two connecting half-circles, is the sign of Aries, which shows 'that [in the practice of this monad] the aid of fire is required'. All of the planets also exist within the hieroglyph since their astrological symbols, Dee explains, are composed

[1] Dee, *Monas*, p. 157.

[2] Dee, *Monas*, p. 157. In a note to this passage Josten suggests, 'It means that, when the cross is considered as formed from four right angles, four pairs of lines containing these angles coincide in one line each.'

[3] Dee, *Monas*, pp. 157–9.

[4] In a later passage (*Monas*, pp. 169–71), Dee speculates again on the symbolism of the cross. He develops some extremely obscure alphabetical and numerological interpretations and invests them all with an arcane meaning.

from those of the sun, the moon, the elements, and Aries.[1]

In the rest of the work, Dee expatiates on his hieroglyph. He emphasizes that everything depends upon 'the Sun and Moon', develops the significance of the sign of Aries, points out that all is contained within the ovular form of the alchemist's egg (which may be meant to recall the Hermetic 'All'), provides detailed mathematical instructions for the proportional construction of the hieroglyph, and so forth. Dee states that in neither the elemental, nor the celestial, nor the supercelestial world is there 'any power, created influential' with which the monad 'is not absolutely enriched and endowed'. He praises 'the most good and great God' for granting men, through the monad, 'such great wisdom, power over other creatures, and large dominion'.[2] It is not difficult to comprehend Dee's excitement about his discovery of this supposedly powerful hieroglyph.

The *Monas Hieroglyphica*, with its attendant symbol, was popular among Dee's learned contemporaries.[3] Since Dee wrote within an oral and secretive alchemical tradition that has probably been permanently lost to us, many aspects of the work must necessarily elude modern interpreters. Despite Meric Casaubon's conclusion that the work is not 'very dark or mystical'. it is saturated with difficult problems of interpretation.[4] Even a cursory reading reveals its esoteric complexity. Nevertheless, it is clear that Dee was attempting to discover a symbol that would embody the entire universe and, when understood and engraved within the psyche, would enable men to achieve that gnostic regenerative experience of which *Nous*

[1] Dee, *Monas*, pp. 159–61. Fire was an essential ingredient in the alchemical process, and one should remember that it also played an important role in the creation described in the *Pimander*.

[2] Dee, *Monas*, p. 217.

[3] See Josten, 'Introduction' to Dee's *Monas*, pp. 85 ff. Among those who admired Dee's treatise and adopted his hieroglyph, Josten mentions Petrus Bongus, Jacob Behmen, Athanasius Kircher, John Winthrop and his son, Wait Still Winthrop, and grandson, John Winthrop. The symbol was also reproduced by Robert Fludd in his answer to Kepler's attack on his philosophical system (*Veritatis proscenium*, in *Utriusque cosmi . . . historia*, II, 33). Michael Maier used the *Monas Hieroglyphica* as a source for his book of emblems (see H. M. E. De Jong, '*Atalanta Fugiens*': *Sources of an Alchemical Book of Emblems* (Leyden, 1969), *passim*).

[4] Meric Casaubon, 'Preface' to *A True & Faithful Relation*, p. 38.

spoke to Hermes Trismegistus. Dee was afraid to let such knowledge become available to ordinary men who might misuse it; he wanted only the most learned magi to understand his daring speculations. Although there was little danger that laymen would grasp the concepts, Dee's fear does account at least partially for the intentional obscurity of the work.

The fact that John Dee was essentially a secretive man can hardly be over-emphasized. When he was in prison in 1555, an unnamed doctor felt that banishment from England would be proper punishment because Dee refused under any circumstances to 'communicate any part, of his learned Talent, by word or writing: But is wholy addicted, to his private commodity only avancing, by his own Studies and practises very secret'.[1] In rebuttal, Dee asserted that he had served his country with his learning and that this doctor's accusation was untrue. The objection is only partially justified. By the time of Dee's imprisonment, it is true, he had already tutored Sir William Pickering, the Earl of Warwick, and Richard Chancellor, the navigator, and he had produced manuscripts for various patrons. By 1555, however, he had not published any books, though his contemporaries clearly expected him to do so. In one part of his mind, John Dee refused to disseminate his knowledge prodigally in print; in another part, he felt obligated to help his countrymen through his immense learning. Miss Yates is probably correct in holding that Dee's position as a late-Renaissance magus helps to explain this ambiguity. He clearly felt the necessity of publishing such works as his augmentation of Robert Recorde's *Grounde of Artes* in 1561, his 'Mathematicall Preface' and annotations to the English *Euclide* in 1570, and his *General and Rare Memorials pertayning to the Perfect Arte of Navigation* in 1577. On other matters, however, the worsening religio-political situation in Europe during the last half of the sixteenth century undoubtedly overpowered claims of patriotism and forced the Renaissance magus to become a secretive type.[2]

A long tradition stood behind Dee's secrecy. The Hermetic texts that spawned the Renaissance magus advocate secrecy,

[1] Dee, 'A necessary Advertisement', in *General and Rare Memorials*, sig. Σ.ii.

[2] Yates, 'The Hermetic Tradition', pp. 263–4.

especially in religious matters. The cabala – an integral part of Renaissance magical theory – was considered to be the oral part of God's revelation to Moses and consequently was so sacred that it could be explained to none but the most learned and pious of men. Pythagoras, another figure who inspired Renaissance magi, never committed his philosophy to writing, and his school was as much a religious society as a philosophical academy. Writing within this secretive tradition, the Abbot Trithemius of Sponheim admonishes Agrippa after reading the *De occulta philosophia*: '*Yet this one rule I advise you to observe, that you communicate vulgar secrets to vulgar friends, but higher and secret to higher, and secret friends only.*'[1] Referring to Ripley's *Compound of Alchymy* (alchemy was the paradigmatic Hermetic science) Dee argues:

> The learned will (no doubt) delight therein,
> And their delight will draw them on to skill:
> Admit the simple force it not a pin,
> So much more the wise embrace it will.[2]

Not only did arcane secrets have to be kept from the 'vulgar', but the overtly magical (and hence dangerous) side of Hermeticism had to be indulged in with the utmost caution. The magical in Hermeticism cannot be separated from the mystical and religious since the gnostic existed in an astro-magical universe.[3] Magic enabled man to become *Aion*. It did more than that, however; it provided conjuring formulae to control the planetary gods and protect the soul during its upward journey.[4]

Renaissance Hermetic magic was an enlightened and refined discipline and quite different from the dark and primitive black magic of the Middle Ages.[5] The medieval church had banned

[1] Agrippa, *Occult Philosophy*, sig. A5.

[2] John Dee, 'Prefatory verses' to *The Compound of Alchymy* by George Ripley, set forth by Ralph Rabbards (London, 1591), sig. *2.

[3] Yates, *Giordano Bruno*, pp. 44–61. Festugière devotes the first volume of his massive *Révélation* to the occult sciences since they form the cosmological framework in which religious gnosticism must be set. Dee refers to his own Hermetic work as a 'magic parable' (*Monas*, p. 135).

[4] Festugière, *Révélation* (1954), IV, 199.

[5] Yates, *Giordano Bruno*, pp. 17–19, 79–81.

magic and therefore forced the magician to practise his proscribed art in secrecy. Magicians of the Middle Ages were persecuted as heretical disturbers of God's order; they were feared as persons who maintained contacts with evil demons and served the devil. Although powerful individuals did employ magicians secretly, they were hardly admired as respectable philosophers and essentially remained social outcasts.

Reformed Renaissance magic was extremely learned and sophisticated and, as has been mentioned, frequently formed an integral part of the thought of esteemed Renaissance philosophers: Ficino, Pico, Bruno, Campanella and Dee, among others.[1] The Renaissance had rediscovered classical magical texts and, as in so many other movements of the period, the classical discoveries instigated refinement. Readers of authors like Plato, Iamblichus, Zoroaster, Orpheus, Synesius, and of such all-important writings as those attributed to Hermes Trismegistus, could hardly view the magician as inferior. Most of the highly esteemed *prisci theologi* were also *prisci magi*. Pico concluded, for example, that Zoroaster's magic 'was none other than the science of the Divine in which the kings of the Persians instructed their sons, to the end that they might be taught to rule their own commonwealth by the example of the commonwealth of the world'.[2]

There was never a complete break between medieval and Renaissance magic.[3] Both were based on similar assumptions. The universe continued to be conceived of as ordered, earth centred and essentially astrological; the stars were thought to be living creatures influencing, though not necessarily determining, the actions of everything below. Both the magicians of the Middle Ages and those of the Renaissance believed in a *spiritus mundi*; this was fundamental to magical operations. Sympathy and antipathy between all things remained an essential tenet of Renaissance magic. Talismans and invocations were also used; though instead of being horrific charms so common in medieval magic, they were more in the nature of

[1] On Renaissance magic, see Walker, *Magic*; Yates, *Giordano Bruno*, *passim*. Also see below, Chapter 5.
[2] Pico della Mirandola, *Oration*, pp. 247–8.
[3] Yates, *Giordano Bruno*, pp. 79–81.

Dee's monad. In effect, the Renaissance absorbed medieval magic and transformed it after the discovery of its classical origins.

Writing to Trithemius, Agrippa discusses one of the most pressing contemporary problems about the status of magic which,

> whereas it was accounted by all ancient Philosophers the chiefest Science, & by ancient wisemen, & Priests was always had in great veneration, came at last after the beginning of the Catholike Church to be alwaies odious to, and suspected by the holy fathers, and then exploded by Divines, and condemned by sacred Canons, and moreover by all laws, and ordinances forbidden.[1]

Dee expresses similar views in the 'Tuba Veneris', but he suggests that magic – essentially an 'Ars pia' – was forbidden by ecclesiastical and secular authorities because chthonic spirits had insinuated themselves into it.[2] The Church, of course, had magical rituals of its own and could not stand by and let its jealously guarded prerogative be infringed upon by magicians.

The rediscovered *prisca theologia* did much to rehabilitate magic during the Renaissance, and no texts of any *priscus theologus* were more important to this purpose than those ascribed to Hermes Trismegistus. Since he had imbibed his religious beliefs from their pristine source – the divine *mens* – it was assumed that the magic that saturates the Hermetic texts and is almost impossible to excise from them was also direct revelation from God. Such magic could not possibly be evil.[3] Thomas Tymme sums up the contemporary attitude among the learned toward the magical Hermetic religion in a preface to an intended translation of the *Monas Hieroglyphica* done in the early seventeenth century. He writes that the Egyptians were

> had in admiracion of all their neighbour Countrys round about them & for yᵉ cause Hermes, who lived about Moses tyme, was truly called trismegistus because he was a King

[1] Agrippa, *Occult Philosophy*, sig. A₂ᵛ.

[2] John Dee, 'Tuba Veneris', Warburg Institute, Warburg MS. FBH 510, fol. 6.

[3] There were those, of course, who took exception to this attitude, most notably in France; on this, see Walker, '*Prisca Theologia*', pp. 204–59.

a Priest & a Prophet, a Magus, & Sophas, a famous Aegiptian Philosopher, excellent in the knowledge of natural things.[1]

This 'knowledge of naturall things' – in other words, magic – had, according to some accounts, been passed on to Moses. In the 'Mathematicall Preface', Dee points out that *'Moses was instructed in all maner of wisedome of the Aegyptians: and he was of power both in his wordes and workes'*. Dee specifically conceives of this wisdom as magical. He concludes, 'You see this philosophicall Power & Wisedome, which Moses had, to be nothing misliked of the Holy Ghost.'[2] If Hermes and Moses could practise magic why not the Renaissance magus?

Hermeticism raised man from the status of a pious and awestruck observer of God's wonders and encouraged him to operate within his universe by using the powers of the cosmos to his own advantage. The Hermetic *Asclepius* contains some remarkable passages in which man is cited with *approval* as the maker of earthly gods. The first is as follows.[3] 'Even as the Lord and the Father or, to give him his most exalted name, God, is the creator of heavenly gods, so is man the maker of the gods who reside in the temples.' Not only does man receive life, 'but he gives it in turn; not only does he progress towards God, but he even creates gods'. Asclepius appears confounded by this pronouncement, and Hermes wonders whether he is admiring 'the true faith', or mocking it 'as most do'. Then Asclepius asks if Hermes refers to the statues in the temples. 'Yes, the statues, Asclepius. See how you yourself lack faith! But these statues possess a soul, consciousness; they are full of vital spirit, and they can accomplish an infinity of marvels.' They are able to predict the future through 'dreams and other good methods', and they can give 'joy or sorrow' to man according to his 'merits'.

Later Hermes explains the process by which man makes gods.[4] He claims that all of man's other abilities are as nothing compared with the one 'that commands the highest admiration,

---

[1] Bodleian, Ashmole MS. 1459, fol. 473.
[2] Dee, 'Mathematicall Preface', sig. A.iiii.
[3] *Corpus Hermeticum*, Nock and Festugière, II, 325–6. My translation. For a complete summary of the *Asclepius*, see Yates, *Giordano Bruno*, pp. 35–40.
[4] *Corpus Hermeticum*, Nock and Festugière, II, 347–9.

which is that man has been made able to discover the nature of gods, and to produce it'. Our earliest ancestors devised the art of making gods by adding to statues 'an appropriate virtue, which they took from material nature'. This virtue consists of a 'composition of herbs, of stones, and of odours, which contain in themselves an occult virtue of divine efficacy'. Also, since 'they could not properly create souls, after having invoked the souls of demons or angels, they introduced them into their idols by sacred and divine rites, in such a way that these idols had the power of doing good and evil'. Finally, Hermes informs Asclepius that, by pleasing these gods with 'numerous sacrifices, hymns, chants of praise', and sweet concerts recalling 'the harmony of heaven', the celestial element that has been introduced into them 'by the repeated practice of celestial rites' will 'joyously' assure that they remain 'long among men'. In this way men make gods.

It is evident that the Hermetic texts not only exalted man as magus, but approved both natural and demonic magic. And though the above passages in the *Asclepius* are in conflict with Biblical strictures against idols and were condemned by Augustine for their idol-making and use of demons, the Renaissance magus brushed these problems aside.[1] After all, the idols commended by Hermes, the most pious of priests who foretold the coming of Christianity, were very different from those condemned in the Bible – the creation of the Egyptian terrestrial gods involved only good demons. Also, Augustine had not known many of the more pious treatises of the *Corpus Hermeticum*, and therefore could not have understood the religious context in which the *Asclepius* must be set. This was the reasoning of the magus. The power of this argument should not be underestimated because Renaissance magi saw a world of difference between dealing with angels and dealing with devils. Such reasoning led, for instance, to Dee's attempts at demonic magic, about which he always protested that his practices were pious and religious because he never dealt with evil demons. One of his chief sources for this argument would have been the approval of demonic magic in the *Asclepius*.[2]

[1] On Augustine, see Yates, *Giordano Bruno*, pp. 9-12, 41-2.
[2] On Dee's angelic magic, see below, pp. 110 ff.

It was out of the Hermetic texts, then, that the Renaissance magus developed his philosophy. The original religious and magical core of Hermeticism underwent many transformations after being introduced to the Renaissance by Ficino, whose own magic was inspired by the *Asclepius*.[1] It was enriched and emboldened at the hands of magi like Pico, Agrippa, Bruno and Dee.[2] Eventually, a philosophy evolved in which Pythagorean numerology, mystical geometry, music, astrology, the cabala, the theory of the four elements, the microcosm-macrocosm relationship and the Lullian art were inextricably tied together with the original Hermetic revelations. The universe was seen as a complex web of interacting forces that man was capable not only of understanding (as had always been the case with Aristotelian science) but of manipulating, even to the point of using God's angels for his own advancement. The belief in the manipulatory ability of man is all-important. The revival of Hermeticism marks the dawn of the scientific age because it unleashed the driving spirit that inspired man to compel natural forces to serve him to an extent never dreamed of before.[3]

The magus envisioned by Pico in the *Oration on the Dignity of Man* and embodied in John Dee combined *magia* with the cabala, joining the Hermetic natural magic introduced by Ficino with the contemplative cabala (which also had its practical side) established by Pico.[4] The magus believed he could operate in the lower worlds of the universe through non-demonic magic, but it was cabalist angel-magic that, he thought, enabled him to operate in the supercelestial or angelic world, the third world of the cabalist universe. A Christian magus like Dee also connected cabalist demonic

[1] On Ficino's magic, see Walker, *Magic*, pp. 3 ff.; and Yates, *Giordano Bruno*, pp. 62–83.

[2] On the development of the Hermetic tradition, see Yates, *Giordano Bruno*. The tradition is appallingly complex, but Miss Yates has outlined it brilliantly in this book. Dee lived near the end of the Renaissance when the tradition was evolving in more extremely occult as well as more overtly scientific directions, and this is why he so often seems to embody contradictory attitudes.

[3] See below, pp. 160 ff.

[4] See below, pp. 111 ff.

operations with the celestial hierarchies of pseudo-Dionysius, thereby cloaking unorthodox demonic magic with the approval of a respected Christian authority.[1] It was not the universe that had changed for the Renaissance magus; it was the role of man that was perceived anew.

[1] On pseudo-Dionysius and magic, see below, pp. 99 ff.

Magic, Science and Religion

Marsilio Ficino, who inspired the widespread Hermetic movement through his translation of the *Corpus Hermeticum* and thus
helped to rehabilitate the magic of the *Asclepius*, practised his
magic within the Chaldean-Ptolemaic framework that had
been accepted throughout the Middle Ages. In this he was
followed by Pico and Agrippa, Dee and Fludd, and a host of
others. The astronomical system within which magi operated
well into the seventeenth century (see Plate 7) put the earth
at the centre of the universe, surrounded by the spheres of the
three other elements – water, air, fire – followed by the spheres
of the moon, two of the planets, the sun, and then the other
three known planets. Then there was the sphere of the fixed
stars, the sphere of the orders of angels and, above them all,
God.

The rediscovered Hermetic texts changed man's view of his
role in this universe (note that the first sphere under God in
Plate 7 is *mens*), and they inspired him, as we have seen, to
attempt to operate with the forces of nature through magic. This
revolutionary attitude had a profound effect on John Dee's
thought. Hermeticism pervades his natural magic, his science
and his religion, all of which can be subsumed under *magia*
in its broadest sense.

Renaissance magic is an extremely complex subject, as is
revealed by Agrippa's survey, *De occulta philosophia*. It should
be mentioned here that certain philosophers like Cardanus –
an extremely learned magus – despised the *De occulta philosophia*
as a trifling affair that deserved to be burned; the astronomer
Tycho Brahe, who was not averse to magic and who admired

Dee, considered Agrippa's work vain and useless.[1] Nevertheless, the book was enormously influential, and was used constantly by John Dee. Since Dee functioned within the Agrippan framework, I shall depend on the *De occulta philosophia* for many of my comments about Renaissance *magia*.

Dee's *Monas Hieroglyphica*, so popular with the *cognoscenti*, is a magical, Hermetic work; it represents the magus at his most abstruse and introverted. His other famous and widely acclaimed work, the 'Mathematicall Preface' to the English *Euclide*, was written primarily for less educated mechanicians, not magi.[2] Among other things, in the preface Dee presents a clear and easily comprehensible outline of his magical philosophy. Though rightly admired for its lucid discussion of practical science, I believe the 'Mathematicall Preface' was inspired by *magia*.

Dee opens the preface with a description of the triadic universe formulated by Plato. For Plato, as for John Dee and other Renaissance magicians, the universe was divided into '*Unum, Bonum,* and *Ens*'. Expatiating on this basic idea, Dee explains:

> All thinges which are, & have beyng, are found under a triple diversitie generall. For, either, they are demed Supernaturall, Naturall, or, of a third being. Thinges Supernaturall, are immateriall, simple, indivisible, incorruptible, & unchangeable. Things Naturall, are materiall, compounded, divisible, corruptible, & chaungeable. Thinges Supernaturall, are, of the minde onely, comprehended: Things Naturall, of the sense exterior, ar hable to be perceived. In thinges Naturall, probabilitie and conjecture hath place: But in thinges Supernaturall, chief demonstration, & most sure Science is to be had. By which properties & comparasons of these two, more easily may be described, the state, condition, nature and property of those thinges, which we before termed of a third being: which, by a peculier name also, are called *Thynges Mathematicall*.[3]

[1] Thorndike, *Magic and Experimental Science*, V, 138. See above, p. 30, n. 1, for works on Agrippa.

[2] On the dispersion of the *Euclide* and the importance assigned to Dee's 'Mathematicall Preface', see below, Chapter 7.

[3] Dee, 'Mathematicall Preface', sig. *v.

In this passage, Dee assumes the same universal structure as Agrippa uses in the *De occulta philosophia*. Agrippa writes that all magic or, as he terms it, 'regulative philosophy' is 'divided into Naturall, Mathematicall, and Theologicall'.[1]

The lowest kind of magic in the universe was natural magic. One of the most influential natural magicians of the Renaissance was John Baptista della Porta whose *Magia naturalis* was first published in 1558 and went through at least six Latin editions before being translated into English in 1658.[2] For della Porta, natural magic 'is nothing else but the survey of the whole course of Nature'.[3] His book, which is really a popularized miscellany of natural magic, includes such diverse chapters as 'Of Beautifying Women' and 'Of Pneumatick Experiments'. The underlying thesis of della Porta's work is that, by studying the antipathies and sympathies of natural objects, one can perform miracles – miracles, by the way, of a distinctly different type from those performed by saints. Natural magic did not violate the laws of nature; rather, it was the discipline by which the magus learned to develop natural powers. It was a thoroughly practical art that enabled man to operate on one level of reality as it was perceived in the sixteenth century. Agrippa defines this lowest realm of magic as the philosophy that 'teacheth the nature of those things which are in the world, searching and enquiring into their Causes, Effects, Times, Places, Fashions, Events, their whole, and Parts, also'.[4] Dee was in complete accord with this definition.

In the broadest terms, natural magic depended on a belief that the effluvia of the celestial bodies affected the lower world. Hermetic philosophers viewed the stars (I use the word to represent all heavenly bodies) as superior organisms through which God channelled his powers. The sun, the planets and the constellations supposedly consisted of eternal fire and, through the energies they emitted, unceasingly influenced those things below. Everything was affected – the natural world as well as

[1] Agrippa, *Occult Philosophy*, I, 3.
[2] Dee had a copy of this book (British Museum, Harleian MS. 1879, art. 5, fol. 39ᵛ).
[3] John Baptista della Porta, *Natural Magick* (London, 1658), p. 2.
[4] Agrippa, *Occult Philosophy*, I, 3.

individuals.[1] The natural magician operated by manipulating the powers of astral bodies. For instance, if one wished to attract the beneficent powers of the sun, one had to know which plants, stones, metals and so forth were particularly sympathetic to it. By forming sun talismans from only those objects that attracted the sun's influence, one could capture its energies and put them to use. The same was true, of course, of all other astral bodies.

A belief in astrology, then, is essential to the theory of natural magic, but only a belief in good astrology. What might well be termed astral magic does not by any means indicate a faith in judicial astrology, or the forecasting of predetermined events. In speaking of the soul of the world, Agrippa explains how astrological magic works:

> There is therefore such a kind of spirit required to be, as it were the *medium*, whereby Celestiall Souls are joyned to gross bodies, and bestow upon them wonderfull gifts. This spirit is after the same manner in the body of man. For as the powers of our soul are communicated to the members of the body by the spirit, so also the Vertue of the Soul of the World is diffused through all things by quintessence.[2]

Dee certainly viewed astrology as an astral magic. In his preface, he defines the science as 'an Arte Mathematicall, which reasonably demonstrateth the operations and effectes, of the naturall beames, of light, and secrete influence: of the Sterres and Planets: in every element and elementall body: at all times, in any Horizon assigned'. Dee explains further, 'We, also, daily may perceave, That mans body, and all other Elementall bodies, are altered, disposed, ordred, pleasured, and displeasured, by the Influentiall working of the *Sunne*, *Mone*, and other Starres and Planets.' As evidence of the type of astrological influence he has in mind, Dee mentions the working of the magnet and the ebb and flow of rivers and the sea. John Dee was, as he terms it, a 'modest *Astrologien*'. He was not, as the definition of astrology in the preface makes absolutely clear, an horrific charlatan who preyed upon deluded men

[1] Festugière, *Révélation*, I, 90.

[2] Agrippa, *Occult Philosophy*, I, 33.

and women like 'the common and vulgare *Astrologien*, or Practiser'. Indeed, he scorned the 'Light Practisers' of the science even more than the 'Light Belevers' and the 'Light Despisers' of it.[1]

There can be no doubt that Dee was deeply immersed in natural astral magic. His earliest full-length publication, *Propaedeumata Aphoristica* (1558), presents a detailed explanation of his theories about the subject.[2] The main body of the text consists of 120 aphorisms that account for the functioning of the physical universe according to magical principles.

Dee begins by stating that everything, against reason and natural laws, was created by God 'from nothing'. Therefore, it is irrational to assume that man can either transform into nothingness things that already exist or create things from nothingness, since the laws of creation were set down by the supernatural God and are under his dominion. Man is capable, however, of performing great miracles through artificial methods (science).[3] Hidden in nature, Dee insists, is another 'Esse' besides those natural traits that are 'conspicuously apparent', and man can employ this hidden energy to his advantage. It is manifested in the 'circular rays' that are emitted from everything and that fill the universe. Substances as well as accidents produce rays, but substantial rays are more efficacious than accidental ones. The powers of the rays are determined by the bodies from which they flow, as well as the ones upon which they act, and the rays are known only through the effects they produce. Each ray, even though similar to another, has a different effect; and without disparities as well as similarities nothing is achieved in the practice of magic: 'Whatever is in the universe has order and harmony in relation to everything else.'[4] Therefore, Dee concludes, the world is like a lyre. He explains that the overall structure of the universe, its harmonies and dissonances, sympathies and antipathies, determines the sweet and infinite variety of the marvellous

[1] Dee, 'Mathematicall Preface', sigs. b.iii–b.iiii.

[2] Dee states that he wrote the treatise at the behest of Gerard Mercator and Antonius Gogava ('Mathematicall Preface', sigs. b.iii^v–b.iiii).

[3] John Dee, *Propaedeumata Aphoristica* (London, 1558; reprinted, 1568), sig. a.i.

[4] Dee, *Aphoristica*, sig. a.i.^r–v. 'Quicquid in mundo est, ad aliud quid ordinem habet & Convenientiam.'

music drawn from the individual strings.[1] This is the cardinal proposition of Dee's *Propaedeumata Aphoristica*. It is the cardinal proposition of all Renaissance magical philosophy.

Man's own senses are not 'causes, but witnesses', even of the sensible effluences of the universe. The senses, along with man's spirit and mind, do form an integral part of the universal system, however; they are all subject to the effluvia from the heavenly bodies. 'Sometimes', celestial powers are transmitted 'through light and sometimes without light: not down to the sight alone, but now and then down to the other senses, and mainly into our imaginative spirit so that they coalesce more intensely, as in a mirror; show us wonders, and work wonders within us'.[2] Thus, marvels are performed through the coalescing of natural forces within man's imagination. Like other Hermetic philosophers (see Plate 8), Dee attaches great weight to the imaginative faculty of the psyche; natural magic and the Hermetic experience both depend on it. The role of the imagination outlined in the *Propaedeumata Aphoristica* is cognate to the functioning of Dee's 'seal of Hermes', his symbol of the monad. As we have seen, this astro-alchemical hieroglyph was supposed to have a powerful unifying effect on the mind, and when understood and engraved in the psyche, it was to cause marvellous transformations within man. Since the hieroglyph is the central feature of the title page of the *Propaedeumata Aphoristica*, Dee perceived his symbol, on one level of interpretation, as the embodiment of his theory of natural magic.

After touching on the role of man's imagination, Dee discusses movement and light. He emphasizes that perfect motion is circular and that light was the first and most sublime creation.

---

[1] Dee, *Aphoristica*, sig. a.ii. 'Sicut lyra constitutio quaedam est tonorum consonantium atque; dissonantium aptissima tamen ad suavissimam & infinita varietate mirabilem exprimendam harmoniam: Sic Mundus iste partes intra se complectitur, inter quas arctissima conspiciatur Sympathia: alias autem inter quas dissidium acre, atque; antipathia notabilis ita tamen, ut tum illarum conspiratio mutua tum istarum lis atque; dissentio, ad Totius consensionem atque; unionem admirandam egregiè faciat.'

[2] Dee, *Aphoristica*, sigs. i.ii^{r-v}. The effluences pour down 'tum lumen tum sine lumine: non ad visum solum, sed ad alios interdum sensus, & praecepuè in Spiritu nostro imaginali, tanquam Speculo quodam coalescunt, seseque; nobis ostendunt, & in nos mirabilia agunt'. Dee seems to be thinking of a concave mirror.

Therefore, organisms composed preponderantly of these two pre-eminent qualities are the most distinguished in the universe; and since celestial bodies possess the most light and perfect movement _they naturally control the motion and order of things in the lower world.[1]

Next, Dee briefly outlines the function of the four elements in the universal hierarchy.[2] In line with the ancient philosophers, he tells the reader that the four elements are the fundamental ingredients of the lower world and, somewhat mysteriously, adds that they have secondary and tertiary 'principles'. By understanding the nature of the elements and by properly using their essences, Dee insists that man can produce diverse and even contrary effects. Combinations of heat, cold, moisture and dryness constitute the true temperaments of everything; following tradition, Dee relates these natural qualities to the bodily humours. He concludes his exposition by stressing that 'the seed contains the power of generation', but the stars always control the development of elemental forces.

At this point in his argument, Dee draws a striking analogy. He compares the invisible natural forces with the visible powers of the magnet which performs at a distance and penetrates matter with its rays.[3] The impressions of celestial bodies on things in the lower world are, Dee contends, like images on seals because the relative 'refinement' and 'strength' of the impressions depend on the material upon which the stars imprint their effluvia, as well as on the power of the penetrating rays.[4]

Much of the subsequent part of the *Propaedeumata Aphoristica* is devoted to pleas for more accurate astronomical observations so that the celestial influences might be better employed. Dee suggests that, by understanding and canalizing the powers streaming from astral bodies, the magus can achieve more with his science than nature does unaided.[5] He cites catoptrics as an example.

Although Dee assumes the Ptolemaic system throughout the

---

[1] *Ibid.*, sig. a.ii^v.
[2] *Ibid.*, sigs. a.ii–a.3.
[3] *Ibid.*, sig. a.3^v.
[4] *Ibid.*, sig. a.iiii.
[5] *Ibid.*, sig. B.iiii^v.

Propaedeumata Aphoristica, the sun, as in the *Monas Hieroglyphica*, is accorded a place of primary importance. Especially potent powers are also ascribed to the moon.[1] The heavenly bodies are consequently more influential than might be apparent to the casual observer, but Dee insists that they are not in themselves evil. Certain stars, he explains, are sometimes called maleficent because they influence the human will' and impel men towards evil; but in such cases the evil is already present in the man's corrupt nature and the stars only allow or promote its development: 'Therefore the stars in themselves never cause evil.'[2] Dee ends the work by invoking the authority of that most ancient of *prisci magi*, Hermes Trismegistus, to support his arguments: 'Ut nos Mercurius ille Termaximus docuit.'

Thus, Dee expounds in the *Propaedeumata Aphoristica* the essential tenets of natural magic, which he only outlines in the 'Mathematicall Preface'. The stars, as he constantly repeats, influence everything, and the magus can perform marvels by manipulating their effluvia. The magician must know the rules of astrology as well as the mechanics of astronomy to practise his art successfully; in the sixteenth century, astrology and astronomy were clearly not separate disciplines. All, as is so frequently stressed in the Hermetic writings, is a unity – 'One'.

Renaissance natural magic cut across several fields of knowledge and involved religion as well as science. Discussing the general theory of natural magic and its effects on the human psyche, D. P. Walker emphasizes that the fundamental operating agents were the cosmic and human spirits. The *vis imaginativa*, or the common imagination of the operator and subject, was the medium through which the magician usually functioned. By using the power of suggestion and employing the celestial effluences pouring down on the subject, the magician could create quite extraordinary psychological effects. The credulity, or faith, of the subject and the operator was understandably very important in the entire process.[3]

Here magic moves into the realm of psychology. And the psychological application of natural magic encroaches upon religion because it was claimed, that without any supernatural

[1] *Ibid.*, sigs. e.i.ᵛ ff.
[2] *Ibid.*, sig. e.iiii. 'Ipsa enim sidera per se nihil operantur mali.'
[3] Walker, *Magic*, pp. 75–84.

help, natural magic could produce effects that were similar to those which resulted from religious experiences. It was possible for the operator to be his own subject. Ficino, for instance, tried to attract solar and other favourable celestial influences through a religious sort of ritual in which he chanted hymns, possibly of Orphic origin, that were supposed to attract desirable celestial powers. During the ritual, he surrounded himself with objects and aromas sympathetic to the particular celestial body whose powers he was trying to capture.[1] Ficino was timid through fear of ecclesiastical censure about practising even this type of harmless natural magic, but such followers as Francesco da Diacetto were much more bold.[2] There were, of course, ancient precedents for Ficino's attempts to attract celestial influences in this way; for example, Orpheus and David were counted among the ancient practitioners of musico-psychological magic. Psychological magic, as I will later suggest, helps to explain John Dee's angelic magic.

Before examining the second world in which the Renaissance magus operated – the mathematical world – we must retrace our steps to the structure of his universe. In 1543, after Ficino practised his magic but before Dee began to implement his own, Copernicus's *De revolutionibus orbium caelestium* (written between 1507 and 1530) was published. The heliocentric theory of Copernicus revolutionized the accepted universal structure, yet we have seen that, like Renaissance magi generally, John Dee used the Ptolemaic-Chaldean framework in his *Propaedeumata Aphoristica* and *Monas Hieroglyphica*. Did Renaissance magic impede the acceptance of heliocentricity? How did a magus like Dee react to this new theory?

Though one might expect Renaissance magi to reject Copernicus's theory, this was not necessarily the case. Dee never discussed the physical reality of the heliocentric theory in print, but he had high praise for Copernicus as an observer of astronomical phenomena. In a prefatory letter to John Feild's

[1] *Ibid.*, pp. 3–24.
[2] Diacetto (see *ibid.*, pp. 31–3) felt that, in order to attract beneficent solar influences, one should clothe oneself in a solar colour like gold, conduct various magical rites propitious to the sun, and perform them in an atmosphere of incense made from solar plants. This, most notably, was to be done before an altar on which a sun talisman was enthroned.

Ephemeris Anni 1557, published at London in 1556, Dee claims that the old tables and canons are no longer in accord with the phenomena to be observed in the heavens, so any accurate *Ephemerides* must be based on the improved calculations of Copernicus, Rheticus and Rheinholdt. Dee had a perfect understanding of the mathematics involved in Copernicanism, but he says, significantly, that this letter is not the proper place to discuss the Copernican hypotheses.[1]

With his first-rate mathematical mind, it is not surprising that Dee admired Copernicus's improved calculations. There was apparently nothing uncommon about accepting the mathematics as accurate and as a necessary improvement on previous calculations while rejecting the heliocentric hypothesis as uncertain, or even as a fiction constructed to explain the observed phenomena.[2] Osiander's spurious preface to the first edition of the *De revolutionibus* encouraged the idea that heliocentricity was only imaginative fiction.[3]

In Dee's case, more facts must be considered before arriving at any conclusion concerning his belief in heliocentricity. He possessed two copies of the *De revolutionibus*, which he had obviously read with some care by 1556.[4] Also, Thomas Digges, the most impassioned English defender of the heliocentric

---

[1] Sigs. Aᵣ-ᵛ. John Dee's three references in this letter are among the first allusions to Copernicus to appear in print in England. On Dee's Copernicanism, see Johnson, *Astronomical Thought*, p. 134.

[2] Thorndike, *Magic and Experimental Science*, VI, 3 ff.

[3] Peter Ramus (see Edward Rosen, 'The Ramus–Rheticus Correspondence', *JHI*, I (1940), 363–8), for example, while praising Copernicus's astronomical observations, just as Dee does, probably agreed with the thesis of Osiander's spurious preface to the *De revolutionibus*. He apparently accepted the preface as a brilliant revelation, since it was in line with his profound desire to develop an astronomy devoid of hypotheses and based solely on mathematical calculations and the observation of phenomena. In his preface, Osiander states that the author of the work is simply completing the task of an astronomer. He is formulating hypotheses that make it possible to calculate the celestial movements, but this by no means suggests that the theories should be accepted as true, or even probable. This spurious preface (see E. J. Dijksterhuis, *The Mechanization of the World Picture*, tr. C. Dikshoorn (Oxford, 1961), pp. 296–7) understandably impeded the acceptance of heliocentricity as a physical reality. It was of course thought to be by Copernicus himself.

[4] British Museum, Harleian MS. 1879, art. 5, fol. 25.

theory during the sixteenth century (see Plate 9), was Dee's pupil and intimate friend and Digges may even have been his ward after the death of Leonard Digges, which occurred in 1559 when his son was only thirteen.[1] Thomas Digges venerated Dee as his 'mathematical father'.[2] The relationship between Dee and Digges suggests that Dee may have been teaching in private what he would not discuss in print – in this case, the heliocentric theory. Another revealing piece of factual information bearing on Dee's Copernicanism has come to light: a marginal note by Dee against a passage about the movement of the sun in John Stadius's *Ephemerides*. Dee writes: 'Revolution is not such an efficient theory.'[3]

The relationship with Thomas Digges and this notation do suggest that John Dee was amenable to the heliocentric theory. Why, then, did he not discuss it in print? To answer this question, we must delve more deeply into the ramifications of heliocentricity because the new theory affected Dee's religion, as well as his magic and science.

Returning to the fount of Renaissance Hermeticism, Ficino, we find his philosophy infused with a preoccupation about the sun. He writes:

> Julian and Iamblichus composed orations to the Sun, Plato called the sun the visible off-spring and image of the supreme God; Socrates, while greeting the rising sun, often fell into an ecstasy. The Pythagoreans sang to the lyre hymns to the rising sun. Concerning the cult of the sun, let them look to that: but undoubtedly 'God has placed his tabernacle in the sun.'[4]

The sun had long been recognized as a Christian religious symbol, but for the Renaissance magus, the most important Christian authority to establish the spiritual significance of the sun was probably Dionysius the Areopagite.[5] It was assumed

[1] Johnson, *Astronomical Thought*, pp. 139, 157, 161 ff.

[2] Thomas Digges, *Alae seu scalae mathematicae* (London, 1573), sig. A₂.

[3] Bodleian, Ashmole MS. 487, p. 17. 'Revolutionum non tam efficax doctrina.' This is the same volume in which he kept his diaries.

[4] As quoted by Walker, *Magic*, p. 18.

[5] On pseudo-Dionysius, see Raymond Klibansky, *The Continuity of the Platonic Tradition during the Middle Ages* (London, 1939), *passim*; on the role of the pseudo-Dionysian writings in the Renaissance, see Yates, *Giordano Bruno*, pp. 117–29.

that Dionysius, who supposedly met Saint Paul at Athens, composed the *Celestial Hierarchy*, a mystical treatise on the angelic orders and their relationship to God and man. Equally crucial, he was regarded as a completely *orthodox* Christian authority and so gave legitimacy to the sun-cult developed in the *prisca theologia*. It is now known that the treatise was composed by an unknown writer profoundly influenced by the Neoplatonic philosophy of Proclus; though he noted the similarities to Proclus, Aquinas accepted the work of the pseudo-Dionysius as authentic, and following a long line of commentators Ficino conceived of the Areopagite as the culmination of Christian and Platonic philosophy.

Like Ficino, John Colet in England exhibited a deep interest in the sun as a religious symbol. Colet was profoundly influenced by the philosophy of Ficino during the earlier part of his life, though he was probably totally unaware that the Italian philosopher was reviving a sun-centred magical religion that diverged from Catholic orthodoxy.[1] Colet also believed that the *Celestial Hierarchy* was written by Dionysius the Areopagite. When he wrote an epitome with the same title, Colet opened his version by all but equating the sun with God (a theme that runs throughout the work):

> When our good and bountiful God would not have them [men] void of his light and truth and grace, it was brought about by the ministry of angels, that to suit their nature and capacity, the ray of the heavenly sun and the truth of God should, as it were, abase itself a little to their condition.[2]

Colet may not have seen this relationship between the sun and God as more than symbolic – he goes on to discuss the orthodox use of symbols in the second chapter – but in magically inspired imaginations like Dee's and Ficino's, symbols often merged with reality. Talismans and seals that had the power to attract celestial influences (Dee's hieroglyph comes immediately to mind) took on the reality of that which they symbolized. The sun, as the visible symbol of God, became a god.[2]

[1] For Ficino's influence on Colet, see Sears Jayne, *John Colet and Marsilio Ficino* (Oxford, 1963), esp. pp. 38–55.

[2] John Colet, *Two Treatises on the Hierarchies of Dionysius*, tr. J. H. Lupton (Ridgewood, New Jersey, 1966), p. 3.

Colet explains that 'the flowing forth from God of a common spiritual and divine light, and its gracious passage through all things, and reception by each, according to each one's capacity' is the underlying principle that unites the universe.

> On the Angels, who are of clear and transparent natures, the light is poured forth in naked simplicity; but for men, according to the wonderful goodness of God, it is administered with folds and coverings, so to speak; that it may not by its excessive brightness dazzle and offend the weak eyes of their mind; that men may be more conveniently drawn, through fit sensible signs, to the truth signified.[1]

The angels imbibe the divine light, which is also divine knowledge, directly from God, whereas man ingests divine light through the intermediary symbol of the sun. The magi would have found it difficult to distinguish when the supercelestial merges with the celestial and when the latter descends to influence the terrestrial. To minds immersed in magic, definite distinctions would be impossible to make. Colet was extremely pious and interpreted the pseudo-Dionysius in an orthodox manner, but the above passage indicates the mystical continuity with which men as different as Colet, Ficino and Dee perceived the universal structure. Also, as we have seen, this type of unified hierarchical structure was conducive to magic.

Hermes Trismegistus was even more important than the pseudo-Dionysius in establishing the religious relevance of the sun for the Renaissance magus. In the *Asclepius*, Hermes specifically calls the sun the demiurge, or the second God.[2] The fact that light, visibly embodied in the sun, is one of the central mysteries of Hermeticism was tremendously significant to Ficino and Dee. To them, the ancient and revered Hermes Trismegistus supported and enriched the ideas of the respected and Christian pseudo-Dionysius on the sun's spiritual role. The sun becomes a part of God through which the magus, by attracting solar influences, can perform magical operations. Only by proper manipulation of the sun's influence (on which the moon is completely dependent) can Dee's Hermetic

[1] Colet, *Hierarchies*, pp. 6–7.
[2] *Corpus Hermeticum*, Nock and Festugière, II, 337.

philosophy in the *Monas Hieroglyphica* be implemented. 'And since,' he writes, 'the Sun occupies the highest dignity, we represent it (on account of its superiority) by a full circle, with a visible centre.'[1] In the mystical religion of the world that developed out of Ficino's Hermetic Platonism – based on the Hermetic conception that the universe is a visible manifestation of God and that there is only one Supreme Being common to all religions – the sun becomes the visible god.[2]

To a mind like John Dee's, heliocentricity must have seemed to corroborate the importance assigned to the sun in the Hermetic religion. In fact, it was in the atmosphere of the Hermetic religion of the world that Copernicus introduced his theory. Although he reached his conclusions concerning the revolution of the earth through a brilliant mathematical achievement, which Dee fully appreciated, both Copernicus's mathematical calculations and his heliocentric theory have frequently been recognized as stemming from the renewed interest in Pythagorean Platonism.[3] Copernicus did not view the theory of a revolving earth as a new doctrine. When he presents heliocentricity in the *De revolutionibus*, he invokes the two *prisci theologi*, Pythagoras and Philolaus, who believed that the earth revolved. More important than this, however, is the fact that directly after diagramming the universe with the sun at its centre, Copernicus quotes from the most ancient and revered *priscus theologus*, Hermes Trismegistus, on the sun-worship of the ancient Egyptians.

In the centre of all rests the sun. For who would place this lamp of a very beautiful temple in another or better place than this wherefrom it can illuminate everything at the same time? As a matter of fact, not unhappily do some call it lantern; others, the mind and still others, the pilot of the world. Trismegistus calls it a 'visible god'.[4]

[1] Dee, *Monas*, pp. 155–7.
[2] The Egyptian magical religion is described in the *Asclepius*. See above, pp. 85 ff.
[3] Debus, *The English Paracelsians*, p. 18.
[4] Nicolaus Copernicus, *On the Revolutions of the Heavenly Spheres*, tr. C. G. Wallis, in *Great Books of the Western World*, ed. R. M. Hutchins, Vol. XVI (London, 1952), pp. 526–7.

Magic, Science and Religion

In brief, Copernicus introduces the centrality of the sun within the framework of the Hermetic religion of the universe in which the sun is perceived as a palpable manifestation of God.[1]

For a Hermeticist like Dee, the sun-centred universe of Copernicus would have been a mysterious, mystical and pregnant religious revelation. This is exactly the type of thing Dee would *not* discuss in print (as he consistently refused to do) since it was matter for the *illuminati*, not the common man.

It should be clear from the above discussion that magic did not impede the acceptance of heliocentricity. Indeed, the Renaissance magus was ready and willing to embrace the Copernican hypothesis. Dee apparently did so, but without fanfare. Thus, we come to the conclusion that, although the Renaissance magus worked his magic within a geocentric system, he had a spiritual affinity with heliocentricity. He accepted it as indicative of his new religion, which he viewed as the revival of the pristine and true religion. Renaissance Hermeticism prepared the way emotionally for the acceptance of Copernicus's revolutionized universal structure. In this case, then, scientific advance was spurred by the renewed interest in the magical Hermetic religion of the world.

We now turn to the second world in which the Renaissance magus operated – the mathematical world, or the world with which Dee's 'Mathematicall Preface' is primarily concerned. Mathematics was necessary to all magical operations, super-celestial as well as elemental, and Agrippa flatly states that nothing can be achieved in magic without mathematics.[2]

To understand fully the role of magic in the Renaissance, and its subsequent influence on thought, there are two basic concepts that must be kept constantly in mind. The first is the Hermetically inspired conviction that man can operate within the cosmos. The second is the *quantitative* approach to the universe that was emphasized in the revival of Pythagorean Platonism. Nicolaus of Cusa (1401–64), the cardinal who is frequently cited as a transitional figure between the philosophy of the Middle Ages and the Renaissance, discusses the significance of mathematics in his *De docta ignorantia*. He says number was

[1] Yates, *Giordano Bruno*, pp. 153–5.
[2] Agrippa, *Occult philosophy*, II, 167. For a fuller discussion of Dee's practical science than will be given here, see below, Chapter 7.

103

always a key to truth among Platonists, and he claims that mathematics leads to an understanding of the universe and, further, he approvingly recalls Boethius's dictum: knowledge of divine things is impossible without mathematics.[1] Cassirer pointed out some years ago that such mathematicism is a distinguishing mark of Renaissance philosophy, and Cusanus was one of the first Renaissance thinkers to revive the study of mathematics as a propaedeutic to philosophy.[2] Dee collected his works.[3]

Quantity, or form, replaced quality, or essence, as the determining factor of perception during the Renaissance. In the case of magicians like della Porta, Campanella or Dee, this 'empiricism leads not to the refutation but to the codification of magic'.[4] Two quite different types of mathematics existed side by side during the period, however: a mystical Pythagorean type (mathesis) and a utilitarian type.[5] Magic provided a common bond between the two types of mathematics, both of which are found in Dee's preface. Dee makes clear his belief that both the mechanician, or utilitarian mathematician, and 'also the *Pythagoricall*, and *Platonicall* perfect scholer, and the constant Philosopher, with more ease and spede, may (like the Bee,) gather, hereby, both wax and hony'.[6] In other words, practical mathematics (the useful wax) and mystical mathematics (the delightful honey) are equally significant components of the 'Mathematicall Preface'. The mechanician did not have to get involved in the mathesis because there was ample useful information in the preface for his benefit, but Dee claimed that the true philosopher would more readily understand the metaphysical implications of number if he did study the preface.

[1] Nicolai Cusae Cardinalis, *Opera* (Paris, 1514; reprinted, Frankfurt, 1962), I, V. 'Boetius illae Romanorum literatissimus: assereret neminem divinorum scientiam/qui penitus in mathematicis exercitio careret/attingere posse.'

[2] Ernst Cassirer, *The Individual and the Cosmos in Renaissance Philosophy*, tr. Mario Domandi (New York, 1963), pp. 7 ff.

[3] Dee's set of Cusanus's works is listed in British Museum, Harleian MS. 1879, art. 5, fol. 22.

[4] Cassirer, *Individual and Cosmos*, p. 152.

[5] Allen G. Debus, 'Mathematics and Nature in the Chemical Texts of the Renaissance', *AMBIX*, XV (1968), 14.

[6] Dee, 'Mathematicall Preface', sig. *v.

Dee views mathematical forms as being in a middle world: they are not completely of the intellectual or supercelestial realm; and although numbers are signified to a certain extent in the sensible world, they cannot be fully 'perceived or judged' by the senses. Mathematics maintains a 'mervaylous newtralitie' between the intellectual and sensible spheres because, as Dee explains, 'In Mathematicall reasoninges, a probable Argument, is nothyng regarded; nor yet the testimony of sense, any whit credited: But onely a perfect demonstration, of truthes certaine, necessary, and invincible'. Recalling that Boethius suggested that number was the pattern in God's mind during the creation, he rhapsodizes, 'O comfortable allurement, O ravishing perswasion, to deale with a Science, whose Subject, is so Auncient, so pure, so excellent, so surmounting all creatures, so used of the Almighty and incomprehensible wisdome of the Creator, in the distinct creation of all creatures.' As proof of the concept that number was used by God in the creation and is the source of knowledge, Dee quotes the eleventh conclusion of Pico della Mirandola: *'By Numbers, a way is had, to the searchyng out, and understandyng of every thyng, hable to be knowen.'*[1] This is, of course, a Pythagorean conclusion.

John Dee thought that number existed in a trinitarian state: 'One, in the Creator: an other in every Creature (in respect of his complete constitution:) and the third, in Spirituall and Angelicall Myndes, and in the Soule of man.' Dee suggests that number is termed *'Number Numbryng'* in the Creator, in the angels and in man's soul, though in all other creatures it is called *'Number Numbred'*. He defines *'Number Numbryng'* as the 'discretion discerning, and distincting of thinges'. Number is therefore connected with creativity, but John Dee distinguishes among the kinds of creativity possible. Following a Platonic tradition that was supported by Augustine, Boethius and Nicolaus of Cusa, Dee explains that God, through his numbering,

produced orderly and distinctly all thinges. For his *Numbryng*, then, was his Creatyng of all thinges. And his Continuall *Numbryng*, of all thinges, is the Conservation of them in being: And, where and when he will lacke an *Unit*: there and then, that particular thyng shalbe *Discreated*.[2]

[1] *Ibid.*, sigs. *v-*.iv.
[2] *Ibid.*, sig. *.iv.

Dee believed that all things have their being in numbers. Objects or creatures exist because they were created (numbered) with what might be termed idea-numbers, or form-numbers, in the mind of God; the form-numbers can be equated with the mathematical formulae that describe things as they are in reality. If the form-number of a certain item becomes lacking in the mind of God, however, that item will be 'discreated'. If the form number of the toad were forgotten, for example, all toads would cease to exist. According to *magia*, the discovery of the form-number that signifies a particular thing gives man power over that thing, just as formulae, according to modern science, give man power over his surroundings.

Mathematical knowledge is man's direct link with God, but Dee adds that man's 'Severallyng, distinctyng, and *Numbryng*, createth nothyng: but of Multitude considered maketh certaine distinct determination'. Dee is not saying that man *cannot* create in the sense of scientifically producing one thing out of some other; rather, he is explaining that God created the universe of his own will out of nothing, and man *cannot* create in that manner.[1] Man's ability to create, even in the glorified account of his origin presented in the *Pimander*, depends on what God has already created. Hermes's definition of man's relationship to science in the *Asclepius* is very similar to Dee's:

> Man investigates with a restless curiosity the differences between things, their qualities, their methods and their quantities, and yet however, encumbered by the weight and evil influence of the body which is too strong for him, he cannot penetrate ultimately the true causes of nature.[2]

Man's creative ability is therefore derivative. He can manipulate natural forces, not create from nothing. However, Dee follows Pythagoras in pointing out that, in man's soul, 'Number beareth such a swaye, and hath such an affinitie therwith: that some of the old *Philosophers* taught, *Mans Soule, to be a Number movyng it selfe.*' The soul of man bears a close resemblance to

[1] *Ibid.*, sig. *.iv. The reader should also recall the opening of the *Propaedeumata Aphoristica*.

[2] *Corpus Hermeticum*, Nock and Festugière, II, 310.

God because the soul possesses the ability to move itself, though this ability is purely accidental and is dependent upon God as the first cause. Because of this accident, Dee explains that man's soul 'had perfect beyng, in the Creator, Sempiternally'.[1]

Dee believed that man could shed his body and approach God through contemplation of number. He especially emphasizes that '(by the infinite goodnes of the Almighty *Ternarie*,) Artificiall Methods and easy wayes are made, by which the zelous Philosopher, may wyn nere this Riverish *Ida*, this Mountayne of Contemplation: and more than Contemplation'. He significantly adds that though number is so 'Immateriall, so divine, and aeternall' man 'by litle and litle' can draw number down to 'grosse and sensible thynges'. Man has the wonderful ability to use number for his 'pleasure and proffit'.[2]

In Dee's Platonically inspired schema, man as magus can use number for his benefit and move up and down the scale of creation; he can operate with number throughout the universe. Dee concludes,

> The Mathematicall minde, [can] deale Speculatively in his own Arte: and by good meanes, Mount above the cloudes and sterres: And thirdly, he can, by order, Descend, to frame Naturall thinges, to wonderfull uses: and when he list, retire home into his own centre: and there, prepare more Meanes, to Ascend or Descend by: and, all, to the glory of God, and our honest delectation in earth.[3]

Dee connects mathematics with a form of gnosticism as well as with practical science, and the implications of this use of number are important indeed.

It has frequently been assumed that the type of mystical mathematicism described by Dee in the opening of the preface did not lead to any useful results.[4] Pythagorean number

[1] Dee, 'Mathematicall Preface', sig. *.iv.

[2] *Ibid.*, sig. *.iv.

[3] *Ibid.*, sig. C.iiiv.

[4] For example, see F. W. Strong, *Procedures and Metaphysics* (Berkeley, 1936), pp. 204 ff.

mysticism did, however, stress number as the key to all knowledge, which in turn led, among other things, to discoveries about prime numbers, perfect numbers and square numbers. It was also the Pythagoreans who first combined geometry and arithmetic.[1] While mathesis had a major role within the scheme of Renaissance *magia*, significance was also assigned to the practical application of mathematics. The full magus realized that he could produce rather amazing mechanical operations through mathematical expertise, and these looked forward to modern applied science.[2] At the beginning of the second book of the *De occulta philosophia*, Agrippa describes what seems to be a form of genuine applied science and states that, by 'Mathematicall Doctrines only', one is able to produce marvels. 'A Magus,' he writes,

> expert in naturall philosophy, and Mathematicks, and knowing the middle sciences consisting of both these, Arithmatick, Musick, Geometry, Opticks, Astronomie, and such sciences that are of weights, measures, proportions, articles and joynts, knowing also Mechanicall Arts resulting from these, may without any wonder, if he excell other men in Art, and wit, do many wonderfull things.[3]

These are exactly the same sciences that Dee discusses in the preface and that Robert Fludd, following in his footsteps, expatiates upon in the *Utriusque cosmi . . . historia*.[4] The special interest that these occult philosophers took in mechanics reflects the practical bent of Hermeticism in England.

Agrippa lists a number of mechanical marvels that had been produced in the past, including the flying wooden dove of Archites, Boethius's brass statue of Diomedes playing a trumpet, and the wonderful statues that Hermes Trismegistus describes in the *Asclepius*.[5] Dee was well acquainted with the machines mentioned by Agrippa and, in the 'Mathematicall Preface',

[1] On this, see Edward A. Maziarz and Thomas Greenwood, *Greek Mathematical Philosophy* (New York, 1968), pp. 10 ff.

[2] Yates, *Giordano Bruno*, pp. 144–56; also see her 'The Hermetic Tradition in Renaissance Science', pp. 255–74.

[3] Agrippa, *Occult Philosophy*, II, 168–9.

[4] Yates, *Theatre*, pp. 20–59. See below, pp. 165 ff.

[5] Agrippa, *Occult Philosophy*, II, 168.

provides a list similar to that in the *De occulta philosophia*. Dee
designates the art of making machines as 'Thaumaturgike' and
defines it as 'that Art Mathematicall, which giveth certaine
order to make straunge workes, of the sense to be perceived,
and to men to greatly be wondered at'. Some of these wonders,
such as the machines of Ctesibus and Hero, are produced by
hydraulic operations; others, including those that Timaeus
mentions, are accomplished by weights; and some rely upon
straining strings or springs. The 'Images of Mercurie: and the
brasen hed, made by *Albertus Magnus*, which did seme to
speake' depended upon other undisclosed devices. All such
marvels are, Dee assures the reader, 'Naturally, Mathematically, and Mechanically, wrought and contrived'.[1] In his *Magia
et Grazia*, Tommaso Campanella terms this form of applied
science 'real artificial magic'.[2]

Only by viewing applied science as 'real artificial magic' can
the Renaissance relationship between *magia* and science be fully
understood and the activities of a man like John Dee be
properly assessed.[3] Practical science can be seen to have
developed, at least in part, out of the renewed interest in
magic. Dee's 'Mathematicall Preface', although utilitarian in
approach, is essentially a magical work – to Dee, as to Campanella, the subjects covered in it were 'real artificial magic'.

The third and most exalted realm of *magia* involved theological, or supercelestial, magic. Only the most intrepid magicians dared to operate on this dangerous level, which might lead
to contact with chthonic spirits.[4] Theological magic, even more
than natural magic, presented a challenge to the Church
because the implication was that man was able to attain
salvation through his innate divine abilities, without the
Church's intercession with God on man's behalf. After all,
Hermes counsels Tat in the *Asclepius* that God distinguished
man from all other living creatures by granting him the

[1] Dee, 'Mathematicall Preface', sigs. A.iʳ⁻ᵛ.

[2] As quoted by Yates, *Giordano Bruno*, p. 147.

[3] Dee himself points out that the 'whole craft of hydraulics and the rest
of Heron's feats' were popularly termed 'magic' (see below, p. 128, n. 3).

[4] Agrippa stresses the danger of practising theological magic: 'Whosoever shall attempt this and not be purified, doth bring upon himself judgement, and is delivered to the evil spirit, to be devoured' (*Occult Philosophy*,
III, 358).

'unique privilege of intelligence and science' through which he could attain 'immortality'.[1] The Egyptian religion described in the *Asclepius* approves of science, or magic, as a means of attaining salvation, or gnosis. But the final key to all 'pure philosophy', Asclepius stresses, 'depends only on piety'.[2] In his most exalted role, therefore, the Renaissance magus usurped the function of the priest.

Dee began his attempts at angel-magic early in the 1580s; the first recorded conference is dated 22 December 1581.[3] He left for the Continent in September 1583 and by September 1584 was in Prague, where he hoped to impress the half-mad Emperor Rudolph II with his great dignity and learning and become the resident *philosophus et mathematicus*. The Emperor granted him an audience, which turned out to be quite extraordinary. Dee writes that he began by declaring:

All my life time I had spent in learning: but for this forty years continually, in sundry manners, and in divers Countries, with great pain, care, and cost, I had from degree to degree, sought to come by the best knowledge that man might attain unto in the world: And I found (at length) that neither any man living, nor any Book I could yet meet withal, was able to teach me those truths I desired, and longed for: And therefore I concluded with my self, to make intercession and prayer to the giver of wisdom and all good things, to send me such wisdom, as I might know the natures of his creatures; and also enjoy means to use them to his honour and glory.

Dee adds that, as a result of his prayers, God's 'holy Angels, for these two years and a half, have used to inform me'.[4]

[1] *Corpus Hermeticum*, Nock and Festugière, II, 324.
[2] *Ibid.*, 312.
[3] British Museum, Sloane MS. 3188, fol. 8.
[4] Dee, *True & Faithful Relation*, p. 231. Dee believed there were trustworthy precedents for his success in communicating with angels. He writes: 'I have often read in thy [God's] books & records, how Enoch injoyed thy favour & conversation; with Moses thou was familiar; And also that to Abraham, Isaack & Jacob, Joshua, Gideon, Esdras, Daniel, Tobias & sundry others thy good angels were sent by thy disposition, to Instruct them' (British Museum, Sloane MS. 3188, fols. 118–19).

Evincing a missionary zeal, Dee claimed he had been sent, like the prophets, to rebuke the emperor for his sins. The emperor was not particularly impressed.

Dee's speech is revealing, however. He passionately describes the desire of the Renaissance magus to operate on all levels of creation. By operating on the angelic level Dee hoped to learn the secrets of nature. It was a way of executing science in a higher sphere. An angel visitant once chided him, '*Ignorance was the nakednesse wherewithal you were first tormented, and the first Plague that fell unto man was the want of Science; . . . the want of Science hindreth you from knowledge of your self.*'[1] Know yourself, discover the star-demon within you through *magia* and science, and become like God. As we have seen, this is constantly reiterated in the Hermetic texts.

In the 'Mathematicall Preface', written long before his attempts at angelic communication, Dee hints at the possibility of angel-magic when he emphasizes that man 'participateth with Spirites, and Angels: and is made to the Image and similitude of *God*'.[2] In actually attempting to deal with the angels, Dee used the cabala, an essentially mystical discipline that supposedly constituted the oral part of God's revelation to Moses.[3] The cabala enabled contemplation of the celestial and supercelestial mysteries through permutations of the sacred Hebrew alphabet, which was thought to contain symbolically the names of God and the entire universe. Use of this system really took two forms – contemplative cabala and its extension and complement, practical cabala, which tried to employ the highest spiritual powers.

Cabalists assigned governing angels to the various parts of the universe and even to time, as in the case of Trithemius's *Steganographia*. It was the angels, the archangels, the sephiroth (who represent the names and powers of God), and God himself that the practical cabalist invoked. Through magical processes, but especially through the powers of the sacred Hebrew language, supercelestial powers could be tapped. The cabalists

[1] Dee, *True & Faithful Relation*, p. 7, section 1.
[2] Dee, 'Mathematicall Preface', sig. C.iiii.
[3] On the cabala, see G. G. Scholem, *Major Trends in Jewish Mysticism* (Jerusalem, 1941); Blau, *Christian Interpretation of the Cabala*; Secret, *Les Kabbalistes Chrétiens*; Yates, *Giordano Bruno*, pp. 84–116.

necessarily created numerous angelic names not found in the Bible, and these names, when invoked or drawn on seals, were thought to be powerful.[1] The Hebrew language was used for more than gathering new angelic names, however. Abbreviations of Hebrew words were formed by a method known as *notarikon*, and another method, known as *temurah*, enabled the development of anagrams; these permutations were naturally considered magically potent. The most complex system involving the use of Hebrew in cabalist magic was *gematria*, in which numerical values assigned to Hebrew letters were subtly and intricately calculated to derive the mysteries of the universe.[2] These cabalist methods could be used as purely contemplative exercises; but in the hands of the practical cabalists, they were bound up with the implementation of angel-magic. Dee was well acquainted with all of these methods and used them in his experiments with demon-summoning.

Since the Renaissance believed that the cabalist texts paralleled those of Hermes, the cabala was absorbed into Hermeticism. When Pico della Mirandola integrated the re-discovered cabala into Hermetic magic, he provided the essential equipment for magical operations in the super-celestial realm. Like the Hermetic philosophy, the cabala was Christianized. This was partially accomplished by equating cabalist angels with the celestial hierarchies outlined by the pseudo-Dionysius, but Lullism was a more significant element in the Christianizing of the cabala. Important similarities unite the Lullist and cabalist systems.[3] Lull's contemplative art may originally have been indebted to the Jewish cabala, but Lullism is completely Christian. Pico was first in explicitly connecting cabalism with Lullism, but he was followed by many others, including Dee. The widespread revival of Lullism during the Renaissance provided a ready-made Christian framework for

[1] Yates, *Giordano Bruno*, p. 193.

[2] Dee was especially addicted to *gematria* as a cabalist method. In the *True & Faithful Relation*, there are pages and pages (see, for instance, pp. 94–153) in which he explores the relationships between angels' names, numbers and the secrets of the universe. This particular branch of practical cabala undoubtedly appealed to him so much because of his belief that mathematics was a key to understanding the universe and a means of approaching God.

[3] On this and Dee's interest in Lullism, see above, pp. 47 ff.

the cabalist philosophy. John Dee was deeply immersed in Lullism and he apparently accepted the traditional attitude toward the Lullist–cabalist synthesis; at any rate, he always practised his angel-magic within the Christian trinitarian framework on which Lullism is based.

It would obviously be difficult to separate cabalist angel-magic from religion. The third book of Agrippa's *De occulta philosophia* (largely dependent on the works of Reuchlin and Trithemius) deals exclusively with religious magic and includes elaborate tables for summoning angels, descriptions of angel-attracting seals, copious lists of angels' names and other material related to practical cabala. Dee used Agrippa's book constantly during his experiments in this realm of magic. He notes in his 'Spiritual Diaries' at one point, 'Agrippa hath so', and at another Uriel is asked: 'Do you mean Agrippa his book? and is it there expressed by the name SALAMIAN?'[1]

Dee's most successful medium, Edward Kelley, was also well-versed in Agrippa's book and its magic.[2] After a particularly frustrating session between Dee and Kelley and some demons, Kelley left in a dour mood. Shortly afterwards, he stormed into Dee's room with a copy of the *De occulta philosophia*. In one chapter of Agrippa's work, Kelley had discovered the names and descriptions of various countries and provinces that

[1] British Museum, Sloane MS. 3188, fols. 11, 13v.

[2] Edward Kelley was born at Worcester on 1 August 1555. For a time he attended Oxford under the alias of Edward Talbot, but he left abruptly after some sort of trouble. A few years later, he was pilloried in Lancaster for forgery. Kelley acted briefly as a secretary for Thomas Allen, who was a magus like Dee, and Kelley may have acquired his knowledge of occult philosophy while in Allen's service. Kelley appeared at Dee's house in Mortlake on 10 March 1582, where he introduced himself as a medium named Edward Talbot. He immediately ingratiated himself because he claimed to see visions in Dee's crystal. Eventually, Kelley admitted that his name was not Talbot. Dee was not bothered by the deception, however, and the close association between the two men lasted until 1589 when Dee left Bohemia to return to England. Kelley remained behind and was eventually knighted by Rudolph II for his alchemical efforts. Rudolph finally lost patience and imprisoned Kelley because he produced no gold. Some time in November of 1595 when trying to escape, Kelley fell from a turret and shortly afterwards died from the injuries incurred. See the article on Kelley in the *Dictionary of National Biography*; and Fell Smith, *John Dee*, pp. 76 ff.

paralleled the instructions about these matters that the angels had just provided Kelley denounced the demons as 'coseners' because they stole their material from books, and he decided he would have nothing more to do with them. Dee was thoroughly alarmed and spent some time calming down the volatile Kelley.[1]

An insoluble problem concerning these actions, or spiritual conferences, presents itself. Did Kelley know Agrippa's work so well that he was able to regurgitate the angel-magic of the *De occulta philosophia* and dupe his pious and credulous master? Or did Kelley have some form of mental illness that made him think he actually did see angel visitants? Though it is somewhat difficult to tell from the way the 'Spiritual Diaries' are written (see Plate 10), most responsible scholars have concluded that John Dee never asserts that he personally saw any of the demons.[2] In his spiritual conferences, Dee always acted through a skryer. It was with Kelley acting as medium that Dee achieved, or believed he achieved, his greatest successes in communicating with angels. The demons supposedly addressed themselves to Kelley who, in turn, would inform Dee of their comments; Dee's questions were apparently heard directly by the demons since the transcripts do not indicate that Kelley ever had to repeat them. The minutes of the actions at which Kelley was the skryer cover hundreds of pages and occur during a period of about eight years. Though Kelley has usually been pictured as a blatant charlatan – even worse than Dee – it is very difficult to believe that he saw nothing at all.[3]

There were other mediums who claimed, at least to some extent, that they could see visions in the showstone that Dee used. Dee's son Arthur saw little, but Bartholomew Hickman, his last skryer, saw a good deal. Although Barnabus Saul, Dee's first medium, said he saw visions, he afterwards denied it. The retraction could have been prompted, of course, by

[1] Dee, *True & Faithful Relation*, pp. 158–9.

[2] Fell Smith, *John Dee*, p. 63; Yates, *Giordano Bruno*, p. 149. The amazing story of these conferences is recorded in: British Museum, Sloane MS. 3188; British Museum, Cotton Appendix MS. XLVI, parts 1 and 2; Bodleian, Ashmole MS. 1790, art. 1. Meric Casaubon published Appendix MS. XLVI; C. H. Josten has recently published Ashmole MS. 1790.

[3] Frances Yates (*Giordano Bruno*, p. 149) concludes that Kelley was a fraud who deluded his pious master'.

Saul's fear of conjuring charges after he left Dee's service. It is hard to accept the accusation that all of these individuals – especially Arthur and Bartholomew Hickman, who returned to serve Dee in his poverty and old age – abused his trust. The mediums probably believed they saw some sort of visions in the crystal. A possible solution to the problem may be found in Dee himself, who was the only person present at all the actions. Dee must have been an extremely magnetic personality, and it is likely that he was able to impress his own enthusiasm and ideas on those around him so profoundly that the susceptible skryers often repeated them as visions. There may have been much deception on the part of Kelley, but psychological magic could produce very strange effects – effects similar to religious experiences. Everything depended upon the power of imagination in the operator and the gullibility of the subject. Operator and subject could be the same person, as we have seen was the case with Ficino in his attempts to attract beneficent celestial influences. Dee's conviction that, as a magus, he could operate in the supercelestial realm must have had its effect on his skryers as well as on him.

The elaborate preparation involved in the 'dignification' of the religious magus was not unlike the exercises that might lead to mystical experiences. Agrippa unequivocally says that the key to operation in the angelic realm is 'the dignifying of men to this so sublime vertue and power'.[1] Only the intellect, the highest faculty of the soul, can work the wonders connected with this level of magical operations. Agrippa gives a detailed formula for attaining a Hermetic gnosis, which is basic to all religious magic. The magus attains proper 'dignification' by two steps. The first, in which he leaves 'carnal affections, fraile sense, and the materiall passions', leads to the second, which is a gnostic ascent through the three worlds 'to an intellect pure & conjoyned with the power of the gods'. In his fullest dignity, the religious magus must perform various ceremonies, expiations, consecrations and holy rites. The end result of all this is that his mind will become 'pure and divine, inflamed with a religious love, adorned with hope, directed by faith, placed in the hight and top of the humane soul'.[2] At his

[1] Agrippa, *Occult Philosophy*, III, 350–1.
[2] *Ibid.*, 357–8.

heights, the religious magus could theoretically change the stars and control the heavenly powers. But the strain would be so great that his body would soon be destroyed and his spiritual essence would be completely absorbed into the Godhead. This great transformation was exactly what Dee was attempting to achieve through his magic.

In an epitome of Dee's system of religious magic gleaned from the 'Spiritual Diaries', Elias Ashmole gives a list of seven steps necessary for successful implementation. One must '3 days before abstaine from Coitus, & Gluttony &c', and it is necessary to 'wash hands, face, cut nailes, shave the beard, wash all'. When the operator is ready for the work, he must say his 'invocations 7 times'. The actions should preferably take place in the sunshine and for a limit of fourteen days at a time. One could work only on even days in the 'increasing hours' – from sunrise to noon, and from sunset to the crowing of the cock (midnight). Finally, the sun must 'be well placed with a beneficent planet reigning'.[1] The importance of prayer as the means of effecting religious magic cannot be over-emphasized. Dee stresses constantly, *'The key of Prayer openeth all things'*; and one is struck by the immense piety and the almost continuous state of prayer that inform the spiritual conferences.[2]

The whole affair was conducted in an appropriately structured atmosphere. Supposedly at the express command and under the guidance of Uriel, Dee constructed a special table for his showstone. The table was painted in brilliant colours, primarily yellow, blue and red, and the sides were covered with *'Characters and names'* written in yellow. Seals were placed under each foot and a great seal was placed in the centre of the table; the centre seal and the table were covered with red silk. The crystal then was set on the great seal.[3]

All the holy seals, made 'of perfect wax', were similar to the great seal, Sigillum Emeth (see Plate 11).[4] Through Kelley, Uriel provided Dee with detailed instructions for making the

[1] Bodleian, Ashmole MS. 1790, art. 3, fol. 39.
[2] British Museum, Sloane MS. 3188, fol. 26.
[3] British Museum, Sloane MS. 3188, fol. 10.
[4] In a marginal note, Dee mentions that both Agrippa and Reuchlin refer to seals by this name.

Most Gratious Soueraine Lady, The God of heauen and earth,
(Who hath mightilie, and euidently, giuen vnto your most excellent
Royall Maiestie, this wunderfull Triumphant Victorie, against
your mortall enemies) be allwaies, thanked, praysed, and glorified;
And the same God Almightie, euermore direct and defend your
most Royall Highnes from all euill and encumbrance: and finish
and confirme in your most excellent Maiestie Royall, the blessings,
long since, both decreed and offred: yea, euen vnto your most
gratious Royall bosom, and Lap. Happy are they, that can
perceyue, and so obey the pleasant call, of the mightie Ladie,
OPPORTVNITIE. And, Therfore, finding our duetie concurrent
with a most secret beck, of the said Gratious Princess Ladie
OPPORTVNITIE, NOW to embrace, and enioye your
most excellent Royall Maiesties high fauor, and gratious great
Clemencie, of CALLING me, Mr Kelley, and our families
boame, into your Brytish Earthly Paradise, and Monarchie
incomparable: (and, that, abowt an yere since: by Master
Customer Yong, his letters,) I, and myne, (by God his fauor
and help, and after the most conuenient manner we can,)
Will, from hencefurth, endeuour our selues, faithfully, loyally,
carefully, warily, and diligently, to ryd and vntangle our
selues from hence: And, so, very deuowtely, and Sowndlie,
at your Sacred Maiesties feet, to offer our selues, and all,
Wherein, we are, or may be hable, to serue God, and your most
Excellent Royall Maiestie. The Lord of Hoasts, be our
help, and Gwyde, therein: and graunt vnto your most excellent
Royall Maiestie, the Incomparablest Triumphant Raigne, and Monarchie
that euer was, since Mans creation. Amen

Trebon: in the kingdome of Boemia
the 10th of Nouebre: A. Dni: 1588: stylo

Your Sacred and most excellent
Royall Maiesties
most humble and dutifull
Subiect and Servant

---

1 Letter from Dee to Queen Elizabeth. British Museum,
Harleian MS. 6986, fol. 45.

The Order of the Inspirati

MAHOMET *receives his Law by Inspiration.*

APPOLONI. TYANEUS *in* DOMITIANS *tyme*

Edw: Kelly *Prophet or Seer to Dr. Dee.*

Roger Bacon *an English man.*

PARACELSUS *Recests from the Inspiration of Spirits.*

Dr. Dee *avoucheth his Stone is brought by Angelical Ministery*

Fran: Clein Inuent.

2 (above)   Frontispiece to Meric Casaubon's *A True & Faithful Relation of What Passed for many Yeers Between Dr: John Dee . . . and Some Spirits* (London, 1659).

3 (opposite)   Figures illustrating the Lullian art. Raymundus Lullus, *Opera* (Mainz, 1729; reprinted, Frankfurt, 1965), V, 1.

PRIMA FIGURA.

SECUNDA FIGURA.

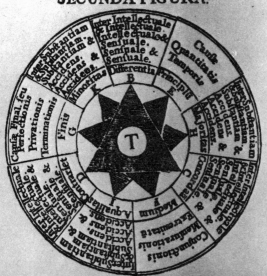

TERTIA FIGURA   # QUARTA FIGURA

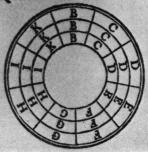

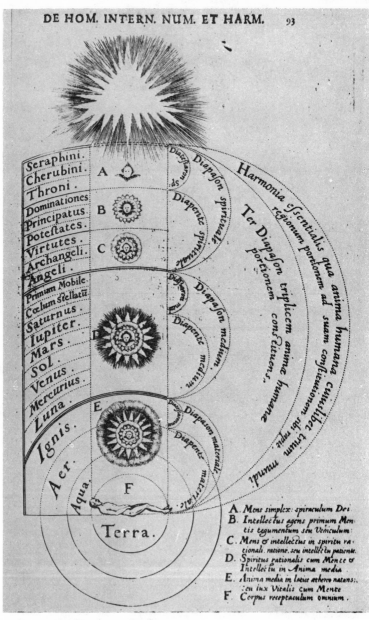

4 The divine *mens* descending into the human body. Robert Fludd, *Utriusque cosmi . . . historia* (Oppenheim, 1619), II, i, 93.

Aptissima regionum & partium Microcosmi cum illis Macrocosmi comparatio.

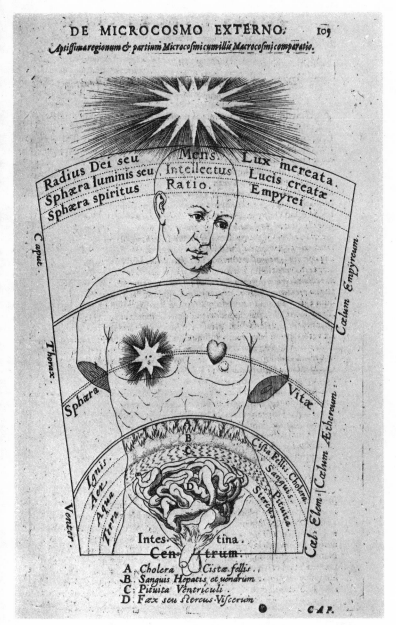

5 Correspondencies between the microcosm and the macrocosm. Robert Fludd, *Utriusque cosmi . . . historia* (Oppenheim, 1619), II, i, 105.

6 Title page of John Dee's *Monas Hieroglyphica* (Antwerp, 1564).

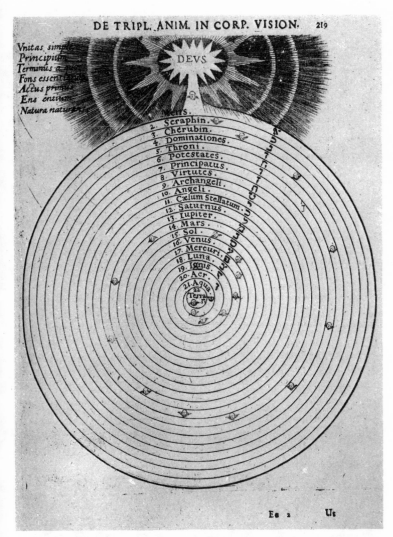

7 The structure of the universe. Robert Fludd, *Utriusque cosmi . . . historia* (Oppenheim, 1619), II, i, 219.

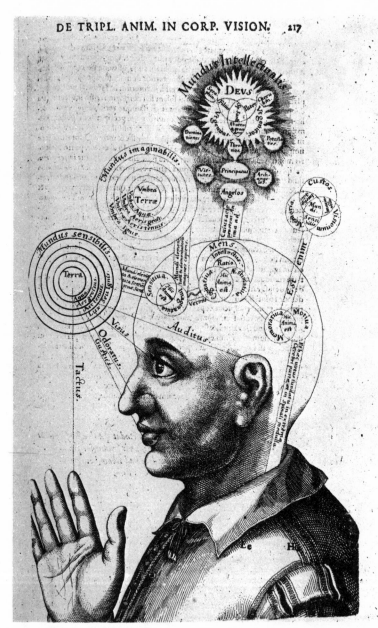

8 The functioning of the senses, imagination and intellect in the mind. Robert Fludd, *Utriusque cosmi . . . historia* (Oppenheim, 1619), II, i, 217.

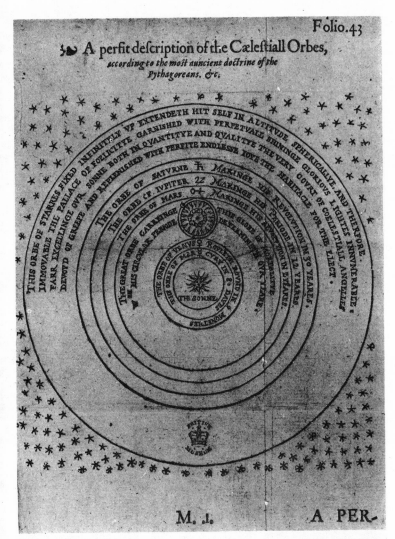

9 The Copernican universe. Thomas Digges, *A Perfit Description of the Caelestiall Orbes* (London, 1576).

10 Dee's minutes of the first angelic conference at which Edward Kelley acted as medium. British Museum, Sloane MS. 3188, fol. 9.

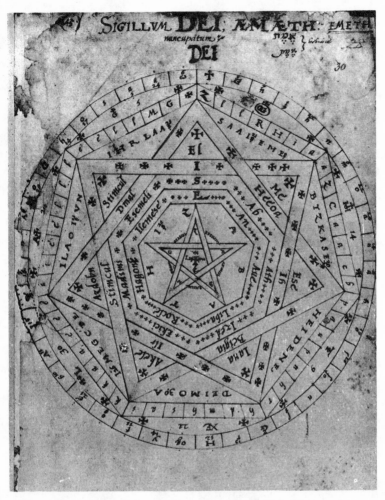

11 Design for John Dee's great seal. British Museum,
Sloane MS. 3188, fol. 30.

Hic autem monochordum mundanum tum fuis proportionibus, confo
nantiis & intervallis exactius compofuimus,cujus motorem extra mundum effe
hoc modo depinximus.

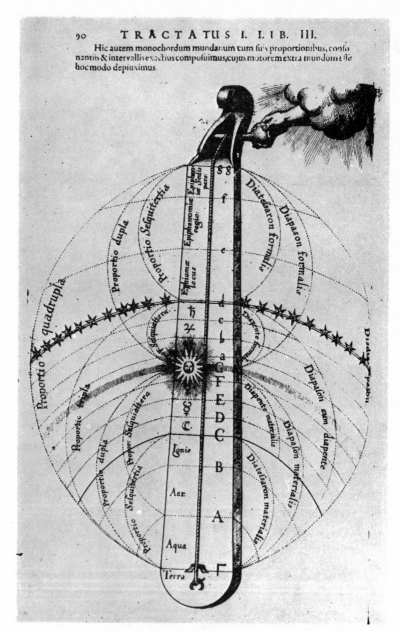

12 Correlation of the *monochordum mundi* with the elemental, planetary and angelic spheres. Robert Fludd, *Utriusque cosmi . . . historia*
(Oppenheim, 1617), I, i, 90.

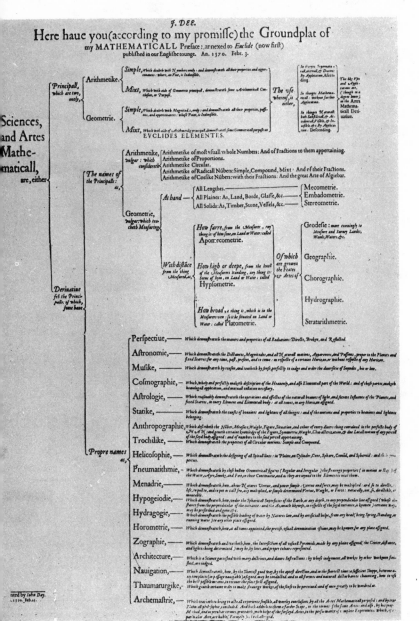

13 John Dee's 'Groundplat' for the English *Euclide* (London, 1570).

14 John Dee's original title page for the *General and Rare Memorials*.
Bodleian Library, Ashmole MS. 1789, fol. 50.

15 A page from John Dee's 'Of Famous and Rich Discoveries'. British Museum, Cotton MS. Vitellius. C. VII, fol. 206v.

16 Letter from John Dee to John Stow. British Museum,
Harleian MS. 374, fol. 15.

great seal.[1] It had to be nine inches in diameter and exactly one and one-eighth inches thick. Unlike the table, 'no respect of cullours' was required. The seal contained the various names for God, names of angels, and signs that were supposed to command the angelic orders. The names to be inscribed on the seal were revealed during a series of actions that took place early in 1582. In his visions, Kelley saw recurrent sets of seven angels, each carrying a tablet with his name written on it. Uriel told Dee how the names should be inscribed on the seal. Dee was then instructed to draw a diagram of forty-nine squares and fill them with letters, from which he drew the seven sacred names of God that are written around the inside of the large

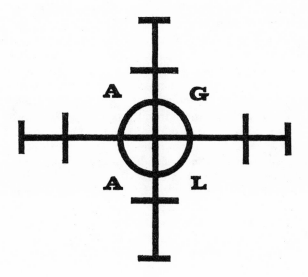

---

[1] British Museum, Sloane MS. 3188, fols. 10, 25 ff. Also see O. M. Dalton, 'Notes on Wax Discs used by Dr. Dee', *Proceedings of the Society of Antiquaries of London*, XXI (1906–7), 380–3. Dalton rightly points out that the designs on the discs are similar to those found on seals pictured in Agrippa's *De occulta philosophia*, but in Agrippa's work the designs are not so complex. The original seals that Dee used are now in the British Museum.

heptagon. The names of the seven most powerful governing
angels – Zabathiel, Zedekiel, Madimiel, Semeliel, Nogabel,
Corabiel and Lavaniel – are written around and in the middle
of the central pentangle. These were also obtained from the
diagram of forty-nine squares. The cross (see diagram) appears
on the back of the seal.

The initials are Roman characters for the Hebrew words
meaning 'Thou art great forever, O Lord', and the device was
regarded as a potent charm in the Middle Ages. The complexity of the conjuring system is abundantly illustrated. Dee
went into his angel-magic very deeply indeed and was fully
aware of the 'dignification' required by a successful operator
in the supercelestial realm. Although it would probably be
possible to reconstruct Dee's system of religious magic completely, I am not qualified for that formidable task and it is not
essential to this study.

It is necessary, however, to understand that practical cabala,
with its attempts to tap the powers of the supercelestial realm,
was an integral part of the philosophy of a Renaissance magus
and represented a logical extension of the desire to operate in
the lower worlds. Dee undoubtedly believed that his angelic
communications were the crowning success of his career. His
gullibility – if that is what one wishes to term it – aside, Dee's
attempts at angelic magic reveal a great deal about the
religious situation in the sixteenth century. Men were no less
devout than they had been in the Middle Ages, but they were
trying to infuse Christianity with new life. Some were turning
away from a Church that had become less catholic and more
Catholic and were directly placing their faith in God alone. To
many, Catholicism had ceased to be the religion of love. Some
people sought to reform and reunite Christendom as the
universal religion of love in extremely esoteric ways. The
establishment of a universal religion was one of Dee's burning
desires, and it was closely linked to his angel-magic.

Of Dee's profound piety there can be no doubt. He viewed
his angel visitants with awe and wonder and was willing in all
humility to do anything that God commanded through them.
The prayer that prefaces his 'De heptarchia mystica'
serves admirably to illustrate his religious sincerity. It
opens:

O Almighty, Aeternall, the True and Living God: Ô King of Glory: Ô Lord of Hoasts: Ô thow, the Creator of Heaven, and Erth, and of all things visible and invisible: Now, (even now, at length,) Among others thy manifold mercies used, toward me, thy simple servant John Dee, I most humbly beseche the, in this my present petition to have mercy uppon me, to have pitie uppon me, to have Compassion uppon me: Who, faithfully and sincerely, of long time, have sought among men, in Earth: And allso by prayer, (full oft, and pitifully,) have made sute unto thy Divine Matie for the obteyning of somme convenient portion of True Knowledg and understanding of thy lawes and Ordonances, established in the Natures and properties of thy Creatures: By which Knowledg, Thy Divine Wisdome, Powre and Goodnes, (on thy Creatures bestowed, and to them imparted,) being to me made manifest, might abondantly instruct, furnish, and allure me, (for the same,) incessantly to pronownce thy praises, to render unto the, most harty thanks, to avaunce thy true honor, and to Wynne unto thy Name, somme of thy due Majesticall Glorie, among all people, and for ever.[1]

Dee's abject humility before God is plentifully apparent. Like Agrippa and Bruno, he had an intense inner piety, and, like theirs, the immediacy of his relationship with the Almighty led to dangerous areas of thought. In his attempts to reach God, Dee became involved to an almost terrifying extent in practically every form of manticism and magic.

Dee must be classed with such unorthodox religious thinkers as Pico, Agrippa and Giordano Bruno. Bruno died as a heretic after trying to get to the roots of all religion by embracing the magical Hermetic religion of the world in its most extreme Egyptian form as outlined in the *Asclepius*.[2] Bruno thought that the revival of the true magical Egyptian religion offered a means of reuniting Christendom, and John Dee's attempts at religious magic reveal a similar concern. By following the counsel of God's angels, and by returning to a pristine but Christian religion of universal love, Dee firmly believed that Protestants and Catholics could be reunited. All of the angel

---

[1] British Museum, Sloane MS. 3191, fol. 45.

[2] On Bruno's religion, see Yates, *Giordano Bruno*, pp. 205–359, esp. 229–31.

visitants, Dee explains, continually exhorted him and Kelley
'to a betterment of our life, to piety, and to the practising of
peace and charity towards our neighbours'.[1] One of the angels
made a rather astounding suggestion, with which Dee heartily
concurred:

> Whosoever wishes to be wise may look neither to the right
> nor to the left; neither towards this man who is called a
> catholic, nor towards that one who is called a heretic (for
> thus you are called); but he may look up to the God of
> heaven and earth and to his Son, Jesus Christ, Who has
> given the Spirit of His abundant and multifarious graces to
> those who live a natural life in purity and a life of grace in
> their works.[2]

This was Dee's position. Doctrinally he never went so far as
Bruno, who took the monumental step of abandoning a
Christian interpretation of the magical Hermetic religion;
Bruno considered Christ only the foremost of the benevolent
religious magi. Actually, Dee's bold attempts at implementing
angel-magic were no less daring.

Dee's religious Hermeticism and eirenic, or as we would say
ecumenical, interests became obvious while he was on the
Continent with Edward Kelley experimenting in practical
cabala. Dee records that, in Cracow on 19 April 1585, 'I took
Ghostly counsel of Doctor *Hannibal*, the great Divine, that had
now set out some of his Commentaries upon *Pymander*, Hermetis
Trismigisti.' On the following day, he 'received Communion at
the Bernardine's, where that Doctor is Professor'.[3] This makes
certain his religious affinities with Hermeticism. Hannibal
Rosseli was an Italian Capuchin who published immensely
long commentaries on the *Pimander* at Cracow from 1585 to
1590. The commentaries include an analysis of the concept of
the seven governors, which Rosseli connects with the angels of
the pseudo-Dionysius's celestial hierarchies. His approach to
Hermeticism is extremely pious, and he probably avoided with

---

[1] C. H. Josten, 'An Unknown Chapter in the Life of John Dee', *JWCI*,
XXVIII (1965), 234.

[2] *Ibid.*, p. 245.

[3] Dee, *True & Faithful Relation*, p. 397.

dread any attempts at the angel-magic with which Dee was so deeply involved.[1] John Dee's choice of a Capuchin monk for his spiritual adviser and his taking of communion in the Catholic rite demonstrate his ability to transcend the religious divisions that split Europe at the time.

The extraordinary segment of the 'Spiritual Diaries' recently published by C. H. Josten fully reveals Dee's religious attitude. In 1586, when the events in this part of the 'Spiritual Diaries' were recorded, Dee and Kelley were in a precarious situation in Prague. Dangerous gossip about the supposed necromancy and dishonesty of the Englishmen had been spreading since 1584, and their presence had to be justified to the ecclesiastical authorities.[2] Since these two philosophers – known to belong to a heretical church – proclaimed that they were having intercourse with angels, the suspicions of successive papal nuncios were aroused.

On 6 May 1586, Dee and Kelley wisely left Prague for Leipzig. Three weeks after their departure, Dee was informed that the papal nuncio had submitted a document to the emperor that accused Dee and Kelley of conjuring and other forbidden practices. The Pope, Sixtus V, also sent a letter commanding Rudolph to arrest the English magicians and send them to Rome for interrogation.[3] Luckily, Dee had escaped

---

[1] Yates, *Giordano Bruno*, p. 179.

[2] Dee, *True & Faithful Relation*, pp. 247 ff.

[3] Francesco Pucci, a friend of Dee's (see Fell Smith, *John Dee*, pp. 166–7; Yates, *Giordano Bruno*, pp. 343–4, 346, n. 1) who had been present at some of the angelic actions at Prague, tried to get Dee and Kelley to return to Rome freely for examination under the nuncio's protection. Pucci was an Italian Catholic who had abjured the Church, become a Protestant, and studied at Oxford where he received an M.A. in 1574. He then went to Cracow where he apparently first encountered Dee and Kelley. Despite the fact that he thought of himself as a Protestant, Pucci appears to have been connected with the nuncio at Prague. It seems possible that he was spying on Dee, for he is eventually recognized by Dee (*True & Faithful Relation*, pp. 430–1) as untrustworthy. His suggestion that Dee and Kelley go to Rome may not have been totally malicious, however. Pucci eventually returned to the Catholic Church and became a priest. Like Dee, he was infused with religious Hermeticism, and when he tried to explain his views to the religious authorities, he was condemned as a heretic and beheaded at Rome in 1605. Clearly, John Dee would have been foolish to submit to examination by a Roman court.

before it was too late, but he and Kelley were expelled from the Emperor's dominions. Shortly afterward they were taken under the protection of the powerful Count Rosenberg of Bohemia, who managed to get the decree of expulsion mitigated so that Dee, Kelley and their families were able to remain as his guests. They resided at one of Rosenberg's castles at Trebona for about two years, beginning on 19 September 1586.[1]

This is the ugly atmosphere that surrounded the description in the 'Spiritual Diaries' of John Dee's ideas on the religious situation in Europe. After much pressure from the papal nuncio, Dee and Kelley went to be interrogated by that prelate before leaving Prague. The nuncio wished to know whether Dee's angel visitants had any cure for the numerous ills affecting the Catholic Church. Dee refused to give counsel, claiming that the angels had not informed him about such matters as of that time. He did confess that the angels had revealed many great mysteries to him and Kelley, but he added, 'For the most part, we lead a monastic life, and it is with great reluctance that we let such manifest evidence of our inward joy be known.'[2]

Kelley refused to let the opportunity slip by, and with Dee's encouragement, he informed the nuncio:

> May . . . the doctors, shepherds, and prelates mend their ways; may they teach and live Christ by their word as well as by their conduct. For thus (in my opinion) a great and conspicuous reformation of the Christian religion would be brought about most speedily.[3]

Although Dee and Kelley were assured by the nuncio that he was most pleased with this counsel, the emperor's secretary informed Dee of the truth not long after. Kelley's speech infuriated the nuncio, who swore after their departure that he would do everything in his power to destroy them; it was only for the sake of appearances that he had not had Kelley immediately 'thrown out of the window'.[4] Dee was amazed by the

---

[1] Dee, *True & Faithful Relation*, pp. 421 ff.; Fell Smith, *John Dee*, pp. 132 ff.
[2] Josten, 'An Unknown Chapter', p. 232.
[3] *Ibid.*, p. 233.
[4] *Ibid.*, pp. 233-4.

nuncio's reaction to what seemed to him the obvious truth, but he was certain that, whatever the nuncio 'or anybody else should have said, or decided to do against us, Almighty God, the Creator of heaven and earth, who is our Lord, our preceptor and guide, this God himself will be our protector and liberator'.[1] Clearly, John Dee's inner spiritual life was incandescent at this time, and his touching faith in the directness of his relationship with God was astonishingly strong. He was filled to overflowing with the 'dignification' of the religious magus and had completely appropriated the role of priest.

Dee's belief that his Hermetic religion of love transcended that of any contemporary church was strikingly illustrated shortly after the conversation with the nuncio. Kelley went to the Jesuits to receive confession and was refused absolution because he would not admit that the spirits with whom he and Dee were conversing were evil. Dee cried in outrage, 'How irreligiously (I will not put it more strongly) E[dward] K[elley] was used, the Catholic Church will certainly find out in good time.' He added,

> Surely, all pious and true catholics will be grieved with us that, whilst pure religion is so very sadly afflicted, so great a scandal should have arisen in the Catholic Church from which the fruit of the true, pure, and very great charity of God (namely a remission of sins and peace of conscience) should have issued.

Dee was still able to retain a balanced attitude toward the Jesuits, however; and considering the hatred most Englishmen had for the members of the society, this is noteworthy in itself. John Dee practised the tolerance he advocated. 'The Jesuits,' he predicts,

> mostly devout and peaceful men, will grieve that, at the centre of almost the most distinguished part of the Christian world, so poisonous an egg should have been laid, whence, one must fear, a most horrid basilisk, a great danger to very many people, will be born if it be hatched much longer and be fomented with further bilious matter.[2]

[1] Josten, 'An Unknown Chapter', p. 234.
[2] *Ibid.*, p. 237.

Dee's marvellously strong metaphor for the state of religion shows that he was unable to accept the idea of a permanently divided Christianity. Revealingly, he hoped the Catholic Church would reform itself, return to pristine sources and once again become the universal church of love. He believed this could be accomplished by accepting the *prisca theologia*, by studying the cabala, and by returning to a Christianized version of the magical Hermetic religion of the world in which all was One and a common God ruled everyone. Dee's grand design for a universal religion even encompassed the widely despised Jews. He hoped that his *Monas Hieroglyphica* would convince the 'Hebrew cabalist' that, 'without regard to person, the same most benevolent God is not only [the God] of the Jews, but of all peoples, nations, and languages'.[1]

Complex political issues were of course involved with any scheme for establishing a universal religion, and Dee may not have fully appreciated this. He was sure, however, that all barriers to religious union would crumble if only charity were practised in the true Christian spirit.[2] He may have been right.

Dee's six-year stay on the Continent had something of a missionary atmosphere about it. In addition to meeting Rudolph II, he propounded his magical philosophy to Stephen Bathori, King of Poland, who granted Dee an audience on 17 April 1585 and received him on two subsequent occasions.[3] Dee was unable to impress either Stephen or Rudolph with the

---

[1] Dee, *Monas*, p. 133.

[2] Dee may have gleaned some of his religious ideas from the secret sect known as the Family of Love. Its members believed in divine illumination and stressed universal charity as the pre-eminent Christian virtue. The Familists were thoroughly undogmatic. They attached no significance to outward religious rituals; thus, their consciences allowed them to observe the rites of any church which happened to be in power. As one contemporary proclaims: 'They may joyne with any congregation or Church, and live under the obedience of any magistrate, be he never so wicked or ungodly: the Turke, the Pope, or whosoever' (J[ohn] R[ogers], *The Displaying of an horrible secte of grosse and wicked Heretiques, naming themselves the Familie of Love* (London, 1578), sig. B.viii). Many famous scholars were associated with the Family, and Dee's friend Ortelius was a member. In London, Dee frequented a bookshop that had Familist connections. See J. A. Van Dorsten, *The Radical Arts: First Decade of an Elizabethan Renaissance* (Leyden, 1970), pp. 26 ff.

[3] Dee, *True & Faithful Relation*, pp. 397, 402, 408.

relevance of his angelic communications, and he finally returned to England in December of 1589.[1]

What *can* one make of a man like John Dee? He was entirely within the Hermetic movement so prevalent during the sixteenth century, but he was one of its most extreme adherents. Having seen too much religious intolerance, he desperately hoped that theological magic could be used to return some semblance of normality to a world that to him seemed mad. Dee was haunted by a Christian spirit of appalling intensity, but he was driven equally by an almost pagan belief in the efficacy of magic, a profound feeling for the presence and importance of everything in the universe, and an unshakeable faith in man's innate divine powers. Magic, science and religion combined in him to form one universal vision animated by Hermetic man. His was very much a Renaissance mentality. Dee thought that all his experiments in magic would prove immensely beneficial to mankind, and those involving mathematical magic assuredly did. Those centring on religious magic perhaps did not; his angel-magic certainly never achieved the practical results he sought. But the words he used in writing of Archimedes might well be applied to Dee himself: 'In great matters it is enough to have had the intention.'

[1] A great deal of work remains to be done on Dee's Continental sojourns. He and his work were well known throughout Europe and had considerable influence within certain circles; I have only touched upon this aspect of Dee's activities.

John Dee and the Sidney Circle

Any interest shown by sixteenth-century Englishmen in the magical Hermetic philosophy that John Dee espoused would have been in private circles since there were no officially sponsored mystical academies comparable, for instance, with Baïf's in France. There were, however, courtiers like the Earl of Leicester who took an interest in recent philosophical developments and who, as we have seen, supported Dee. John Dee was close to the powerful group of men who were largely responsible for the amazing renaissance in the arts and sciences that took place during Elizabeth's reign. Since he was sought out by so many of the individuals promoting the exciting developments of the English Renaissance and since these people listened respectfully to his views on many subjects, it is not unreasonable to assume that they also heard about his Hermetic philosophy.

Dee's continuous lifelong intimacy with the Sidneys and their friends has, to my knowledge, never been given careful consideration. The relationship started during the reign of Edward VI when Dee was a tutor to the Duke of Northumberland's children.[1] Among them was the future Earl of Leicester, Robert Dudley, with whom Dee remained on very close terms. As is commonly known this earl's favourite nephew was Philip Sidney. Before leaving for Bohemia in 1577, Sidney travelled to Mortlake in the company of Leicester and Edward Dyer for consultations with Dee.[2] Each of these men had at some time been taught by the English magus, and they continued to value his knowledge. Mary Dudley, Robert's sister, had married Sir

[1] See above, pp. 32–4.
[2] Dee, *Diary*, pp. 2–3.

126

Henry Sidney in 1551, shortly before Dee entered the service of her father, and Dee was almost immediately introduced to the household of Sir Henry Sidney whose close friends included many of the men connected with Northumberland as well as the Duke himself.[1] Dee always recalled Sir Henry and Lady Sidney with great affection and respect; he apparently corresponded with them frequently. Lady Sidney wrote to Dee especially often in 1571, a year when her son Philip was probably studying with him.[2] Finally, John Dee was also a close friend of Sir Francis Walsingham whose house at Barn Elms was not far from Mortlake and was a place where Dee was often invited. This was the home, of course, of Frances Walsingham, whom Philip Sidney eventually married.[3] Dee's path obviously crossed those of the Sidney group recurrently.

It has long been known that Dee taught chemistry to Philip Sidney. Thomas Moffett, who was chief physician to the Earl of Pembroke's family, says of Sidney:

> Not satisfied with the judgement and reach of common sense, with his eye passing to and fro through all nature, he pressed into the inner-most penetralia of causes; and by that token, led by God, with Dee as teacher, and with Dyer as companion, he learned chemistry, that starry science, rival to nature.[4]

As Moffett intimates, chemistry, or alchemy, embraced a good deal. To a Paracelsian and Hermeticist like John Dee, chemistry included the study of the entire cosmos.[5]

Alchemy was by no means limited to the art of trying to transmute base metal into gold; in fact, its essential function was to transmute the human spirit through gnosis. We have

---

[1] Taylor, *Tudor Geography*, pp. 142–3.

[2] Dee, *Rehearsal*, p. 11.

[3] After she became the Countess of Essex, Frances Walsingham Sidney Devereux became the godmother of one of Dee's children (Dee, *Diary*, p. 53).

[4] Thomas Moffett, *Nobilis, or A View of the Life and Death of a Sidney*, tr. and ed. Virgil B. Heltzel and Hoyt H. Hudson (San Marino, Calif., 1940), p. 75.

[5] Debus, *The English Paracelsians*, pp. 22 ff.

seen this view expressed in Dee's *Monas Hieroglyphica*.[1] In his introduction to a proposed translation of that work, Thomas Tymme explains: 'This noble science is the way to celestiall & supernaturall things, by wch the ancient Wisemen were led from the works of Art & Nature to understand, even by reason the wonderfull powre of God in the creacion of all things.'[2] Alchemy, being the paradigmatic Hermetic art, was for the Paracelsian a means of understanding the miracle of creation. Since the creation of the cosmos was a chemical action, the Paracelsian believed that the universe continued to operate according to chemical laws. Therefore, if he studied the chemistry of creation, he thought he would learn not only about nature, but about the Creator as well.[3]

Dee held these generally accepted views about chemistry, and he must have taught Philip Sidney, Edward Dyer and possibly other members of the Sidney circle accordingly. Dyer, an intimate friend of Philip and his sister throughout his life, remained one of Dee's closest disciples and constant patrons.[4] Dee notes that he was acquainted with Dyer as early as 1566, about the time that Dyer first came to court. In 1576, when rumours were rampant about Frobisher's return from one of his exploratory voyages with a sample of gold, Edward

---

[1] See above, Chapter 4, esp. pp. 76 ff.

[2] Bodleian, Ashmole MS. 1459, fol. 478.

[3] This type of chemical philosophy also had its practical aspects; for instance, it may have stimulated an interest in hydraulics. In his letter of dedication to the Emperor Maximilian, Dee writes, 'Likewise, those who have most diligently examined the condition of space occupied [by matter] and void (a problem which has been controversial from the very beginnings of philosophy) and who have seen that the surfaces of neighbouring elements are so coordinated, cohering, and joined together by a law and (almost indissoluble) bond of Nature ([decreed] by God) that in fire, air, and water, [going] upwards and downwards, and in all directions (according to their natural tendencies) wonderful things may most confidently be displayed to people who are to be guided or stimulated (by various devices; [devices] that are also useful to the state, as is shown by the whole craft of hydraulics and the rest of Heron's feats of magic, as it pleases nowadays to call them)' (Dee, *Monas*, p. 133). Bracketed insertions are Josten's.

[4] Ralph M. Sargent, *At the Court of Queen Elizabeth: The Life and Lyrics of Sir Edward Dyer* (London and New York, 1935), pp. 56–71, 88–90, 97–122. On 16 July 1579 (Dee, *Diary*, p. 6), Dyer became the godfather of Dee's eldest son, Arthur.

Dyer put his instructions from Dee to practical use and helped to test a sample of the ore for Walsingham. Anthony Wood claims that it was only at an advanced age that Dyer delved deeply into chemistry, but Dee must have inspired his great enthusiasm for the science.

Mary Sidney also retained a lifelong interest in chemistry, and after her marriage to the Earl of Pembroke, in whose father's household Dee had once served, she moved to Wilton where she kept Adrian Gilbert as her laborator, or chemist.[1] Gilbert was the half brother of Sir Walter Ralegh and the brother of Sir Humphrey Gilbert, whom Dee instructed in navigational matters. Adrian Gilbert and John Dee were on close terms: Gilbert often visited Dee at Mortlake, and he was one of the few men in England allowed to witness Dee's attempts at practical cabala.[2] Here, then, is another link in the chain connecting John Dee and the Sidney circle, and Gilbert's presence at Wilton draws the group closer to the Hermetic philosophy that Dee espoused. Whether or not the Countess of Pembroke received instruction in chemistry from Dee is uncertain, but it seems decidedly possible. She had more than a passing acquaintance with the science, for Aubrey comments that the countess was a 'great chymist, and spent yearly a great deale in that study'.[3]

Chemistry with its philosophical implications was not, of course, the only abstruse subject that John Dee taught, and apparently it was not the only subject in which he instructed Philip Sidney; a curious horoscope cast for Sidney emphasizes his precociousness in cognate occult disciplines.[4] In the horo-

[1] Aubrey, *Lives*, p. 139.
[2] British Museum, Sloane MS. 3188, fols. 103 ff.
[3] Aubrey, *Lives*, p. 139.
[4] Bodleian, Ashmole MS. 356, art. 5. On this horoscope, see James Osborn, '*Mica, mica, parva stella*: Sidney's Horoscope', *TLS* (1 January 1971), pp. 17–18. The casting of this horoscope has been assigned to John Dee because it was thought to be in his handwriting. It is not. Osborn plausibly argues that it was prepared by Thomas Allen (1542–1632), although it does not seem to be in his handwriting either. While circumstantial evidence does indicate that Allen might well have cast the horoscope, I do not think that Dee can be completely eliminated as the astrologer in question. Whoever the astrologer was, Osborn's conclusion that Sidney had no more than a 'polite' interest in astrology and other occult sciences is misleading.

scope, Sidney is addressed directly as 'Nobilissime Juvenis', or 'Philippe', indicating that it was prepared for him to read personally. This fact suggests that Sidney had more than a perfunctory interest in the occult sciences, as did his uncle, the Earl of Leicester.[1] If this had not been so it is improbable that Sidney would have studied chemistry under Dee because that science was often termed *astronomia inferior*. Moffett asserts that Sidney 'could never be so far misled as to taste' astrology, 'even with the tip of his tongue'.[2] Since Moffett was a chemist, one assumes that he was referring to reckless judicial astrology, which Dee also scorned, rather than astral magic. The following sonnet, even if taken somewhat ironically, does show that Sidney had some understanding of the workings of the type of astrological magic that Dee favoured:

> THOUGH dustie wits dare scorne Astrologie,
> And fooles can thinke those Lampes of purest light,
> Whose numbers, wayes, greatnesses, eternitie,
> Promising wonders, wonder do invite,
>   To have for no cause birthright in the skie,
> But for to spangle the blacke weeds of night:
> Or for some brawle, which in that chamber hie.
> They should still daunce to please a gazer's sight,
>   For me, I do Nature unidle know,
> And know great causes, great effects procure:
> And know those Bodies high raigne on the low.
> And if these rules did faile, proofe makes me sure,
>   Who oft fore-judge my after-following race,
>   By only those two starres in *Stella's* face.[3]

Although Sidney's horoscope carries no date, internal references indicate that it was prepared after Sidney had attended and probably left Oxford but before he started his Continental travels in 1572. Thus, the horoscope was cast in 1570 or 1571 when Sidney was about sixteen; in it, the astrologer commends Sidney's frequently demonstrated abilities in

[1] Taylor, *Tudor Geography*, p. 138.
[2] Moffett, *Life and Death of a Sidney*, p. 75.
[3] Philip Sidney, *The Poems*, ed. William A. Ringler, Jr. (Oxford, 1962), pp. 177–8.

grammar, rhetoric, dialectic, natural philosophy and ethics. More revealingly, he describes Sidney as a promising youth 'who is intended by nature for the study of the mathematicals, and by birth for learning celestial philosophy'.[1] Sidney had not been afforded the opportunity to develop these particular talents at Oxford, but according to the astrologer he displayed an 'eager and ardent' ('studiosa et ardens') interest in astronomy and he could discuss 'mathesis' ('Mathesi') intelligently.[2] Renaissance mathesis, a philosophy of number in the three worlds, was involved with astrology, and it was an integral part of chemical philosophy, especially as chemistry was interpreted, for instance, by John Dee.[3]

Had Sidney already started to receive some instruction in philosophy from Dee? We know from Thomas Moffett that Sidney, in late adolescence and after attending Oxford, 'devoted the greater share of his time and energy to philosophy and to the arts of observation'; in a few years he excelled in these subjects. Occult philosophy and the 'arts of observation' were unavailable at Oxford and were the very subjects that John Dee taught. Moffett elaborates on Sidney's performance as Dee's pupil: 'So far did he have an unexhausted eagerness for complete (or rather for only the accepted) learning that he leaped over all . . . obstacles [to the study of chemistry] at one bound. . . . With the same alacrity he proceeded in other subjects of abstruse learning.'[4] Even though Moffett's biography is an encomium meant to impress the youthful William Herbert, and in spite of the biographer's curious modification of his statement about Sidney's desire for 'complete' knowledge, this passage proves Sidney's enthusiasm for his studies under Dee's guidance.[5] And Moffett makes it quite clear that these studies were not circumscribed by chemistry, even in its broadest sense. (Edward Dyer presumably received the same kind of

[1] Bodleian, Ashmole MS. 356, art. 5, fol. 26: 'qui a Natura ad Mathematicum studia conformatus & Celestem Philosophiam discendam natus.'
[2] Bodleian, Ashmole MS. 356, art. 5, fols. 26–7. See Osborn, 'Mica, mica, parva stella', for lengthy quotations from the horoscope.
[3] See Debus, 'Mathematics and Nature', 1–28.
[4] Moffett, Life and Death of a Sidney, p. 75.
[5] The correction may have been made because Moffett recalled Dee's notorious attempts at angel-magic.

information as Sidney.) So, the fragmentary data provided by the astrologer who cast Sidney's horoscope are corroborated by Thomas Moffett – a creditable witness.

The success of Dee's teaching of Philip Sidney is reflected in other contemporary comments. In his *Life* of Sidney, Fulke Greville certifies that, '*even in the most ingenuous of Mechanicall Arts*', Sidney would have been able to perform wonders.[1] The mechanical arts, as we have seen, were an integral part of the knowledge of a Renaissance magus, and Dee was particularly well-versed in this branch of knowledge which was avoided at the English universities.[2] Sidney makes his delight in the mathematical sciences apparent when he writes to his brother Robert, who is travelling on the Continent, and advises, 'Now (deere brother) take delight likewise in the mathematicalls.'[3]

The ramifications involved in Dee's close association with Sir Philip Sidney and his circle are significant. Dee was promulgating a Hermetic philosophy that was widely accepted in Continental Europe but had not yet been openly acknowledged in England. This philosophy was diametrically opposed to the openly approved new humanism of men like Roger Ascham. What effect did Dee's ideas have on the thought of Philip Sidney and the members of the so-called Areopagus?

James Phillips has recently suggested that Sidney's group of courtiers may have been indulging in the same speculations that characterized the sixteenth-century French academies.[4] Phillips bases his conjecture on the role that the diplomat and neo-Latin poet, Daniel Rogers, played as a link between the Areopagus and the Pléiade, and I believe that his surmises are correct.[5] Although he is aware that John Dee's philosophical Hermeticism was known to the group that I loosely term the

[1] Fulke Greville, *The Life of the Renowned Sr Philip Sidney* (London, 1652), pp. 20–1. My italics.

[2] See above, pp. 24, 108 ff.

[3] Sidney, *Correspondence*, in *Complete Works*, III, 132.

[4] James E. Phillips, 'Daniel Rogers: A Neo-Latin Link Between the Pléiade and Sidney's "Areopagus"', in *Neo-Latin Poetry of the Sixteenth and Seventeenth Centuries*, William Andrews Clark Memorial Library (Los Angeles, 1965), pp. 5–28. On the French academies see Frances A. Yates, *French Academies of the Sixteenth Century* (London, 1947).

[5] Dee refers to Daniel Rogers as 'my friend' (Taylor, *Tudor Geography*, p. 262).

Sidney circle, Phillips admits that he does not know what effect it might have had. I will follow Phillips's lead in comparing the possible interests of the Areopagus with the known interests of the Pléiade, but my comparison will be made in the light of what we have learned about Dee's philosophy, to which important members of Sidney's group were exposed. Through this approach, I think we can come closer than ever before to understanding the real concerns of the Englishmen.

The first question that usually comes to mind when the Areopagus is mentioned is whether or not it actually functioned as a formal society. For the present analysis the question is purely academic. I must stress emphatically that my purpose is not to re-examine the historical evidence concerning the existence of the Areopagus as a formal club; nor is it to try to designate specific individuals as members. Rather, I will attempt to suggest the ideas that might have inspired the men who are usually associated with it. I use the name only to designate an amorphous group of individuals with Philip Sidney as the focal point. In other words, I wish to uncover the spirit of the Areopagus. This approach introduces new avenues for research, whereas the historical argument about the society's formal existence (unless new evidence is discovered) leads to a dead end.

To summarize, however, practically all the evidence suggesting that the Areopagus was an organized academy is contained in well-known letters between Gabriel Harvey and Edmund Spenser written in 1579 and 1580. In one letter, Spenser informs Harvey that Philip Sidney and Edward Dyer

> have proclaimed in their *Areopagus*, a generall surceasing and silence of balde Rymers, and also of the verie beste to: in steade whereof, they have by autho(ri)tie of their whole Senate prescribed certaine Lawes and rules of Quantities of English sillables, for English Verse: having had thereof already great practise, and drawen mee to their faction.[1]

Harvey replies to Spenser: 'Your new-founded *Areopagus* I

---

[1] *Two other very commendable Letters*, in *Poetical Works*, ed. J. C. Smith and E. De Selincourt (London, 1966), p. 635. I have used the Latin instead of the Greek for the name Areopagus.

honoure more, than you will or can suppose: and make greater accompte of the twoo worthy Gentlemenne, than of two hundreth *Dionisii Areopagitae.*'[1] This is obviously very little on which to base a theory about the makeup of the group.

But, as has frequently been pointed out, it is completely unsatisfactory to think that these men were drawn together solely for the sake of 'Dranting' English verse. It seems unlikely that men like Sidney, Spenser, Dyer, Greville, Daniel Rogers and Dee did not have more to discuss than counting syllables. Although they probably never organized an academy like Baïf's in Paris, these men undoubtedly were conscious of themselves as a group interested in philosophical and religious, as well as literary, ideas.[2] New evidence from Daniel Rogers makes this certain. Especially singling out Dyer and Greville, Rogers says of Sidney, 'With them you discuss great points of law, God, or moral good.'[3] Rogers, most curiously, never mentions that this group even spoke of literature.

The Areopagus, then, had rather broad interests. We have already seen the main tenets of Dee's philosophy, but it remains to outline very briefly the concerns of the sixteenth-century French academies, which will provide a useful guide for considering the subjects that engaged the men who composed the Areopagus.

The most widely known preoccupation of certain members of the Pléiade was the attempt to revive measured verse. In fusing the proper words with the right music, the French academicians believed that they could produce beneficial effects on the psyche of the auditor, effects that would lead to a purification of the mind and an initiation into a higher realm of truth.[4] This idea rested on stories about the magical effects produced by Orpheus and David; the same sources were used by Ficino for his musical magic, but the more overtly magical implications were avoided in the Pléiade.[5]

The attempt by the academicians to revive measured verse was really a Hellenic interest and was part of a broad philosophical outlook that had little to do with the primarily

---

[1] *Two other very commendable Letters*, p. 639.

[2] Phillips, 'Daniel Rogers', p. 7.

[3] J. A. Van Dorsten, *Poets, Patrons, and Professors* (London, 1962), p. 66.

[4] Yates, *French Academies*, pp. 36 ff.

[5] Walker, *Magic*, pp. 119–26.

philological and textual concerns of Latin humanism. Hellenism was largely concerned with science and philosophy, Platonism and Hermeticism, as they were jointly developed in the Italian academies.[1] Magic and mysticism were involved in this Hellenic philosophical outlook, but the extent varied among individuals. The French academicians who followed the Italian tradition also discussed mathematics and natural philosophy, both of which were, of course, tied to magic. And Copernicus's theory of heliocentricity was not excluded from consideration. Thus, the early French academies have some right to be designated as the precursors of later scientific groups.[2]

The Frenchmen were also interested in religious Hermeticism, though they once again avoided the overtly magical implications of the Egyptian religion.[3] Attention was paid to the cabala, but the French would never have tried to use it for angel-summoning as John Dee attempted to do: the cabala was seen as a possible way of reuniting the Christian religion. The principal exponent of this use of the cabala in France was Guillaume Postel, among whose disciples was Guy Le Fèvre de la Boderie, a prime-mover of the Pléiade.[4]

One of the most pressing concerns of the French academies, and possibly of the Areopagus, was eirenicism. There was a widespread movement to reunite a fragmented Christianity through the use of the *prisca theologia*.[5] The experiments in measured verse were even tied to this goal because it was thought that the mystico-magical powers inherent in chanted verse (which is obviously closely related to magical incantations) would work on the hearer's highest faculties and lift him above mundane religious divisions. It was in the Platonic academies succeeding Ficino's that hopes were nurtured of religious reunion being accomplished through the revival of a mystical religion of the world. Within an academy like Baïf's, where

[1] See above, pp. 21 ff.

[2] Yates, *French Academies*, pp. 95–104.

[3] Walker, 'Prisca Theologia', 234–40.

[4] F. Secret, 'L'Humanisme florentin du Quattrocento vu par un kabbalist français, Guy Le Fèvre de la Boderie', *Rinascimento*, V (Florence, 1954), 105–12; *Les Kabbalistes Chrétiens*, pp. 151–217. Also see Walker, *Magic*, pp. 119–26.

[5] Yates, *French Academies*, pp. 199–235; *Giordano Bruno*, pp. 169–89.

Protestants and Catholics amiably intermingled, the theological differences of the time must have seemed less than unbreachable.

John Dee may have been the only exponent in sixteenth-century England of a philosophy encompassing all of the concerns outlined above. Largely because of his overt acceptance of the power of magic, his own philosophy differed somewhat from that which pervaded Baïf's academy. Dee was more in line with the ideas propounded by the Italian academicians, who were less hostile to the magical implications of Hermetic Platonism than the French. Even in France, however, Jacques Gohory, who was a Paracelsian, an occult philosopher and a friend of Du Bellay and Baïf, set up a mystical academy very near Baïf's house where the Pléiade met. Gohory was on close terms with many members of Baïf's academy, but never joined that group. There were actually, then, two academies functioning in the same place in France at the same time. Both descended from Ficino's academy, but they developed in different directions: Baïf's was encyclopedic but concentrated on music and poetry; and Gohory's 'Lycium philosophal San Marcellin' was also encyclopedic and included poetry and music among its concerns but was essentially oriented towards magic.[1] Gohory thought that Ficino's spiritual magic had not gone far enough. A fusion of the interests of these two academies, with certain individualistic variations, best summarizes Dee's concerns.

As we have seen, Sidney and Dyer both remained interested in subjects that Dee taught them, and other men associated with the Areopagus were also familiar with his philosophy. He was friendly, for example, with Daniel Rogers.[2] Gabriel Harvey must have been fully cognizant of Dee's ideas because he comments in a letter to Spenser, 'Would to God in heaven I had awhile . . . the mysticall and supermetaphysicall philosophy of Doctor Dee.'[3] One must assume that Spenser knew what his friend meant by the reference and therefore also had some acquaintance with Dee's philosophy.

[1] Walker, *Magic*, pp. 96–101.
[2] Dee, *Diary*, p. 4.
[3] Gabriel Harvey, *Letter Book. A.D. 1573–1580*, ed. E. J. L. Scott, *Camden Society Publications*, XXXIII (London, 1884), 71.

There is little doubt that one of the prime interests of the Areopagus, as well as of the Pléiade, was measured verse. In the case of the Englishmen, the attempts to revive classical prosody have been considered a disastrous affair. These experiments too often have been attributed to a resurgence of classicism such as was sponsored by humanists like Roger Ascham, who thought the rhyming of vernacular poetry a rather beggarly innovation introduced by the barbarians when they invaded Italy.[1] John Buxton, though he conceives of the Areopagus as a light-hearted group, thinks that Sidney was following the attempts of Ronsard and Baïf in trying to imitate the ancient custom of chanting verses, rather than following the more pedestrian attempts of the humanists to quantify meter.[2] One must realize that musical accompaniment was an essential requisite of the experiment; this is reflected, for example, in Sidney's introduction of the eclogues in the *Arcadia* with musical directions. Sidney also explains in the *Apology* that the poet 'cometh to you with words set in delightful proportion, either accompanied with, or prepared for, the well enchanting skill of music'.[3] In the same work, he emphasizes that poetry is 'the only fit speech for Music (Music, I say, the most divine striker of the senses)'.[4] He apparently had a higher, more mystical role in mind for measured verse than the mere counting of syllables. After referring to the Sibylline prophecies, he concludes, 'That same exquisite observing of number and measure in words, and that high flying liberty of conceit proper to the poet, did seem to have some divine force in it.'[5] Poetry is able to move the reader, to initiate him into a higher realm of truth, to encourage him to action.

Many of Sidney's comments on poetry, and especially its relationship to music, are reminiscent of the role John Dee assigns to music in his 'Mathematicall Preface'. Comparing music with astronomy, Dee explains, 'As *Astronomie* hath a more divine Contemplation, and commodity, then mortall eye can

[1] John Buxton, *Sir Philip Sidney and the English Renaissance* (London, 1954), p. 116.

[2] *Ibid.*, pp. 102, 116.

[3] Philip Sidney, *An Apology for Poetry*, ed. Geoffrey Shepherd (London, 1965), p. 113.

[4] *Ibid.*, p. 122.

[5] *Ibid.*, p. 99.

perceive: So, is *Musike* to be considered, that the Minde may be preferred, before the eare.' He goes on to suggest the possible effects of measured verse:

> And what is the cause of the apt bonde, and frendly felow-ship, of the Intellectuall and Mentall part of us, with our grosse & corruptible body: but a certaine Meane, and *Harmonious Spiritualitie, with both participatyng & of both (in a maner) resultyng? In the Tune of Mans voyce, and also the sound of Instrument*, what might be sayd, of *Harmonie*: No common Musicien would lightly beleve.

Dee cites the usual ancient authorities who were supposed to have performed marvellous feats with music, including Ter-pander, Orpheus, Amphion, David, Pythagoras and Timo-theus. He ends by saying that, if he explained the mysterious effects that could be achieved by music, 'I should finde more repreevers, then I could finde privy, or skilfull of my meaning.'[1] Whether in fact Dee greatly influenced Sidney or not, both were clearly working on the same assumptions. Measured verse – music and words – has something divine about it, and produces amazing effects.

The theory expounded by Dee and Sidney can be traced back to the musico-magic of Ficino. To him, the combination of words and music was exceptionally potent because it affected the entire human being: the musical sound worked on the human spirit, which links the body with the soul, and the text influenced the intellect, or mind. Ficino aimed at creating an effect either on an auditor or on himself, and he quite definitely perceived the effects created as having a moral character.[2] He thought that, by chanting verses in which the perfect words were placed in exactly the right order, one could attract bene-ficent planetary influences and attain the energies of the astral bodies. This type of Ficinian musico-magic inspired the experi-ments with measured verse of the French academicians; it was one source for Dee's comments on music; and I believe it may have been instrumental in forming Sidney's attitude towards measured verse. This would help to explain the quantitative experiments of the Areopagus.

[1] Dee, 'Mathematicall Preface', sigs. b.iiᵛ–b.iii.
[2] Walker, *Magic*, pp. 1–23; see above, pp. 96 ff.

The theory was based on stories of the peculiar effectiveness of ancient music. Using a list of ancient musicians similar to Dee's in the preface, Sidney recalls: 'As Amphion was said to move stones with his poetry to build Thebes, and Orpheus to be listened to by wild beasts – indeed stony and beastly people – so among the Romans were Livius Andronicus, and Ennius.'[1] Sidney also uses David's psalms as a religious example of the miraculous effects of music. Sidney is speaking in metaphorical terms, but so is Dee in his preface, and so are the other people who have been cited as concerned with measured verse. The suggested transformations take place within the imaginative faculty of the mind, which the Hermeticists had exalted to new heights in their attempts to understand the mysteries of creation and comprehend the truth of human existence.

The sources that Sidney used for his ideas about the structure of ancient music cannot be documented, but he necessarily knew Boethius, and the two most influential contemporary works on the subject were at his disposal. Zarlino's well-known *Institutioni Harmoniche*, first published at Venice in 1558, and Glareanus's *Dodecachordon*, published at Basel in 1547, were both in Dee's library.[2] These were works on which the French academicians depended. The presence of these volumes in Dee's library, together with his superb collection of classical poets, indicates that Dee had more than a passing interest in measured verse himself.

Dee also owned a copy of Francesco Giorgi's *De harmonia mundi*.[3] This massive work, first published at Venice in 1525, exerted an influence within the French academic movement and was translated by Guy Le Fèvre de la Boderie and published at Paris in 1579. Giorgi develops the theme of the universal harmonic relationship between the microcosm and macrocosm. This concept had been held throughout the Middle Ages and is a prominent feature of Boethius's musical

[1] Sidney, *Apology*, p. 96.

[2] British Museum, Harleian MS. 1879, art. 5, fols. 21v, 22. On these works, see Walker, *Magic*, pp. 18–19; Yates, *French Academies*, pp. 47–8.

[3] British Museum, Harleian MS. 1879, art. 5, fol. 25. On Giorgi, see Wittkower, *Architectural Principles*, *passim*; C. Vasoli, 'Francesco Giorgio Veneto', in *Testi umanistici su l'ermetismo*, ed. E. Garin *et al.*, pp. 79–104; Walker, *Magic*, pp. 112–19.

theory, but among Renaissance Hermeticists (see Plate 12)
the theory was fully, and often fantastically, developed. Giorgi
constantly integrates ideas from the Hermetic writings to fill
out the original theory.[1] He also absorbs the complexities of
cabalist doctrine into the basic analogy of *musica mundana*,
humana and *instrumentalis*, which permeates the whole work.[2]
Giorgi thus infuses an old idea with new richness. After him, a
deeper awareness of universal harmony enveloped the Renaissance.

Giorgi's approach to musical theory brings us very close to
Dee's mystical conception of music. When he compares the
universe with a musical instrument on which the knowledgeable
musician can create new harmonies, Dee implies that music
puts man in tune with the universal structure; it permeates his
inner being and lifts him to new heights of perception. As is
unfortunately the case with so many other subjects, Dee never
published a detailed version of his theories about music, but
since he was so deeply interested in music – he considered proportion and harmony essential to all art – he must have discussed its philosophical implications with Sidney along the
lines I have outlined.[3]

[1] Vasoli ('Francesco Giorgio Veneto', pp. 91–104) reproduces many
passages from the *De harmonia mundi* that reveal Hermetic influence.

[2] The translation of the *De harmonia mundi* by Guy Le Fèvre de la Boderie
is prefaced by an explanation of cabalist doctrines (sigs. ēii ff.) by Nicolas
Le Fèvre de la Boderie. There is also a prefatory poem (sigs. õ–õii) concerning the principles of the *Pimander*.

[3] In the 'Mathematicall Preface' (sig. C.iii) under the science 'Anthropographie', Dee stresses the microcosm–macrocosm relationship. He refers
the reader to Vitruvius, Dürer and Agrippa who develop the harmony
between man and the cosmos. Robert Fludd, who followed Dee's lead in so
many instances, expounds the theory of the musical relationships among the
parts of the universe at great length (as well as Plate 11, see Plate 5) in the
Utriusque cosmi . . . historia, on the publication of which, see above, p. 76,
n. 1. P. J. Ammann has shown ('The Musical Theory and Philosophy of
Robert Fludd', *JWCI*, XXX (1967), 198–227) that music was one of the
pre-eminent components of Fludd's philosophy and that he was very much
in the Ficino–Giorgi tradition. This is also the tradition in which Dee was
working. Since Fludd covered most of the same subjects that Dee outlines
in the preface, including music (see Yates, *Theatre of the World*, pp. 54–9),
and approached them in a similar manner, we can be fairly certain that his
musical philosophy was an expansion with variations of the type that Dee
promulgated.

Mathematics is naturally incorporated in the study of measured verse, since harmonic intervals are based on quantity and proportion; Dee always stressed the mathematical origins of music. He writes of Euclid's fifth book: 'It entreateth of proportion and Analogie, or proportionalitie, which pertayneth not onely unto lines, figures, and bodies in Geometry: but also soundes & voyces, of which Musike entreateth.'[1] In a passage that recalls Dee's definition of music in the preface, Sidney says in the *Apology*:

> If *oratio* next to *ratio*, speech next to reason, be the greatest gift bestowed upon mortality, that cannot be praiseless which doth most polish that blessing of speech: which considers each word, not only (as a man may say) by his forcible quality, but by his best measured quantity, carrying even in themselves a harmony – without, perchance, number, measure, order, proportion be in our time grown odious.[2]

Throughout the Middle Ages and Renaissance, music was placed among the quadrivial subjects. The French academicians showed considerable interest in the mathematical sciences, with Baïf writing works on mathematics and the mathematician, Peter Ramus, showing marked concern about the Pléiade's experiments with measured verse and suggesting possible syllabic reforms for the quantification of French poetry. Mauduit, who after Baïf's death in 1589 moved the academy to his house, studied the sciences, including mechanics.[3]

The French academicians' involvement with the sciences is especially intriguing because these were the subjects that Dee particularly studied. In this area, perhaps more than any other, he connects the concerns of the Pléiade with those of the Areopagus. Sidney was of course immersed in the sciences, and Moffett even claims that Sidney 'himself made corrections upon various authors of scientific works, and by his methods led sundry to writing more correctly – or at least to observe more correctly'.[4] Whether or not science was discussed by the associates

[1] Dee, *Euclide*, fol. 125ᵛ.   [2] Sidney, *Apology*, pp. 121–2.
[3] Yates, *French Academies*, pp. 30, 104.
[4] Moffett, *Life and Death of a Sidney*, p. 75.

of the Areopagus together (and it is hard to believe that it was not), Dee was largely responsible for establishing interest in this area of knowledge among members of the group. Vincent Hopper has suggested, for instance, that Spenser's House of Temperance, that exceptionally complex image in Book II of the *Faerie Queene*, is directly indebted to Dee's *Euclide*.[1] Perhaps Spenser's abstruse numerological imagery is also, at least in part, a result of Dee's attempts to integrate the medieval English mathematical tradition with the philosophy of the Renaissance.[2]

Since Dee's philosophy developed directly out of the Hermetic Platonism of the Florentine academies and looked forward to the scientific spirit of the Royal Society, he parallels the French academicians in attempting to transform medieval magic into Renaissance science. Dee, we have seen, was one of the few men in England, and perhaps the most important, who tried to absorb medieval traditions into English Renaissance thought after the excesses of the Edwardian reformers. On the Continent, where the iconoclasm that marked the English Reformation was not so rampant, this transition occurred effortlessly – the aforementioned case of Giorgi's work on harmony is a perfect example.

This difference between England and the Continent raises an important question about the Sidney circle. Were its members such ardent Puritans and Ramists – as has often been assumed – that they were willing to ignore the philosophical and scientific traditions of England because they were considered papistically inspired? Though the English universities did so, I believe the case was rather different with Sidney and many of the men who surrounded him. I suggest that they were attracted to Ramism but that they incorporated it in a broader system that had definite Hermetic and magical overtones. These men were not willing, any more than Dee, to abandon their heritage.

Ramus was essentially an educational reformer, a simplifier, a utilitarian mathematician who wished to break with the past

[1] Vincent F. Hopper, 'Spenser's "House of Temperance"', *PMLA*, LV (1940), 958–67.

[2] See A. Kent Hieatt, *Short Time's Endless Monument: The Symbolism of the Numbers in Edmund Spenser's 'Epithalamion'* (New York, 1960); and Alastair Fowler, *Spenser and the Numbers of Time* (London, 1964).

scientifically, philosophically and religiously.[1] That he was a friend of Dee's there is no doubt. Dee collected a number of Ramus's works, and Ramus considered Dee the most suitable man in England to hold a mathematical chair at either of the universities; he even petitioned Elizabeth to establish such a chair. The two men also corresponded about mathematical texts.[2] When Dee gave his well-attended lectures at Paris in 1550, Ramus displayed an interest in his ideas. It seems almost impossible that Dee, who taught Sidney the mathematical sciences, did not introduce him to Ramistic thought, and there is certainly no reason to assume, as Buxton does, that Sidney had little if any acquaintance with Ramus's work before leaving England for his tour on the Continent in 1572.[3] It is quite possible that it was with Dee's encouragement that Sidney sought out Ramus.

This does *not* mean that Sidney was a Ramist any more than it means that John Dee was. Dee left Ramus far behind as a speculative philosopher. Ramus was totally uninterested in the theoretical philosophy that was so absorbing to Dee, and the Pythagorean mystical mathematics that form one of the cornerstones of Dee's magical philosophy were inimical to Ramus's thought. To portray Sidney as a Ramist does not give adequate consideration to other very important movements of Renaissance thought, movements with which Sidney, through Dee, must have been well acquainted. There is ample evidence to show that Sidney, like Dee, was quite capable of accepting Ramism simply as a part of a much more complex whole in which practical science and utilitarian education were integrated with magical philosophy.[4]

---

[1] Hookyaas, *Humanisme, Science et Réforme*, pp. 29, *et passim*.

[2] P. Rami and A. Telei, *Collectaneae* (Paris, 1577), pp. 204–5.

[3] Buxton, *Philip Sidney*, p. 46.

[4] There is also no reason to assume that, just because De Banos dedicated his life of Ramus to Sidney, the Englishman was completely Ramistic in his outlook. Sidney was able to charm everyone, and even Giordano Bruno, the volatile Hermetic magician to whom Ramus was the greatest pedant in France, dedicated several of his works to Sidney and was well received in his circle. In his introduction to the *Apology* (pp. 33 ff.), Shepherd provides a brief outline of Sidney's connections with the Ramists; Rosemond Tuve (*Elizabethan and Metaphysical Imagery* (Chicago, 1947)) has made much o Sidney's association with them.

Sidney makes a most curious reference that touches on this point in the *Apology*. 'We know', he writes,

> a playing wit can praise the discretion of an ass, the comfortableness of being in debt, and the jolly commodity of being sick of the plague. So of the contrary side, if we will turn Ovid's verse, *Ut lateat virtus proximitate mali*, that 'good lie hid in nearness of the evil', Agrippa will be as merry in showing the vanity of science as Erasmus was in commending folly. Neither shall any man or matter escape some touch of these smiling railers. But for Erasmus and Agrippa, they had another foundation, than the superficial part would promise.[1]

What a revealing comparison! Sidney makes it clear that he perceived Agrippa's *De incertitudine & vanitate scientiarum declamatio invectiva* for what it really was, a kind of satire. He had a complete understanding of Agrippa and his magical philosophy if he knew that this work, which was meant to fool the authorities, was a sham.[2]

The magically attuned mind, with its emphasis on the imagination, saw symbolism everywhere, whereas the Ramistically oriented mind, with its stress on charts and schemata, did not. Ramism abandoned visual imagery as the basic mode of mental perception and replaced it with dialectical order, which, to put it succinctly, proceeded from the most general to the most specific examples.[3] This procedure supposedly took advantage of natural mental processes. Ramism is not quite so elementary, of course, but it should be remembered that Ramus's aim was to *simplify* logic so that it might be used by everyone, and not just by university scholars. The first English translator of his *Logic* certainly stressed simplicity as the great benefit of Ramus's method; he triumphantly insists:

> The forme and methode which is kept in this arte, commaundethe that the thing which is absolutely most cleare, be first placed: and secondly that which is next cleare, & so forthe

[1] Sidney, *Apology*, p. 121.

[2] See above, pp. 52–3.

[3] On Ramus's method, see Ong, *Ramus*, pp. 171–213; also Yates, *Memory*, pp. 231–42.

whith the rest. And therefore it continually procedethe from
the general to the speciall and singular.[1]

This method was thought by the Ramists to be practical,
totally utilitarian.[2]

Sidney's influential *Apology* represents a form of thought very
different from Ramism. As I have already suggested, certain
tenets of magical philosophy clearly underlie the conception of
measured verse delineated in the *Apology*, but Hermetic magical
thought may have played an even greater role in the formula-
tion of the document. Distinct similarities exist between the
assumptions on which Sidney bases his concept of the poet and
the abilities ascribed to the Renaissance magus by Pico in the
Oration on the Dignity of Man. Sidney was certainly cognizant of
the exalted role that Renaissance magi had assumed; witness
John Dee, his friend and tutor. Could Sidney have usurped this
role and assigned it to the poet?

Following ancient tradition, Sidney goes out of his way to
stress the fact that the poet is a *maker*; however, the Renaissance
magus also appropriated this role. 'The Greeks', Sidney
stresses,

> called him 'a poet', which name hath, as the most excellent,
> gone through other languages. It cometh of this word *poiein*,

[1] M. R. Makylmenaeum Scotum, tr., 'The Epistle to the Reader', *The
Logike*, by Peter Ramus (London, 1574), p. 12.

[2] There is also a mystical way of looking at Ramism, for it was supposedly a method that could be applied to all subjects and a means of
gaining universal knowledge. In this, it is similar to Lullism, and there are
other superficial similarities (see Yates, *Memory*, pp. 237 ff.) between the
two systems; but the basic uniting factor is that they are both attempts to
delineate method. During the period, the Lullian art and Ramus's dialectic
were often linked together. George Hakewill (*An Apologie of the Power and
Providence of God in the Government of the World* (Oxford, 1627), p. 244), for
example, cites them both as modern short-cuts to knowledge. Thus Dee may
have interpreted Ramism as a sort of everyman's introduction to Lullism.
Besides the fact that he was interested in anything concerning mathematics, this may be why Dee collected Ramus's works. Unless everything
I have written so far is wrong, however, Dee could never have accepted the
Ramist method as the final key to knowledge. I shall continue to interpret
Ramism like the Ramists of the period: as a simplified and completely
utilitarian logical method.

which is 'to make': wherein I know not whether by luck or wisdom, we Englishmen have met with the Greeks in calling him 'a maker': which name, now high and incomparable a title it is, I had rather were known by marking the scope of other sciences than by my partial allegation.[1]

He then compares the value of other sciences that, with poetry, 'lead and draw us to as high a perfection as our degenerate souls, made worse by their clayey lodgings, can be capable of'. Sidney points out that men have tried various ways to achieve this goal:

> For some that thought this felicity was principally to be gotten by knowledge, and no knowledge to be so high and heavenly as acquaintance with the stars, gave themselves to Astronomy; others, persuading themselves to be demi-gods if they knew the cause of things, became natural and super-natural philosophers; some an admirable delight drew to Music; and some the certainty of demonstration to the Mathematics.

At the end of this list, Sidney once again stresses, 'But all, one and other, having this scope – to know, and by knowledge to lift up the mind from the dungeon of the body to the enjoying of his own divine essence.'[2] One immediately recalls the most basic concept of Hermeticism: man must know himself and recover his divine essence by reuniting with the divine *mens*. Sidney denigrates the ultimate value of all the sciences he mentions, but his purpose is not so much to dismiss their worth, which he did fully appreciate, as it is an attempt to exalt the role of poetry. After all, he readily admits that the admirable goal of these sciences is a type of *Hermetic gnosis*. To Sidney, how-ever, the aim of poetry is 'not *gnosis* but *praxis*'.[3] Through his verse, the poet can move the hearer; but the magus thought he could do the same thing through his magic. This was con-stantly in Ficino's mind, and Dee repeatedly stressed that he

---

[1] Sidney, *Apology*, p. 99.
[2] *Ibid.*, p. 104.
[3] *Ibid.*, p. 112.

wanted supernatural knowledge in order to *act* for the benefit of man.

According to Sidney's argument, the poet does have one advantage over the magus – he does not have to depend on nature and her laws to create. As Sidney says,

> Only the poet, disdaining to be tied to any such subjection [as the laws of nature], lifted up with the vigour of his own invention, doth grow in effect into another nature, in making things either better than Nature bringeth forth, or, quite anew, forms such as never were in Nature.[1]

Thus, the poet has divine creative powers – powers which the magus seeks to regain by reuniting with the divine *mens* – and the poet does not have to remain dependent on the creation of God. The magus seeks to control the heavens and the angels, but he does not create out of nothing, even when he has recovered his divine powers. (In the *Pimander*, it might be recalled, magus-man creates by 'embracing' nature.[2]) The ability to create 'anew' without regard to nature's laws is the only major difference between the Hermetic definition of the magus and Sidney's description of the poet.

Sidney's poet and the Hermetic magus are extraordinarily close in their conceptions of the imagination: both – and this is crucial – worked through images operating within the psyche.[3] Poet and magus were often one, as in the case of Giordano Bruno, who was in England espousing his magical philosophy to Sidney and his circle while writing the *De gli eroici furori* (the series of love poems he dedicated to Sidney) about the time the *Apology* was being composed. Needless to say, magi were not necessarily good poets; Dee's poetry, for instance, is abominable.

Something can be learned about the genesis of Sidney's theory of imagination through comparison with the theory championed by the Renaissance magus. In both cases, the imaginative faculty is accorded a divine function. The place to begin is with a brief recapitulation of the art of memory.[4]

[1] *Ibid.*, p. 100.
[2] See above, p. 73. For John Dee's conception of magus-man's creative ability, see above, pp. 93, 105–6.
[3] See above, p. 94.
[4] For my comments on mnemonics, I have depended on Yates, *Memory*, *passim*.

Ramus had abandoned the art of memory as a part of logic and replaced it with dialectical order, charts and schemata; in doing so, he abandoned imagery and the creative imagination. The old system of mnemonics, one very different from Ramus's, was supposedly invented by the Greek poet Simonides of Ceos. The classical art of artificial memory assigned facts and ideas to be remembered to various *loci*, for instance, the various parts of a room, a house or even a town. Then, when the particular fact or idea had to be recalled, it was only necessary to remember the part of the room, the house or the town to which it had been assigned for recollection in the proper order. Naturally, this system encouraged the use of imagery because facts and ideas were represented in the mind by the particular *locus* to which each was assigned.

During the Renaissance, the classical art of memory underwent transformation at the hands of occult philosophers like Giulio Camillo, who actually constructed a complete wooden theatre for the purpose of illustrating his mnemonic system; he associated the parts of the theatre with the zodiac.[1] Camillo was attempting to develop a memory system that would, in the Hermetic manner, reflect the universe internally through memory. Because based on celestial powers, the memory would be activated magically and would thus inspire the speech of the orator, or poet, with the divine harmony of celestial proportions. Giordano Bruno followed this basic concept of Camillo's theatre and expanded it in more extremely magical directions.[2] To the Hermeticists, therefore, memory images were paramount forces in activating the psyche, and, consequently, in changing man.

Sidney's poet could hardly afford to ignore this mnemonic system since it would provide the means of achieving his goals. And Sidney apparently realized this for he writes:

Even they that have taught the art of memory have showed nothing so apt for it as a certain room divided into many places well and thoroughly known. Now, that hath the verse

[1] Dee had a copy of Camillo's *L'Idea del Theatro* (British Museum, Harleian MS. 1879, art. 5, fol. 35). On Camillo's theatre and its fame during the Renaissance, see Yates, *Memory*, pp. 129–72.

[2] Yates, *Memory*, pp. 199–230, 243–65.

in effect perfectly, every word having his natural seat, which seat must needs make the words remembered.[1]

Sidney here refers to the old, imagistic, art of memory in formulating his theory of the poetic imagination and *not* to the iconoclastic memory system of Peter Ramus. Did Sidney know the art of memory in its occult Renaissance transformation – memory as magic? It seems likely. Dee was interested in mnemonics and was of course aware of its occult forms and may well have introduced Sidney to Camillo's *L'Idea del Theatro*.[2] At any rate, it is clear that occult mnemonics, with its tremendous emphasis on efficacious images, provides a more complementary background for Sidney's theory of visual images working in the psyche than does Ramist dialectic.

Sidney is defending, after all, the imaginative mode of thinking as opposed to the purely utilitarian one. The major connection which Sidney sees between the poet and the painter is their common *creative imagination*. Both the painter and the poet, he suggests, are able to present in a striking form that which philosophical speculation may not be able to bring to life for the imagination; thus, powerful changes are brought about in the psyche of the viewer, auditor or reader. At his best, the philosopher is also able to invest his ideas with imaginative life, and Sidney reverences Plato above all thinkers as the most poetical of philosophers. He quite rightly suggests that in the *Ion*, at least according to the Renaissance interpretation, Plato gives 'high and rightly divine commendation to poetry'.[3] Plato banishes the abuse of poetry from his republic, but not poetry itself, and Sidney completely agrees with Plato that the true end of poetry is to promote good and not to hinder it, which can happen if poetry's powerful effects are misused.

According to Sidney, poetry – *ut pictura poesis* – has two important functions. First, it strikes the imaginative faculty by

[1] Sidney, *Apology*, p. 122.

[2] Sidney may also have learned about magical mnemonics from Giordano Bruno, who was in England from 1583 to 1585. It appears that Sidney was not averse to the occult memory system, for he allowed Alexander Dickson, Bruno's foremost disciple in England and a master of 'the art of memory' (Yates, *Memory*, p. 283), to attend him. This fact was recently discovered by John Durkhan in the Scottish State Papers.

[3] Sidney, *Apology*, p. 129.

manipulating images within the psyche. Second, it attempts to create pictorial images that impress the imagination of the hearer, or reader, with the truth of spiritual or intellectual structures that are paralleled in the human and universal minds. The Renaissance poet imitated both the sensible world and the intellectual world and did not believe – as post-Romantics so often do – that truth was made manifest by sense impressions. With other Renaissance poets, and in line with Renaissance magical philosophy, Sidney did not pretend to project intelligibility into the universe.[1] The designs that Renaissance artists perceived were not projections of their sensibility; rather, they were significant structures inherent in the cosmos. In this sense, Dee's symbol of the monad is a perfect example of a sensible image that supposedly contained the power of the divine *mens* and possessed the ability to transform man by revealing higher truths.

Such imagery was used by painters, sculptors, architects and poets, but the greatest artists were also philosophers. All of the artists, in their fullest roles, presented sensible images reflecting the immaterial world. Recall, for example, that the essential ingredient lacking in the Bower of Bliss, which Sir Guyon destroys in Book Two of the *Faerie Queene*, is a spiritual correlation to the sensual images – the bower does not have a place in the natural cosmic structure. Of the artist's achievement, Sidney writes:

Now doth the peerless poet perform both: for whatsoever the philosopher saith should be done, he giveth a perfect picture of it in some one by whom he presupposeth it was done, so as he coupleth the general notion with the particular example. A perfect picture I say, for he yieldeth to the powers of the mind an image of that whereof the philosopher bestoweth but a wordish description, which doth neither strike, pierce, nor possess the sight of the soul so much as that other [the artist's] doth.

[1] Pico della Mirandola (*Oration on the Dignity of Man*, p. 249) states: 'As the farmer weds his elms to vines, even so does the *magus* wed earth to heaven, that is, he weds lower things to the endowments and powers of higher things.'

How different is this theory from that which inspired the magical use of talismans and images of all kinds to effect transformations within the psyche? I suggest that the difference is not very great, as becomes clear when Sidney elaborates:

> For as in outward things, to a man that had never seen an elephant or a rhinoceros, who should tell him most exquisitely all their shapes, colour, bigness, and particular remarks; or of a gorgeous palace, the architecture, with declaring the full beauties might well make the hearer able to repeat, as it were by rote, all he had heard, yet should never satisfy his inward conceits with being witness to itself of a true lively knowledge; but the same man, as soon as he might see those beasts well painted, or the house well in model, should straightways grow, without need of any description, to a judicial comprehending of them: so no doubt likewise the philosopher with his learned definition – be it of virtue, vices, matters of public policy or private government – replenisheth the memory with many infallible grounds of wisdom, which, not withstanding, lie dark before the imaginative and judging power, if they be not illuminated or figured forth by the speaking picture of poesy.[1]

For Sidney, then, poetry is an art by which images are vivified in the imagination, and these images, in turn, have the power to move the hearer.

John Dee's comments on the art of 'Zographie', or painting, apply to the plastic arts to which Sidney compares poetry. Dee readily admits, 'A notable Arte, is this: and would require a whole Volume, to declare the property thereof: and the Commodities ensuing.' Recognizing this limitation, we can regard Dee's comments on 'Zographie' in the preface as only an indication of what he may have discussed with Sidney in person. Dee writes:

> For, the most excellent Painter, (who is but the propre Mechanician, & Imitator sensible, of the Zographer) hath atteined to such perfection, that Sense of Man and beast, have judged thinges painted, to be things naturall, and not

[1] Sidney, *Apology*, p. 107.

artificiall; alive, and not dead. This Mechanicall Zographer
(commonly called the Painter) is mervailous in his skill: and
seemeth to have a certaine divine power: As, of frendes
absent, to make a frendly, present comfort: yea, and of
frendes dead, to give a continuall silent presence: not onely
with us, but with our posteritie, for many Ages. And so
procedyng, Consider, How, in Winter, he can shew you, the
lively vew of Sommers Joy, and riches: and in Sommer,
exhibite the countenance of Winters dolefull State, and
nakednes. Cities, Townes, Fortes, Woodes, Armyes, yea
whole Kingdomes (be they never so farre, or greate) can he,
with ease, bring with him, home (to any mans Judgement) as
Paternes lively, of the thinges rehearsed. In our little house,
can he, enclose (with great pleasure of the beholders,) the
portrayture lively, of all visible Creatures, either on earth, or
in the earth, living: or in the waters lying, creping, slyding,
or swimming: or of any foule, or fly, in the ayre flying. Nay,
in respect of the Starres, the Skie, the Cloudes: yea, in the
shew of the very light it selfe (that Divine Creature) can he
match our eyes Judgement, most nerely. What a thing is
this? thinges not yet being, he can represent so, as, at their
being, the Picture shall seame (in maner) to have Created them.[1]

Dee includes both sculpture and architecture under the creative arts – those arts that, under the guidance of the 'Zographie'
of universal forms, present sensible images readily compre-
hended by the imagination.[2]

Considering Dee's comments on the magical effects produced
by music, especially in combination with words, and knowing
his attitude toward visual imagery, there is little doubt that he
would have endorsed Sidney's defence of the poetic imagination.
Dee does not specifically discuss poetry when outlining his
theory of the creative arts, but we know that he was deeply
concerned with the magical power of language. Moreover, he
possessed that superb collection of classical poets.[3] And he had
several works by more recent poets, including Du Bartas's
History of the World, Sansovino's *Chronology of the World*, the

[1] Dee, 'Mathematicall Preface', sig. d.ii^v.
[2] Dee bases his theory of the creative arts on Alberti and Vitruvius.
[3] See above, p. 57.

Romance of the Rose, Petrarch's *Sonnets*, the *Mirror for Magistrates*
(1574 edition), and Giambullari's study of Dante's *Inferno*, as
well as various poetical dictionaries and French works on
poetry.[1] In addition, Dee attempted to write poetry himself.
His verse is doggerel, but his efforts may well reflect a belief in
poetry as the most efficacious means of using words to stamp
ideas on the imagination. Dee was really the 'Zographer'
behind the artist; he was trying to outline the cosmic implications of the arts and to stress the burden placed upon the artist
who, in his highest function, was a 'Zographer' of the divine *mens*.

The image-conscious magical imagination clearly predomi-
nated over the charts and schemata of Puritan Ramism in the
theories of Dee and Sidney. Aesthetic images assumed a magical
role because of the powerful effects they produced in the mind.
Both men refused to abandon the essential concept that the
first stage in man's comprehension of the universe is through
visual images, and both believed that imaginative use of language could transform visual images into potent and essentially
magical verbal images. Dee and Sidney, then, conceived of the
painter, the architect, the poet and the philosopher – at their
greatest – as very much the same; all were painting images in
the mind that reflected the form of the immaterial universe.
The philosopher, poet, artist and architect were often combined,
of course, in individual Renaissance men: Leonardo da Vinci
and Michelangelo naturally come to mind.

It is possible that Sidney did not have Dee's ideas on the
creative arts specifically in mind when he wrote the *Apology*;
but on the other hand, he may well have known far more of
Dee's theory of the artistic imagination than is expressed in the
'Mathematicall Preface'.[2] Although the evidence that has been

[1] British Museum, Harleian MS. 1879, art. 5; for Du Bartas, see fol. 88;
for Sansovino, see fol. 29; for *Romance of the Rose*, see fol. 46; for Petrarch,
see fol. 52v; for the *Mirror for Magistrates*, see fol. 73; for the *Inferno*, see
fol. 46v; for dictionaries and French poetic works, see fols. 43v, 70v, *et passim*.

[2] Miss Yates has pointed out (*Memory*, pp. 252–3) that, in one of his works
on memory, Bruno propounds a theory in which he, like Dee and Sidney,
conceives of the philosopher, poet and painter as the same: all paint images
in the mind. Bruno overtly ties his interpretation to magical mnemonics.
She wonders (*Memory*, pp. 262–3) whether Sidney had read Bruno's work
before formulating his own theory of *ut pictura poesis*. This is, of course,
decidedly possible since Bruno was involved with the Sidney circle. Clearly
the three men were basing their ideas on similar assumptions.

cited thus far does not show how deeply Sidney was immersed in the occult Hermetic philosophy that Dee espoused, it does prove that he was not working within the confines of Ramistic thought.[1] The Hermetic and magical context of Sidney's *Apology* would have been abundantly evident to men like the Earl of Leicester, Edward Dyer and Gabriel Harvey, the men who were meant to read it. They all knew something of Dee's 'mysticall and supermetaphysicall philosophy'. In fact, when Gabriel Harvey writes about the relationship between magical philosophy and poetry, he pointedly says that 'it is not sufficient for poets, to be superficial humanists: but they must be exquisite artists, & curious universal schollers'.[2] Dee's type of philosophy was as conducive to art as it was to science.

If Sidney was opposed to Puritan attitudes towards the arts, may he not also have been less than an ardent Puritan in his religion? It was suggested earlier that the interests that informed the sixteenth-century French academies could be taken as a guide for considering the concerns of the Areopagus. With one exception, the preoccupations of the Frenchmen have now been considered and related to the Sidney circle. The final subject that must be examined – eirenicism – may have been the most consequential of all to the men of the period.[3]

[1] Sidney also heard Giordano Bruno espouse his magical philosophy at Oxford (Yates, *Giordano Bruno*, pp. 205–56), where Bruno was scorned by the scholars whom he, in turn, despised. The debates in which Bruno participated were performed before the Polish Prince, Albertus Alasco, who was visiting Elizabeth. After what Bruno claims was an idiotic showing on the part of the Oxford 'pedants', Alasco and Sidney went to visit Dee, who made the following notation in his *Diary* (p. 20): 'June 15th, abowt 5 of the clok cam the Polonian Prince Lord Albert Lasky down from Bissham, where he had lodged the night before, being returned from Oxford wither he had gon of purpose to see the universityes, wher he was very honorably used and enterteyned. He had in his company Lord Russel, Sir Philip Sydney, and other gentlemen: he was rowed by the Quene's men, he had the barge covered with the Quene's cloth, the Quene's trumpeters, &c. He cam of purpose to do me honor, for which God be praysed!' Alasco and Sidney visited Dee because he embodied in its Renaissance form the medieval philosophy that had flourished at the university but had become despised there. He was the principal representative of traditional English philosophy as modified to reflect ideas of the Continental Renaissance.

[2] Gabriel Harvey, *Marginalia*, ed. G. C. Moore-Smith (Stratford-upon-Avon, 1913), p. 161.

[3] On the religious situation and the attitudes of the French academicians, see Yates, *French Academies*, pp. 99 ff.

The divisions between Catholics and Protestants were exceedingly deep in the sixteenth century. Yet, the prospect of a permanently divided Christianity struck most concerned men as horrible. Appallingly, the alternative that took precedence over reunion attempts was for each side to try to exterminate the other. We have observed that John Dee feared the prospect of a divided church and foresaw the 'horrid basilisk' that would result if reunion and reform were not achieved, but his solutions – like those of Giordano Bruno – were extremely esoteric. There were many schemes for reuniting the church, however, and the eirenic movement had such various adherents as Melancthon, Cardinal Pole, the Cardinal of Lorraine (uncle to Mary Stuart), Michelangelo, Turnebus, Postel, the members of Baïf's academy and, I suggest, the members of the Areopagus.

Daniel Rogers and Henry Constable, who were both involved with the Sidney circle, were actively working for reunion. Rogers's father had been the first of the Marian martyrs, and the very fact that his Protestant son was still working for Christian reunion indicates the appeal of that dream. Justus Lipsius, the famous Dutch scholar, and Jean Hotman, a Frenchman who served as Leicester's secretary for a time, were both intimate with Sidney and his circle and tried to promote eirenicism.[1] Gabriel Harvey was also concerned with the subject, as was Paul Melissus, the German poet-humanist who was friendly with Rogers and connected with Sidney's group.[2] Further, when Philip Sidney went to the Continent in 1577 to attempt to cement a union between the Protestant princes of Europe, some of his friends there, including Languet, perceived his efforts as a first step towards a reunion of all Christians. Just before leaving for Bohemia in 1577, Sidney, the Earl of Leicester, and Edward Dyer visited Mortlake to consult John Dee, an apostle of eirenicism.[3]

Many men – Reginald Pole and Sadoleto among them – thought that a general council of the Church would reunite Christendom. The Council of Trent thus took place, but it did not make Christian reunion a fact. The Council having failed, men continued to search for other ways of reuniting Christendom.

[1] Van Dorsten, *Poets, Patrons, and Professors*, pp. 83 ff.
[2] Phillips, 'Daniel Rogers', p. 25.
[3] Dee, *Diary*, pp. 2–3.

Among the most prevalent of the alternative methods was religious Hermeticism, which contained doctrines common to both Protestants and Catholics, and therefore offered a unifying bond.[1]

In the *Oration on the Dignity of Man*, Pico della Mirandola traces the tenets that, in his opinion, unite all religions.[2] Following Ficino, Pico uses the *prisca theologia* to form a Christian religious synthesis in which it is possible to see gentile philosophy pointing toward Christianity; Pico also incorporates the cabala in his synthesis. With the pseudo-Dionysius behind him as one important authority, Pico contends that the deepest religious truths are handed down 'from mind to mind, without writing, through the medium of speech'.[3] It was believed that any of the ancient seers who had had to put their revelations in writing did so cryptically, and the cabala especially emphasizes the fact that new truths can be discovered through meticulous exegesis. This naturally fostered the belief that the profoundest truths in the Bible, and in the *prisca theologia*, might not yet have been uncovered and that new revelations awaited the skilful interpreter. It was hoped that, once understood, the occult, divinely inspired wisdom of the most ancient sages would lead to a new era of Christian unity and a universal religion of love. To us, looking back on events, this may seem a fantastic dream; to the sixteenth-century philosopher this seemed a realizable hope.

It was mainly among the various successors of the Platonic academy of Florence that thoughts of a religion of the world were nurtured, and the Hermetic religious movement was widespread in France. In the Pléiade, men like Tyard, Baïf and La Boderie all had an interest in eirenicism and religious Hermeticism. By understanding the mysteries of thrice-great Hermes and contemplating the doctrines of the divine Plato, believers in the new and essentially mystical religion felt that one could move beyond scholastic rationalism and reach new levels of hidden truth. To the academicians, universal harmony was an accepted fact, and the broken harmony of a divided Christen-

---

[1] Yates, *Giordano Bruno*, pp. 169–89.
[2] Pico, *Oration on the Dignity of Man*, pp. 245 ff.
[3] *Ibid.*, p. 251.

dom must have disturbed them deeply, especially since they believed that the harmony could be restored.[1]

When Turnebus, the French Catholic classical scholar, published his influential edition of the *Hermetica* in 1554, he included a preface by Vergerius that emphasized the resemblance between the Hermetic religion and Christianity.[2] Guillaume Postel, the famous French cabalist who influenced La Boderie, dreamt of a reunited Christendom, based on the new revelations of the *prisca theologia* and the cabala. He also called for a united world under one universal monarch – the French king.[3] In 1574, François de Foix de Candale, Bishop of Aire, published an edition of the *Corpus Hermeticum* based on Turnebus's earlier one. He believed that Hermes had attained to a knowledge of religious matters greater than that of the Hebrew prophets and equalling that of the apostles and evangelists.[4]

The Hermeticists listed above were all Catholics, but Philip Sidney's friend and seemingly favourite theologian was Phillipe Du Plessis-Mornay, a Protestant. In the *De la vérité de la réligion chrétienne* published in 1581, Du Plessis-Mornay makes considerable use of Hermetic doctrines, and Sidney began a translation of this work before leaving for the Low Countries.[5] The essence of the Hermeticism that saturates the treatise is summed up early in the third chapter. Since Sidney translated some of this work, the following may be in his own words: '*Mercurius Trismegistus*, who (if the bookes which are fathered uppon him be his in deede, as in trueth they bee very auncient) is the founder of them all, teacheth everywhere, That there is but one GOD.' Du Plessis-Mornay continues by saying that Hermes

[1] Yates, *French Academies*, p. 235.

[2] This work was on Dee's shelves: British Museum, Harleian MS. 1879, art. 5, fol. 29ᵛ.

[3] Both Postel and Turnebus knew Dee personally; see above, p. 31. On Postel's philosophy, see Secret, *Les Kabbalistes*, pp. 171–217; and Van Dorsten, *The Radical Arts*, pp. 21–2.

[4] Yates, *Giordano Bruno*, pp. 172–3.

[5] The translation was completed by Arthur Golding, published in 1587 as *A Woorke concerning the Trewnesse of the Christian Religion*, and dedicated to the Earl of Leicester.

calleth him father of the world, the Creator, the Beginning, the Glorie, the Nature, the Ende, the Necessitie, the Renewer of all things, the worker of all powers, and the power of all works, the onely holy, the onely unbegotten, the onely ever-lasting, the Lord of everlastingnesse, and the everlasting-nesse it selfe; the onely one, and by whome there is but onely one worlde; alone, and himselfe alonly all; namelesse, and more excellent than al names.

Finally, Du Plessis-Mornay wonders 'if it bee possible for us to say any thing, either more, or better for the setting forth of the sayd unitie?'[1] This passage conclusively proves the reverence in which the *Hermetica* was held and clearly illustrates the type of religion that intellectual Europe saw as a basis for a reunion of the faiths. It seems impossible that Sidney, the student of John Dee and the favoured acquaintance of the great Hermeticist Bruno, was not impressed by these passages.[2]

There has always been some question as to the direction in which Philip Sidney turned for spiritual consolation on his deathbed at Flushing. He appears to have turned to his own personal religion of the world, which was probably not unlike that described by Du Plessis-Mornay. D. P. Walker has suggested that Fulke Greville, in his *Life* of Sidney, throws some light on the subject when he asserts that Sidney, during his last moments, asked first about the opinions that the ancients – the *prisci theologi* – had about the soul and its immortality. Sidney wanted to know what knowledge the human soul innately possessed concerning eternal life, and only then did he wish to know what parallels there were with the biblical writers.[3] He undoubtedly believed that the authors of the Bible were divinely inspired, and it would seem as though he gave the same authority to the *prisci theologi*. Philip Sidney had great hopes that a universal religion could be established. As we have seen was the case with John Dee and other religious Hermeti-

---

[1] *A Woorke concerning the Trewnesse of the Christian Religion*, in *Complete Works*, III, 232–3.

[2] On Sidney's use of the *prisca theologia*, see D. P. Walker, 'Ways of Dealing with Atheists: A Background to Pamela's Refutation of Cecropia', *Bibliothèque d'Humanisme et Renaissance*, XVII (Geneva, 1955), 252–77.

[3] Walker, 'Ways of Dealing with Atheists', p. 255; Greville, *Life*, p. 137.

cists, Sidney was not the type of person to adopt a narrow religious attitude.

In summary, Sidney had been exposed to at least three types of religious Hermeticism. He had studied with Dee and associated with Bruno – who were both magi and religious Hermeticists – and he had favoured the theology of Du Plessis-Mornay. Sidney was far more liberal religiously than has often been assumed: it was he, after all, who viewed Musidorus, Pamela and Pyrocles as enlightened pagans who would be saved.

Sidney and his circle were concerned with many subjects: measured verse, science, Hermeticism, occult philosophy and eirenicism. The concerns and the spirit of the men who formed the Areopagus were the same as those espoused in England by John Dee and similar to those that invested Continental academies. Like others in his circle, Philip Sidney seems to have been neither a complete Ramist nor a complete Puritan, though both positions have often been ascribed to him. He was susceptible to the magical Hermetic philosophy of Dee and Bruno. Indeed, John Dee was probably the only person in England who could have prepared the Sidney circle for the arrival of that wild but brilliant ex-friar.

Although most of the topics covered in this chapter are subjects for further investigation, it is clear that some of the old assumptions are simply too restrictive. The fact that men like Dee and Sidney and Dyer were interested in mystical Platonism, in Hermeticism and alchemy, in magic, cannot be dismissed as a despicable remnant of medievalism, for these subjects had all been transformed by the genius of the Renaissance mind, and continuing analysis of such topics will bring us ever closer to a full understanding of the English Renaissance.

John Dee and the
Mechanicians: Applied Science
in Elizabethan England

Being a magus in the most complete sense of the term, John Dee was deeply involved in mathesis, the mystical aspects of number, but his interest in mathematics was practical as well as theoretical. It was Dee's concern for the advancement of applied science that inspired him to write a treatise on the great benefits to be gained from everyday use of mathematics. To make this part of his philosophy readily available to his less learned contemporaries – those mechanicians who would use mathematics in their trades – Dee wrote his 'Mathematicall Preface' to *Euclide* in the vernacular.

Dee conceived of the mechanician as one 'whose skill is, without knowledge of Mathematicall demonstration, perfectly to worke and finishe any sensible worke, by the Mathematicien principall or derivative, demonstrated or demonstrable'.[1] Builders, mechanics, navigators, painters, surveyors, and makers of optical glasses were among the mechanicians whose arts, in Dee's mind, were applied mathematics. Although mechanicians were not held in especially high esteem by most Elizabethan university graduates, Dee respected practical craftsmen and perceived clearly the role they would play in the advancement of knowledge.

The attitude of Dee and others like him represented a basic change in the scientific outlook, and this change was largely responsible for the tremendous advances in technology that occurred during the Renaissance. It is commonly known that,

[1] Dee, 'Mathematicall Preface', sig. a.iiiᵛ.

despite their first-rate scientific minds, the Greeks never fully applied their discoveries.[1] As a consequence, they never even achieved the technological sophistication of the ancient Egyptians. S. Sambursky suggests that, though they invented the scientific method, the Greeks never fully understood its ramifications. 'Logic and deduction', he explains, 'were more important than induction and experience, and the teleological view of nature hampered the increase in physical knowledge.'[2] The Greeks lacked the impulse to operate with their cosmos; instead, they wished primarily to understand it. Given this tradition, what was it that inspired Renaissance men like John Dee to *apply* their scientific philosophy? The Hermetic texts that influenced Renaissance philosophy so profoundly and emphasized magical operation may also have fostered practical application of scientific knowledge; at least this possibility must be considered.[3] We have seen that the Hermetic texts encouraged a basic psychological change that released the human spirit and thus prompted magi like Dee to experiment with the powers of the universe, in spite of the dangers involved.[4] Also, as Festugière has stressed, Hermetic science was diametrically opposed to Aristotelian science, which was essentially disinterested, did not attempt to seek practical applications, and neglected the particular for the general. Hermetic science, on the other hand, attempted to study the specific characteristics of everything in nature.[5] The mysticism and secrecy involved with Hermetic science originally made it a science of the

[1] Samuel Sambursky, *The Physical World of the Greeks*, tr. Merton Dagut (London, 1956), pp. 222 ff.

[2] *Ibid.*, p. 225.

[3] See Yates, 'The Hermetic Tradition', pp. 225–74. Walter Pagel (*William Harvey's Biological Ideas* (Basel and New York, 1967), pp. 113–19) points out that Harvey, the protagonist of modern biological science, was not averse to Hermetic speculation about his discoveries; he was also the friend of Robert Fludd. It is well known that both Boyle and Newton were interested in Hermetic alchemy and that, in terms of volume, Newton's mystical writings far exceed his practical scientific ones. The masons believed that Hermes Trismegistus, not Euclid, first taught geometry to the 'sons of princes', and there are curious similarities between James Anderson's *Constitutions of the Free-masons* (London, 1723) and Dee's 'Mathematicall Preface'.

[4] See above, Chapters 5 and 6.

[5] Festugière, *Hermétisme*, pp. 40–4.

cognoscenti, but the urge to experiment, to examine particulars, was none the less inherent in it.

Paolo Rossi has demonstrated that Francis Bacon's ideas on utilitarian science were rooted in the magical tradition.[1] Dee's were even more so. The desire of the Hermetically inspired Renaissance magus was to control nature, to use it for the benefit of mankind; and, as in Dee's case, this hope frequently prompted an interest in technology. Dee expostulates:

> My entent in additions is not to amend *Euclides* Method, (which nedeth little adding or none at all). But my desire is somwhat to furnish you, toward a more general art Mathematical then *Euclides* Elementes, (remayning in the termes in which they are written) can sufficiently helpe you unto. And though *Euclides* Elementes with my Additions, run not in one Methodicall race toward my marke: yet in the meane space my Additions either geve light, where they are annexed to *Euclides* matter, or geve some ready ayde, and shew the way to dilate your discourses Mathematicall, or to invent and practise things Mechanically.[2]

When coupled with an increased familiarity with the mechanical arts, the attempts of the theoretical scientists – the magi – to understand and use nature drew attention to the gap between traditional scientific learning and the practical potential of science.

Francis Bacon, who is often portrayed as the first English exponent of the experimental method, was by no means original in his call for experimentation, as Rossi has shown. Indeed, almost every magician of the sixteenth century advocated some sort of methodological experimentation, and the forms suggested were often more meaningful than Bacon's. Perhaps in reaction to Aristotelianism, Bacon never fully accepted the role that hypotheses play in a truly productive experimental process. After all, the successes of modern science are based on an interplay between induction and deduction. As F. R. Johnson pointed out some time ago, John Dee proposed a viable theory of experimental science considerably before

[1] Paolo Rossi, *Francis Bacon: From Magic to Science*, tr. Sacha Rabinovitch (London, 1968), pp. 1–35. Thomas Fuller compares Dee and Bacon as natural magicians (*The History of the Worthies of England*, ed. P. Austin Nuttall (London, 1840; reprinted, New York, 1965), II, 205-6).

[2] Dee, *Euclide*, fol. 371.

Francis Bacon formulated his own.[1] It is quite possible that Bacon knew of Dee's treatise in which he terms experimental science 'Archemastrie', an art that 'teacheth to bryng to actuall experience sensible, all worthy conclusions by all Artes Mathematicall purposed, & by true Naturall Philosophie concluded'. Dee continues to explain, 'Bycause it procedeth by *Experiences*, and searcheth forth the causes of Conclusions, by *Experiences*: and also putteth the Conclusions them selves, in *Experience*, it is named of some, *Scientia Experimentalis*.'[2] Dee's entire 'Mathematicall Preface' is a paean to the fusion of theoretical knowledge with mechanical application. Though he was secretive about religious matters and speculative science because of being in the Hermetic tradition, Dee tried desperately to help his countrymen make progress in their knowledge of applied science.[3] He wanted people to understand how they could use the powers of the cosmos for their benefit.

Dee's first published effort along this line appeared in 1561 when he produced an augmentation of Robert Recorde's *Grounde of Artes*, an arithmetic textbook in English that was originally published in 1540.[4] Recorde's series of mathematical

[1] Johnson, *Astronomical Thought*, pp. 151–2. Haydn (*The Counter-Renaissance*, pp. 193–5) does not believe Dee really understood the scientific method. Although Haydn defines experiment in the tradition of Roger Bacon, that is to perceive as experience rather than to experiment, I do not believe he has refuted Johnson's claim. Dee does refer to Roger Bacon as an expert on experimentation, but Dee's words reveal that he was thinking of a method involving induction and deduction. Also, Dee's deep interest in applied science shows that he was fully cognizant of the benefits of experimentation.

[2] Dee, 'Mathematicall Preface', sigs. A.iii ff.

[3] See above, pp. 81 ff.

[4] Recorde was an outstanding scholar. Born about 1510, he was educated at Oxford and received a B.A., and perhaps an M.A., after which he was elected to a fellowship of All Souls in 1531. At some point he went to Cambridge, where he received an M.D. in 1545, returning briefly to Oxford to teach before moving to London. From 1551 until his death in 1558, Recorde acted as the general surveyor of mines. His scholarly interests, like Dee's, were extremely broad. He had mastered mathematics, but he was also a learned physician, a recognized Greek scholar, and an antiquarian-historian who was one of the first Elizabethans interested in the Anglo-Saxon language. As a teacher, he was able to present mathematics in a clear and concise way that could be easily grasped by the student. On Recorde and his work, see Francis R. Johnson and Sanford Larkey, 'Robert Recorde's Mathematical Teaching and the Anti-Aristotelian Movement', *HLB*, VII (1935), 59–87; see also Johnson, *Astronomical Thought*, pp. 120 ff.

textbooks was the first in English to present coherently and simply the newly developing subject of algoristic mathematics, or that based on Arabic numbers. The changeover to Arabic mathematics was very slow in taking effect, and government accounts, for instance, continued to be kept in Roman numerals throughout the Tudor period. Recorde's works, like Dee's preface, were aimed specifically at mechanicians, or non-university men, as is indicated in the introduction to the *Grounde of Artes*: 'Therefore gentle reader, though this boke can be but small aide to the learned sort, yet unto ye simple ignorant (which nedeth most helpe) it may bee a good furtheraunce and meane to knowledge.'[1] Mathematical education was so elementary that Recorde had to assume little or no knowledge on the part of his reader and consequently had to start with the most basic concepts and gradually work up to the more complex and difficult aspects of mathematics.

Recorde's various scientific works had extremely practical aims: he wished to arouse the interest of his pupils and encourage them to use mathematics in everyday affairs. The secret of Recorde's method of teaching is to combine, in clear and concise prose, the theoretical and applied aspects of mathematics. He does not condone a system that simply presents the empirical side of the mathematical sciences without giving the student a comprehensive understanding of the principles underlying the application. Using a dialogue form in which the master answers questions and corrects observations made by the student, Recorde leads the pupil through the subject in a carefully ordered fashion. Recorde's series of textbooks was thus meant to give the reader a solid understanding of the subject, and it appears that the books were also meant to be studied in the sequence in which they were published, beginning with the *Grounde of Artes* and ending with his fourth work, the *Castle of Knowledge*, which was first printed in 1556.[2] The *Grounde of Artes*, which Dee augmented after Recorde's death, went through no less than twenty-six editions before 1662; it was the standard arithmetic text of the period.[3]

[1] Robert Recorde, *Grounde of Artes*, augmented by John Dee (London, 1561), sig. V.

[2] Johnson and Larkey, 'Robert Recorde's Mathematical Teaching and the Anti-Aristotelian Movement', pp. 61–4.

[3] Hill, *Intellectual Origins*, p. 17.

Dee revised some of Recorde's text, improving and correcting
it in various details, but he also enlarged the volume by adding
a section entitled, 'The Second Part of Arithmetike Touching
Fractions, briefly sette forthe'. Dee may have based his additions to the *Grounde of Artes* on an existing treatise on fractions
which is in his hand.[1] The treatise, however, is not in dialogue
form, which is one of the notable features of Recorde's work
and is continued by Dee in his augmentation. We can be fairly
sure that Dee viewed his work on the *Grounde of Artes* as preparation for the first English *Euclide*. In conjunction with John
Mellis, a Southwark schoolmaster, Dee produced another
edition of the *Grounde of Artes* in 1582, and this edition included
some verses by Dee addressed to 'the earnest Arithmetician'.
Though not published in the earlier volume, the verses were
apparently written while Dee was working on the 1561 edition
because he mentions that there is not yet an English *Euclide*.
They express his conception of the relationship between
arithmetic and geometry:[2]

> My loving friend to Science bent,
> Something thou hast by this booke woone
> But if thou wilt be excellent,
> Another race thou must yet runne. . . .
>
> The famous Greeke of Platoes lore,
> EUCLIDE I meane Geometer:
> So true, so plaine, so fraught with store,
> (as in our speach) is yet no where.
>
> A treasure straunge, that booke wil prove,
> With numbers skil, matcht in due sort,
> This I thee warn of sincere love,
> And to proceede do thee exhort.

The first English *Euclide* was translated by Sir Henry
Billingsley, an alderman and later Lord Mayor of London, and
was printed as a beautiful folio volume by John Day in 1570.

[1] Bodleian, Ashmole MS. 242, art. 44, fols. 160v–156. This treatise is
bound backwards and upside down in the volume.
[2] John Dee and John Mellis, eds, *Grounde of Artes*, by Robert Recorde
(London, 1582), sig. Yy.viv.

The earliest translation of Euclid into Latin was made by Adelard of Bath around 1130, and this version, to which Campanus of Novara added commentaries, became the popular one. It has usually been assumed that the English *Euclide* of Dee and Billingsley was based on the Adelard–Campanus version, which was first published at Venice in 1482. It seems almost certain, however, that the first English *Euclide* was translated from the Greek edition of the *Elements* produced by Simon Grynaeus and published at Basel in 1533 by John Hervagius. Though Billingsley probably had the Latin version before him, it appears that he used it only for reference.[1] To Billingsley's admirable translation, Dee added his important and influential 'Mathematicall Preface', as well as annotations throughout the body of the text, and the introductions which appear before the various books.[2]

In the Preface, which he claims was hurriedly written under constant pressure from the publisher, Dee manages to outline the entire state of science (see Plate 13) as it was known in the sixteenth century. The Preface opens with a discussion of philosophical mathematics and its mystical implications, which was of interest to magi; but when Dee begins to explain the practical applications of the mathematical sciences, he pointedly states:

> From henceforth, in this my Preface, will I frame my talk, to *Plato* his fugitive Scholers: or, rather, to such, who well can, (and also wil,) use their utward senses, to the glory of God, the benefite of their Country, and their owne secret contentation, or honest preferment, on this earthly Scaffold. To them, I will orderly recite, describe & declare a great Number of Artes, from our two Mathematicall fountaines [arithmetic and geometry], derived into the fieldes of *Nature*.[3]

This he clearly does.

In the text accompanying the 'Groundplat', Dee explains the

---

[1] See George B. Halsted, 'Note on the First English Euclid', *American Journal of Mathematics*, II (1879), 46–8.

[2] Some of the notes for Dee's annotations are found in British Museum, Sloane MS. 15.

[3] Dee, 'Mathematicall Preface', sig. a.iii.

natures of the various sciences, the relationships among them, and the levels of advancement achieved in each. The explanations are usually trenchant rather than detailed.[1] Dee also makes suggestions, which are sometimes prophetic, for future scientific developments. As an example, under 'Pneumatithmie', he discusses the power of a vacuum and says that, by understanding its force, 'two or three men together, by keping Ayre under a great Cauldron, and forcying the same downe, orderly, may without harme descend to the Sea bottome: and continue there a tyme &c'.[2] The most striking of the scientific suggestions offered in the preface is that architecture henceforth be based on classical rules of harmony and proportion, in other words that the architects in England follow the lead of their Continental counterparts and institute a neoclassical revival.[3] The essential point to be remembered about Dee's preface is that it is a revolutionary manifesto calling for the recognition of mathematics as a key to all knowledge and advocating broad application of mathematical principles.

One major aspect of the 'Mathematicall Preface' must be discussed in more detail. Dee advocates an essentially utilitarian form of education based on the quadrivial subjects and thus is very much in the mainstream of educational reformers of the sixteenth century. His thoughts on the subject are similar to those of Robert Recorde, whom he succeeded as the leading scientist and scientific teacher in England, and they parallel those that Peter Ramus, Dee's friend, was advocating in France.[4] In their idea about educational reform and their interest in practical mathematics, Dee and Ramus had an intellectual meeting ground. The two corresponded about mathematical texts; but as I argued earlier, it is likely that Dee

[1] Many of the sciences which Dee discusses have already been considered in this study, and others will be discussed. With the 'Groundplat' reproduced, it hardly seems necessary to add detailed textual descriptions.

[2] Dee, 'Mathematicall Preface', sig. d.i.

[3] *Ibid.*, sigs. d.iii–d.iiii*v*; see also above, pp. 57 ff. In the preface Dee spends more time on architecture than on almost any other subject. As was mentioned, one of his basic sources for the preface was Vitruvius, who discusses in his *De architectura* many of the same arts and sciences that Dee covers in the preface.

[4] On this area of Ramist thought, see Hookyaas, *Humanisme, Science et Réforme.*

perceived of Ramus's approach merely as an introduction to method.[1] On this account, the theories of the Frenchman would have been acceptable to Dee, but they would not have provided a means of exploring the higher – and to Dee all-important – philosophical and mystical aspects of thought. It is improbable that Dee would have found much in Ramus's works that would have improved on the pedagogical method of Recorde. As Johnson and Larkey have shown, Robert Recorde's ideas on education, though in some ways similar to those of Ramus, were arrived at quite independently.[2] Dee carried on the tradition of educational reform that Recorde introduced in England during the 1540s, before Ramus published anything. It seems logical to assume, therefore, that Dee was most indebted to Recorde and only secondarily indebted, if at all, to Ramus.[3]

Like Dee, Recorde was by choice primarily a mathematician and scientist, whereas Ramus, until quite late in his career, remained chiefly a logician wishing to reform and simplify dialectic in relation to the Aristotelian system. Ramus turned to mathematics principally to apply his logical method to the restructuring of its subject matter, but before he was able to apply the dialectical method that marks his system, Ramus had to learn the mathematical sciences. He never approached Dee's profundity as a mathematician, and it is a minor irony that Ramus should have recommended Dee to Elizabeth as worthy of holding a mathematical chair at either of the English universities.

Ramus's textbooks present a revision and simplification of old mathematical knowledge rather than a critical remodelling of material in light of the latest discoveries. The textbooks of Recorde and Dee also simplify the subject matter, but they reflect a much more comprehensive understanding of the mathematical sciences than do the comparable works by Ramus.

[1] See above, pp. 142 ff.

[2] Johnson and Larkey, 'Robert Recorde's Mathematical Teaching and the Anti-Aristotelian Movement', pp. 80–7.

[3] Dee's schematic outline of the sciences might strike many as Ramistically inspired; however, even a cursory glance through the works of Lull shows that he constantly used the same type of diagrammatic outline to demonstrate his ideas. Since Dee had an extensive collection of Lull's works, I believe it is to him, rather than to Ramus, that Dee was chiefly indebted for the idea of using a schema.

This is probably why Ramus's works on geometry and arithmetic, though translated into English, had little success in England, though use of his dialectical system was fairly widespread in the last part of the sixteenth century.[1] The mathematical works of the Englishmen were simply better.

To Peter Ramus, for example, 'Geometrie is the Arte of measuring well'.[2] To John Dee, this is only one aspect of the science's complex function:

> But, well you may perceive by *Euclides Elementes*, that more ample is our Science, then to measure Plaines: and nothyng lesse therin is tought (of purpose) then how to measure Land. An other name, therefore, must nedes be had, for our Mathematicall Science of Magnitudes: which regardeth neither clod, nor turff: neither hill, nor dale: neither earth nor heaven: but is absolute *Megethologia*: not creping on ground, and dasseling the eye, with pole perche, rod or lyne: but liftyng the hart above the heavens, by invisible lines, and immortall beames: meteth with the reflexions, of the light incomprehensible: and so procureth Joye, and perfection unspeakable.[3]

Their diverse conceptions of the role of geometry exemplify the difference between the minds of Dee and Ramus. The latter would have nothing to do with the theoretical aspects of mathematics; for example, he thought Euclid's tenth book on irrational magnitudes was useless.[4] Dee and Recorde, on the other hand, both considered theory necessary for any real

[1] *Elementes of Geometrie* was translated by Thomas Hood and published in 1590, and *The Art of Arithmeticke in whole Numbers and Fractions* was translated by William Kempe and published in 1592. These appear to be the only English publications of Ramus's mathematical texts during the period.

[2] Peter Ramus, *Elementes of Geometrie*, tr. Thomas Hood (London, 1590), p. 1.

[3] Dee, 'Mathematicall Preface', sig. a.ii^v. Dee bases this on Plato's authority.

[4] Dee admits that Euclid's tenth book 'is yet thought & accompted, to be the hardest booke to understand of all the bookes of *Euclide*', and he adds that many people believed it could not be understood 'without the knowledge of that most secret and subtill part of Arithmetike, commonly called Algebra', but he did not think it any more difficult to comprehend than the other books, and he recognized its value (fol. 228^{r-v}).

understanding of the subject. In his study of Ramist attempts at educational reform, Hookyaas outlines its purpose: 'They wanted to make education easier, more interesting, and more concrete by inserting into it examples borrowed from everyday practices because, in Ramus's opinion, the natural method is also, inevitably, the easiest method.'[1]

Recorde, Ramus and Dee all published their mathematical texts in the vernacular, which was necessary to the furtherance of their attempts at educational reform. Dee was fully aware of the revolutionary aspects of presenting an edition of Euclid's *Elements* in English, and at the end of the preface he defends himself against possible attack by disapproving university men. Dee assures the universities that they really have nothing to fear and comments: 'great Comfort, with good hope, may the *Universities* have, by reason of this *Englishe* Geometrie, and Mathematicall Praeface, that they (hereafter) shall be the more regarded, esteemed, and resorted unto.'[2] He was probably not quite so solicitous about the universities as might be imagined since he did leave them because they were so backward in the teaching of science, and he did make it plain in other writings that they had nothing to offer in the profounder sciences.[3] Dee makes his attitude somewhat clearer when he adds:

Besides this, how many a Common Artificer, is there, in these Realmes of England and Ireland, that dealeth with Numbers, Rule, & Cumpasse: Who, with their owne Skill and experience, already had, will be hable (by these good helpes and informations), to finde out, and devise, new workes, straunge Engines, and Instrumentes: for Sundry purposes in the Common Wealth? or for the private pleasure? and for the better maintayning of their owne estate? I will not (therefore) fight against myne owne shadowe. For, no man (I am sure) will open his mouth against this Enterprise. No man (I say) who either hath Charitie toward his brother (and would be glad of his furtherance in vertuous knowledge): or that hath any care & zeale for the bettering of the Common state of this Realme.[4]

[1] Hookyaas, *Humanisme, Science et Réforme*, p. 29.
[2] Dee, 'Mathematicall Preface', sig. A.iiii.
[3] See above, pp. 22 ff.
[4] Dee, 'Mathematicall Preface', sigs. A.iiii^r-v.

There is, of course, one particularly strong reason why the universities would have been annoyed with Dee's preface: not only does it implicitly attack the standard Oxford or Cambridge education, but it is definitely *not* Aristotelian in spirit.

Like Recorde, but unlike Ramus, Dee was not particularly anti-Aristotelian. It is well known that Ramus, for his M.A. at Paris, defended the notorious thesis that everything Aristotle said was wrong. In contrast, Dee accepted and used the doctrines of Aristotle that he felt had validity; he did not denounce Aristotle indiscriminately. Dee's attitude was one that tended to destroy rigid Aristotelianism from within rather than from without by a vicious onslaught. In his attempt to give the English mechanicians the means to think for themselves about the sciences, Dee advocated testing old beliefs by experiment in the Platonic tradition supported at medieval Oxford, which was more hospitable to science than the predominating Aristotelianism of Renaissance Oxford and Cambridge.[1] This was hardly an approach that the universities would condone, but it did lead to the establishment of scientific method and did encourage the practical application of the mathematical arts.

The centre of English science during the sixteenth century was in London, not at the universities. In the capital, numerous non-university people, as well as university men like Dee and Recorde, formed a kind of amorphous third university.[2] Functioning at Syon House, along with Dee's circle at nearby Mortlake, was the group that gathered around Henry Percy, the 'Wizard Earl', during the latter part of the sixteenth and the early seventeenth centuries. Some of the greatest intellects in England were in this circle; Anthony Wood includes Thomas Hariot, John Dee, Walter Warner and Nathaniel Torporly – 'the Atlantes of the mathematical world'.[3] To these should be added Thomas Allen, a mathematician who in many ways resembled Dee, Christopher Marlowe, John Donne and Walter Ralegh. There was apparently considerable communication between Dee's circle and that of Percy. Ralegh did favours for Dee at court and had considerable respect for the man who

[1] See above, pp. 26–7.
[2] Hill, *Intellectual Origins*, pp. 14–84; Johnson, *Astronomical Thought*, *passim*.
[3] Wood, *Athenae Oxoniensis*, II, 542.

directed the exploratory voyages of his half-brothers, Adrian and Humphrey Gilbert.[1] Thomas Hariot, who was educated at Oxford and was subsequently employed by Ralegh as a mathematical tutor, has been neglected, but his substantial contributions to science are beginning to be recognized. His biographer claims with good reason that Hariot was as great a mathematician and scientist as Galileo; Hariot was certainly studying the moon with a telescope by July of 1609.[2] One of Hariot's primary interests was optics, which was also a preoccupation of Dee's; in fact, the interests of these two scientists usually coincided.[3] And there is no doubt that they were good friends.[4]

Besides the Dee and Northumberland circles, the first formal scientific academy in England, Gresham College, was situated in London. The methods of teaching and the orientation towards the quadrivial subjects at the college were in direct contrast to the educational system at Oxford and Cambridge.[5]

It was particularly among extra-university mechanicians and scholars living in the capital, that Dee's 'Mathematicall Preface' enjoyed popularity. Since it was so commonly known and so highly respected, it is probably almost impossible to estimate its true influence on the development of scientific and philosophical thought in England during the Renaissance. Dee's

[1] Dee, *Diary*, pp. 20, 21, 54.

[2] Henry Stevens, *Thomas Hariot: The Mathematician, the Philosopher and the Scholar* (London, 1900), p. 114. On Hariot, see also R. H. Kargon, *Atomism in England from Hariot to Newton* (Oxford, 1966), pp. 18 ff. Kargon's conclusions are rather suspect. For a summary of current work being done on Hariot, see A. C. Crombie *et al.*, 'Thomas Harriot (1560–1621): an Original Practitioner in the Scientific Art', reprint from *TLS* (23 October 1969).

[3] Dee writes that the science of optics makes 'thynges, farre of, to seeme nere: and nere, to seme farre of. Small things, to seme great: and great, to seme small. One man, to seme an Army. Or a man to be curstly affrayed of his owne shadow' ('Mathematicall Preface', sig. b.iv). William Bourne testifies to Dee's pre-eminent knowledge of optics (*A Treatise on the Properties and Qualities of Glasses for Optical Purposes*, in *Rara Mathematica*, ed. J. O. Halliwell (London, 1841), p. 45).

[4] In the British Museum copy of *El viaje que hizo Antonio de Espejo en el anno de ochenta y tres*, the following notation by Dee appears on the title page: 'Joannes Dee: Ao 1590. Januarii. 24 Ex dono Thomas Hariot, Amici mei.'

[5] F. R. Johnson, 'Gresham College: Precursor of the Royal Society', *JHI*, I (1940), 413–38.

personal role as a teacher and adviser to mechanicians and scientists may have been even more important. Yet, Dee and his treatise have often been neglected by historians of science. A brief history of the dispersion of the preface subsequent to its publication in 1570 will demonstrate its popularity.

When George Gascoigne decided to publish Sir Humphrey Gilbert's *A Discourse of Discoverie for a new passage to Cataia* in 1576, he claimed that one reason for publication was Dee's approval:

> Now let mee say that a great learned man (even *M. Dee*) doth seeme very well to like of this *Discoverie* and doth much commende the Authour, the which he declareth in his *Mathematical* preface to th'english *Euclide*, I refer thee (Reader) to peruse the same, and thinke it not strange though I be encouraged by so learned a foreleader, to set forth a thing whiche hee so well like of.[1]

This is one of the earliest printed indications of the respect that contemporaries afforded Dee's preface.

William Bourne, a popularizer, a Londoner, a self-educated individual, and the first of a series of non-university teachers and writers, published *A Booke called the Treasure for Traveilers*. Though Bourne terms his borrowing from Dee, 'A briefe note, taken out of *M. Dees* mathematical preface that goeth before *Euclides Elementes* nowe extant in our Inglishe tongue, as touching what the *Mathematical* sciences are', he reproduces the entire breakdown of the sciences offered by Dee.[2] Edward Worsop, another Londoner and popularizer of practical mathematics, styles Dee the foremost mathematician in Europe. He adds that Dee

> hath put unto these englished elements, many scholies, annotations, corollaries, and expositions which give great light, and facilitie to the understanding of them. Also his mathematical preface unto these elements, is a worke of such

---

[1] George Gascoigne, 'The Epistle to the Reader', in *A Discourse of Discoverie*, sig. qq.iiii.

[2] William Bourne, *A Booke called the Treasure for Traveilers* (London, 1578), sigs. ***.ii–***.iii.

singularitie and necessitie to all students of the Mathematicals, that I wish them to make it a manuel.[1]

One of the most glowing contemporary tributes accorded Dee's 'Mathematicall Preface' was made by Thomas Hylles in *The Arte of Vulgar Arithmetic*. Hylles was also a Londoner and a popularizer and translator of practical scientific works; he published on everything from gardening to the interpretation of dreams. Hylles exhorts the reader,

> I refer you to the prefaces of *M. Rob Record* in his Ground of artes and Whetstone of wit, & to the notable preface of *M. John Dee* prefixed to *Euclid*, where you shal finde matter aboundant touching that argument, delivered with such grace & sweetnes of stile that the very memory thereof forceth my rustick pen, as quite abashed, all amased & astoined, here sodenly to stop, & abruptly to stay.[2]

Hylles suggests, interestingly, that the frenzied and emotionally charged prose that Dee uses in the preface is of considerable merit. Dee certainly rises to heights of lyrical enthusiasm in his praise of the mathematical sciences, and his contemporaries apparently found this extremely effective, though the style now seems at first obscure and alien. In his own century Dee's preface fully achieved the objectives which he had in mind: it did impress on his compatriots the significance of the mathematical sciences and the benefits to be gained from their study.

The fame of Dee's 'Mathematicall Preface' continued well into the seventeenth century. In his edition of the first six books of Euclid's *Elements* printed in 1651, Thomas Rudd does not bother adding any significant comments of his own in evaluation of the mathematical sciences. Instead, he reprints the preface of 'that pious and learned Mathematician M^r. JOHN DEE . . . (which deserves perpetual commendations) having beene so large in the explanation and use of all the parts' of the mathematicals.[3]

---

[1] Worsop, *A Discoverie of sundrie errours*, sig. G3^v.

[2] Thomas Hylles, *The Arte of Vulgar Arithmetic* (London, 1600), sig. B4^v.

[3] Euclide, *Elements of Geometry: The first VI Books*, ed. Thomas Rudd (London, 1651), sig. A3^v; the 'Mathematicall Preface' covers sigs. B–N4. Thomas Rudd was steeped in Hermeticism, and he admired Dee's *Monas Hieroglyphica*. British Museum, Harleian MS. 6486, is a Hermetic treatise ascribed to Rudd; a copy of Dee's hieroglyph of the monad appears on fol. 4^v.

Perhaps the most telling evidence of the widespread admiration that the preface continued to command is found in the correspondence between John Worthington, who was Master of Jesus College, Cambridge, during the Protectorate, and Samuel Hartlib, an educational reformer and friend of John Milton. Writing to Worthington on 20 November 1655, Hartlib begs him to have some outstanding Latinist translate Dee's preface because, as he says:

> M^r. Dee's large Preface before his Commentary upon Euclid (wch hath been epitomized and printed last year as I take it with the s^d Preface) is deservedly extolled as a Substantial, solid, and learned discourse to shew the Necessity and Excellency of Mathematicks, I should think, if this were added also to Jungius's Discourse, it would put many more young Scholars throughout the world, into a Mathematical Conversation. That great Scholar of *Christ's Coll.* in Camb. (I mean Sr W. Boswell,) was pleased to attribute all his proficiency in learning whatever it was, to the goodness of the fore-mentioned Preface of Dee's. Methinks, this should be a sufficient Incentive to stir up some able pen at Camb. to turn it in Latin.[1]

Apparently nothing came of this suggestion because Hartlib comments to Worthington on 12 December 1655: 'You say nothing whether any body may be found, that will undertake the translating of Dee's mathematical preface. I pray be pleased to answer categorically to this particular.'[2] Hartlib obviously considered this a project of some moment. It is, none the less, slightly ironic that he was so anxious to see the preface in Latin when Dee had so pointedly avoided that language.

About the same time that Hartlib wrote to Worthington, John Webster, the Puritan divine, was examining the state of education at the universities and, in the course of his study, had special praise for Dee's preface. When recommending the introduction of a form of education very like that which Dee envisages in the 'Mathematicall Preface', Webster says,

[1] John Worthington, *The Diary and Correspondence*, ed. James Crossley, *Chetham Society Publications*, XIII (Manchester, 1847), 59–60. Sir William Boswell was ambassador to The Hague from 1633 until his death in 1649.
[2] Worthington, *Diary and Correspondence*, p. 66.

What shall I say of *Staticks*, *Architecture*, *Pneumatithmie*, *Stratarithmetrie* and the rest enumerated by that expert and learned man, Dr. *John Dee* in his Preface before *Euclide*? What excellent, admirable and profitable experiments do every one of these afford? truly innumerable, the least of which is more use, benefit and profit to the life of man, than almost all that learning that the Universities boast of and glory in.[1]

It is revealing that, in his attack on the Aristotelians, Webster defends natural magic, apparently understanding that there is a close relationship between magic and the development of science; this relationship is, of course, especially exemplified by Dee. One cannot help but wonder if that other Puritan, John Milton, who was so deeply interested in mathematics, also had Dee's preface in mind when he wrote *Of Education*. Certainly Milton knew the edition of the *Grounde of Artes* with Dee's augmentation, and it is highly probable that he knew the English *Euclide*, or at least the 'Mathematicall Preface', in one of its reprintings since it was also a standard mathematical work.[2]

Almost a hundred years after it was written, the preface was reprinted in an edition of Euclid published in 1661. The editors assert, 'We have thought good to insert . . . that full and learned Preface of the famous Mathematician *John Dee*, then which nothing of that nature can be more ample or satisfactory.'[3] As much as Bacon's *Advancement*, Dee's 'Mathematicall Preface' is a milestone in the history of English scientific thought.[4]

The role played by Dee and his preface in spurring develop-

---

[1] John Webster, *Academiarum Examen* (London, 1654), p. 52. Seth Ward published *Vindiciae Academiarum* (Oxford, 1654), which is a refutation of Webster's attack on the universities. On this controversy, see Allen G. Debus, *The Chemical Dream of the Renaissance* (Cambridge, 1968), pp. 28–32.

[2] On Milton's mathematical studies, see Harris Francis Fletcher, *The Intellectual Development of John Milton* (Urbana, Ill., 1956), I, 355–83, esp. 359–62. Fletcher does not realize that the 'Mathematicall Preface' was reprinted several times, though he recognizes the fact that the 1570 *Euclide* was the standard edition during the period.

[3] Euclid, *Elements of Geometry*, ed. John Leeke and George Serle (London, 1661), sig. A; the 'Mathematicall Preface' covers sigs. (a)–A.

[4] The very real possibility of Dee's preface influencing Francis Bacon has never, so far as I know, even been considered.

ments in each branch of science should be examined, but that would require a book in itself. There was one particular group of mechanicians, however, upon which John Dee and the English *Euclide* were peculiarly influential – the navigators. Dee energetically promoted voyages of exploration, and until 1583 when he left for the Continent with Edward Kelley and the Polish Prince Albertus Alasco, he was perhaps *the* major guiding spirit behind the glorious saga of English expansion.[1] A current expert on the history of navigation, D. W. Waters, states flatly that no other single work was so influential in encouraging the development in England of mathematics, navigation and hydrography – in spurring the practical application of mathematics generally – as Dee's 'Mathematicall Preface' and the English *Euclide*. He concludes that Dee's handling of the mathematical sciences as a whole is masterful in the preface, but Waters contends that his analyses of navigation and hydrography have never been surpassed.[2]

John Dee displayed his eager interest and thorough capability in the geographical sciences from his earliest trips to the Continent. He was in contact with Gemma Frisius, at one time cosmographer to the Emperor Charles V, and another of Dee's close friends was Pedro Nuñez, the Cosmographer Royal of Portugal and Professor of Mathematics at Coimbra. It is possible that Dee and Nuñez never met in person; but in 1558, when Dee was worn by illness and anxiety as a result of his brief detention for heresy, he wished Nuñez to be his literary executor in the event of his death. Dee could also count among his close friends Gerard Mercator, the greatest cosmographer, globe-maker and producer of navigational instruments in Europe. Oronce Finé also knew Dee well. Finé was Professor of Mathematics at the Collège de France, and he was one of the most important contemporary French geographers; Dee spent time discussing science with him while in Paris in 1550 and 1551. Finally, as I have mentioned previously, Dee and Abraham Ortelius of Antwerp, one of the most influential cosmographers of the day, kept in close contact. They exchanged

[1] Like everyone who studies Dee as a geographer I am deeply indebted to the work of E. G. R. Taylor, especially *Tudor Geography*, pp. 76 ff. For her other contributions to the study of Dee's geographical influence, see the bibliography at the end of this book.

[2] Waters, *Art of Navigation*, p. 131.

visits, and through Daniel Rogers, Dee's friend and Ortelius's nephew, had an effective means of continuous communication.[1]

Dee was one of the principal advisers in the early English attempts to find a north-eastern passage to Cathay.[2] To further this special interest of the Duke of Northumberland and the London wool merchants, the Muscovy Company was formed and Richard Chancellor, a brilliant young seaman, was chosen to pilot the first voyage. While Chancellor was staying in the household of Sir Henry Sidney, Dee placed himself at the disposal of the young pilot, teaching him the fundamentals of navigation and working with him on a new *Ephemerides*. Sebastian Cabot and Richard Eden were also involved in the preparations for the voyage, and they often conferred with Chancellor; though there is no direct evidence, they must have come into contact with Dee. After the death of Richard Chancellor, Stephen Borough and his younger brother William took over the piloting of the exploratory voyages for the Muscovy Company. The shareholders of the company asked Dee to educate the brothers, who had little or no mathematical or technical training; Dee's instructions were probably in preparation for the Muscovy voyage of 1559. The discovery on this voyage of the desirable Muscovy trade and a new route to Persia led to the abandonment of the search for a new route to Cathay itself, though the company continued to hold the patent for such explorations.

After searching for a north-eastern passage to Cathay, Englishmen sought a north-western route to the Orient. In 1576, 1577 and 1578, Martin Frobisher made attempts at finding such a passage under Dee's guidance. These voyages caused a good deal of excitement because Frobisher brought back from his first voyage an Eskimo, who was believed to be a native from the Asian mainland because of his Mongolian characteristics. Frobisher also returned with a sample of ore that he thought contained gold. As a result, Dee and others invested money in the subsequent voyages, but the ore was found to be worthless after extensive investigation, and Frobisher's voyages ended.

[1] Taylor, *Tudor Geography*, pp. 83 ff.
[2] On the following, see Taylor, *Tudor Geography*, pp. 119–21.

Over approximately the same period, Sir Francis Drake was involved in his epic-making voyage around the world, and there is strong evidence to suggest that Dee may have been behind Drake's voyage.[1] The promoters of Drake's explorations included Sir Francis Walsingham, the Earl of Leicester, Sir Christopher Hatton, and Sir Edward Dyer, who were all intimate friends of Dee's. Entries in Dee's *Private Diary* reveal visits from these principal backers at about the same time Drake left England in 1577. Drake returned late in 1580, and Dee was visited in June of 1581 by John Hawkins, one of Drake's companions on the voyage; it may have been from Hawkins that he received the story of Drake's adventures.[2]

During the 1580s, Dee's influence in geographical matters was beginning to wane, but he remained the chosen adviser of older men like Sir Humphrey Gilbert. In September of 1580, Gilbert entered an agreement, in the presence of witnesses, that granted Dee the rights to all newly discovered land north of the 50th parallel.[3] This would have given Dee the largest part of what is now Canada, but when the voyage was finally undertaken, it failed. After Gilbert arrived in Newfoundland, his flagship – the *Delight* – which contained most of his provisions, was wrecked while attempting to reach the American mainland. On the return to England, the ship *Squirrel* sank and Gilbert was drowned.

The last geographical adventure in which Dee is known to have been directly involved was a plan in 1583 to form a company – with Adrian Gilbert and John Davis (the last seaman Dee ever taught) – to carry out the colonization, conversion and general exploitation of Atlantis, as Dee termed America.[4] At this time Dee was still following up the prerogative granted to him by Humphrey Gilbert several years before. Dee was already deeply involved with his attempts at practical cabala;

[1] The material supporting Dee's influence on Drake is assembled by Miss Taylor in *Tudor Geography*, pp. 110–19.

[2] Dee, *Diary*, p. 11; British Museum, Lansdowne MS. 122, fols. 22–8v, is a record in Dee's handwriting of Drake's voyage.

[3] Dee, *Diary*, p. 8; see also Humphrey Gilbert, *The Voyages and Colonising Enterprises of Sir Humphrey Gilbert*, ed. D. B. Quinn, *Hakluyt Society Publications*, LXXXIII–LXXXIV (London, 1938–9), II, 483. ·

[4] Gilbert, *Voyages*, I, 96–9; II, 483–9. Both of these men were also involved with John Dee in his magical exercises.

and he made inquiries of the angels, in Adrian Gilbert's presence (with Kelley as medium), concerning the planned voyage and the intended conversion of the natives, the latter point being of particular importance to Dee.[1] Before Gilbert left for the New World, Dee had slipped away to the Continent.

The above outline of Dee's genuine contributions to English navigation is cursory, but it provides direct evidence of his influence on contemporary events. As one might expect, Dee's enthusiasm for promoting English exploratory voyages was inspired by a number of motives. First, he hoped to find a way to the East, for traditionally (and he accepted this tradition) it represented one of the great repositories of occult knowledge. Second, John Dee had an apocalyptic vision of England's future in which he perceived the formation of an 'Incomparable BRYTISH IMPIRE' – both religious and political – with Elizabeth as empress. The possible material wealth to be gained for the country through exploration was not overlooked, but it was only a secondary factor. [2]

The first of Dee's primary objectives is made clear in several ways. As early as 1570, in his discussion of navigation in the 'Mathematicall Preface', he refers to the unfulfilled English attempts to reach the Orient. He implores,

Some one, or other, should listen to the Matter: and by good advise, and discrete Circumspection, by little, and little, wynne to the sufficient knowledge of that Trade and Voyage: Which, now, I would be sorry, (through Carelesnesse, want of Skill, and Courrage,) should remayne Unknowne and unheard of. Seyng, also, we are herein, halfe Challenged, by the learned, by halfe request, published. Therof, verely, might grow Commoditye, to this Land chiefly, and to the rest of the

[1] British Museum, Sloane MS. 3188, fols. 103 ff. The angels, not surprisingly, were particularly unco-operative about supplying any useful information.

[2] Dee was most desirous of improving England's economic situation. As early as 1570, he outlined (British Museum, Cotton Charter XIII, art. 39) a plan to 'MAKE THIS KINGDOME FLOURISHING, TRIUMPHANT, FAMOUS AND BLESSED'. Among other things he suggests that it would be wise 'to make England both abroad and at home to be Lord and ruler of the Exchange', a task that Sir Thomas Gresham accomplished and that produced great benefits for England. The plan is quite thorough and covers most of the areas of England's economy, such as tin production and cloth trade.

Christen Common wealth, farre passing all riches and worldly Threasure.[1]

The challenge that Dee refers to was indirectly expressed by Mercator and Ortelius, who thought that the English navigators were obliged to complete the explorations of Asia that they had started with some success and then halted with the Muscovy voyage of 1559. The concluding promise of benefits surpassing all worldly riches is no exaggeration on Dee's part, for it pertains directly to his hope of gaining knowledge of occult mysteries from the East.[2] Dee and other philosophers like Guillaume Postel interpreted cosmography as a science of intellectual as well as geographical discovery; they thought Oriental wisdom might reveal a means of establishing a *concordia mundi* and a universal faith.[3]

Dee's interest in Oriental matters was prodigious, which in itself implies an objective for exploration beyond the mere discovery of new trade routes. It seems that he was actually planning to travel to Asia in 1577, and in 1581 he conferred with the German John Haller, whom he claims to have inspired to journey to China.[4] Contemporaries apparently regarded Dee as something of an expert on Far Eastern affairs, and his manuscript, 'Of Famous and Rich Discoveries', is largely devoted to Oriental matters.[5]

Dee formed his ideas about any little known region by first collecting all the data available. He constantly cites ancient and medieval authorities like Roger Bacon, Dionysius Alexandrinus, Marcus Paulus and Cornelius de Plano Carpini; he also used the most up-to-date geographical works. In addition, he gathered as much information as possible from contemporary travellers. When he had exhausted these sources, he extrapolated his own conclusions and evaluated the possible advantages to be gained by further exploration. Dee's method is made

[1] Dee, 'Mathematicall Preface', sig. A.i.
[2] Taylor, *Tudor Geography*, p. 105.
[3] Van Dorsten, *Radical Arts*, pp. 21–2.
[4] Dee, *Diary*, pp. 3, 11.
[5] British Museum, Cotton MS. Vitellius. C. VII, art. 3. This manuscript is badly burnt and parts of it are missing. A list of its contents made by Elias Ashmole is found in the Bodleian, Ashmole MS. 1788, art. 4.

amply evident in 'Of Famous and Rich Discoveries', and he describes it as 'discovering after my manner of large conjecture, & general enquiry'.[1] One of Dee's most curious attempts at implementing his method was his effort to determine the exact details of Solomon's Ophirian voyages. The full description of Dee's thesis is contained in a manuscript section that is presently lost, but Samuel Purchas apparently had it before him when he wrote his influential epic on navigation, *Purchas his Pilgrimes*. Early in that work, when he discusses the Ophirian voyages, Purchas refers constantly to Dee's conclusions about them, and one can fairly safely reconstruct Dee's approach.[2]

Dee mingles the literal acceptance of scripture with a broad interpretation that takes modern geographical discoveries into consideration. There is no doubt that Purchas took Dee's speculations quite seriously and had high respect for them. He gives the reader Dee's account of the voyages:

> Doctor *Dee* allows fiftie miles a day of requisite way, that is 1200. miles every foure weekes, resting on the Sabbath, and forty miles a day within the Gulfe or Red Sea: the miles he computeth 9155. 3/4, and the whole Voyage to be performed in seven moneths and six and twenty dayes outward, and as much homeward; one fortnight of rest after their landing before they fell to their Mine-workes, to be spent in mind-workes of devout thankfulnesse, prayers and festivall rejoycing; as much before their shipping for returne, the rest in their workes and purveying of commodities.[3]

Though Dee's conclusions at first appear rather unscientific, they are perfectly legitimate if one takes the Bible literally. In a valid archaeological manner, Dee considered recent geographical data and he also took into account the social habits of Solomon and his people, which is necessary for a complete reconstruction of the voyages.

Dee published his *General and Rare Memorials pertayning to the Perfect Arte of Navigation* in 1577, but it is only a fragment of a much larger work, which was to include 'Of Famous and Rich

---

[1] British Museum, Cotton MS. Vitellius. C. VII, art. 3, fol. 94ᵛ.
[2] Samuel Purchas, *Purchas his Pilgrimes* (London, 1625), I, 35 ff.
[3] Purchas, *Pilgrimes*, I, 42.

Discoveries'. The whole work was meant to cover the philosophy and history of navigation and was originally to be in four parts. The first section is the one that was published, and the last is contained in the manuscript, 'Of Famous and Rich Discoveries', but the two central segments no longer exist. One of them included navigational tables for Elizabethan seamen. The other was burned, possibly because it was politically dangerous. It is of course impossible to know exactly what was contained in the missing parts of Dee's grand work, but they were almost certainly concerned with ways of establishing a British Empire, as the surviving sections are. One clue to the goal that Dee had in mind for the complete opus is his illustration (see Plate 14) at the beginning of *General and Rare Memorials*. This beautiful drawing, which Dee produced himself, is impregnated with symbolism, and it may reasonably be assumed to represent the theme – imperialism – which underlies Dee's entire project. In the published section of *General and Rare Memorials* entitled *The Brytish Monarchie*, Dee proposes building a powerful navy, which is a farsighted plan, but in the context is only a means to an end.[1]

Dee's title page elucidates his overall scheme.[2] The inscription in Greek that surrounds the picture explains that the whole is a British hieroglyph and that a more complete explanation of the picture's symbolism is to be found in the text itself. The reference is to the following passage:

> Why should not we HOPE, that, RES-PUBL. BRYTANICA, on her knees, very Humbly, and ernestly Soliciting the most Excellent Royall Majesty, of our ELIZABETH, (Sitting at the HELM of this Imperiall Monarchy: or, rather, at the Helm of the IMPERIALL SHIP, of the most parte of Christendome: if so, it be her Graces Pleasure) shall obteyn, (or Perfect Policie, may perswade her Highnes,) that, which is the Pyth, or

[1] On the basis of this work, Thomas Fulton claims that Dee 'must be recognized as the literary pioneer of the claims to the sovereignty of the sea which were put forth by England in the seventeenth century' (*The Sovereignty of the Sea* (Edinburgh, 1911), p. 99). Dee's book exerted a considerable influence on other men who wrote on the subject of a closed sea policy in the seventeenth century.

[2] On this illustration, see Joseph Ames, *Typographical Antiquities* (London, 1785), I, 660–2.

Intent of RES-PUBL. BRYTANICA, Her Supplication? Which is,
That, *ΣΤΟΛΟΣ ΕΞΩΠΛΙΣΜΕΝΟΣ*, may helpe us, not onely,
to *ΦΡΟΥΡΙΟΝ ΤΗΣ ΑΣΦΑΛΕΙΑΣ*: But make us, also,
Partakers of Publik Commodities Innumerable, and (as yet)
Incredible. Unto which, the HEAVENLY KING, for these many
yeres last past, hath, by MANIFEST OCCASION, most Graciously,
not only invited us: but also, hath made, EVEN NOW, the Way
and Means, most evident, easie, and Compendious: In-
asmuch as, (besides all our own sufficient Furniture, Hability,
Industry, Skill, and Courage) our Freends are become
strong: and our Enemies, sufficiently weake, and nothing
Royally furnished, or of Hability, for Open violence Using:
Though their accustomed Confidence, In Treason, Trechery,
and Disloyall Dealings, be very great. Wherein, we besche
our HEAVENLY PROTECTOR, with his GOOD ANGELL to Garde
us, with SHIELD AND SWORD, now, and ever.[1]

Turning to the illustration, we can see that Elizabeth is seated
at the helm of the ship of state, which contains members of the
nobility, bears the name 'Europe', and has the arms of England
emblazoned on its rudder. Elizabeth's hand is outstretched to
grasp the blowing hair of a naked figure of opportunity, who is
offering the Queen a laurel crown. The 'Occasio' stands on a
fortified citadel, and a figure of Britannia kneeling on the shore
implores Elizabeth to develop a strong royal navy. Two of the
figures in the foreground seem to be amicably agreeing on a
treaty, and the ship in the river flies the Dutch flag, which may
suggest that Dee advocated an open alliance with the Netherlands.

In Dee's illustration, there is also a stem of wheat, full-eared
and upside down, and nearby – just at the edge of the picture –
a skull. Wheat is a Hermetic symbol for man, and its inverted
position here could represent the disrupted state of Europe at
the time.[2] The nearby skull may therefore be intended to sym-
bolize the troubles that Dee envisions if Elizabeth does not grasp
the hair of opportunity and establish a strong British navy and
empire. Ten stars, the moon, and the sun appear together in the
heavens, thus indicating favour toward the enterprise. There is

[1] Dee, *General and Rare Memorials*, p. 53.
[2] Pagel, *Harvey's Biological Ideas*, p. 112.

also a radiant sphere that bears the Hebrew Tetragrammaton (the sacred four-letter name of God) and emits beneficent influences; and Michael, with sword and shield, appears in the sky to protect the undertaking. The mixture of favourable religious and astrological portents implies that Elizabeth has a sacred obligation to implement Britannia's entreaties and that no forces on earth can thwart her if she undertakes the task. The practical moral of this elaborate allegorical drawing, as well as of the text of *General and Rare Memorials*, is that the Queen must seize opportunity and strengthen her 'Imperiall Brytish Monarchy', and perhaps become the pilot of the foundering ship of Christendom as well.

The ideal of imperialism was very much alive during the middle and late sixteenth century. On the Continent was the dazzling figure of Charles V and later his son, Philip II, England's archrival. The advocates of English imperialism found a new impetus in the country's religious troubles because many people – John Dee among them – believed that, with the resumption of religious authority by the Queen, England was returning to the earlier days of an empire independent of Rome. The Pope had been granted his temporal authority by devout emperors early in the history of Christendom. (Actually, even papal apologists based their arguments on the spurious donation of Constantine, which by the application of philological criticism, Valla had proved a forgery.) Popes had abused their privileges, so it was reasoned that the emperors were within their rights if they rescinded their gift of power. In the *Actes and Monuments*, Foxe presents Elizabeth as returning to pre-Constantinian imperial Christianity, free from the burdensome authority of the Pope.[1] He asserts that the English received a pure form of Christianity early in their history and kept it undefiled longer than any other nation: it was not until John that an English king was forced to submit to the unfair demands of a pope. Rome, not England, had veered from the true church. Foxe sought to convince Englishmen that they were a chosen people with imperial rights, and Dee did the same, though his approach was extremely different from Foxe's.

Dee makes his attitude towards English imperialism quite

[1] On this, see Frances A. Yates, 'Queen Elizabeth as Astraea', *JWCI*, IX (1946), 27–82.

185

clear when he admiringly refers to Cicero's *De officiis* as an example of a philosopher setting forth rules for government and then offers the following advice:

> I have oftentymes, (Sayd He,) and many wayes, looked into the State of Earthly Kingdoms, Generally, the whole World over: (as far, as it may, yet, be known to Christen Men, Commonly:) being a Study, of no great Difficulty: But, rather, a purpose, somewhat answerable, to a perfect Cosmographer: to fynde hym self, *Cosmopolites*: A Citizen, and Member, of the whole and only one MYSTICALL CITY UNIVERSALL: And so, consequently, to meditate of the Cosmopoliticall Government thereof, under the King Almighty: passing on, very swiftly, toward the most Dreadfull, and most Cumfortable Term Prefixed:
>
> And I finde (sayd he) that this BRYTISH MONARCHY, wold heretofore, have followed the Advantages, which they have had, onward, They mought, very well, ere this, have surpassed (By Justice and Godly, sort) any particular Monarchy, els, that ever was on Earth, Since Mans Creation.[1]

To bolster his case, Dee uses the two orations on ways of improving the economy and defence of the Greek islands that the Byzantine philosopher Gemistus Pletho addressed to the Emperor Manuel and his son Theodore about 1415.[2] Feeling that Pletho's orations offer a valuable lesson about imperialism, Dee reprints, at the end of *General and Rare Memorials*, the Latin version of most of the first oration and all of the second with his own commentary in the margins. His conclusion: the advice given to the Byzantine emperor by Pletho is also good advice for Elizabeth, Empress of Britain.

John Dee, the Hermetic magus and mystic, it is now clear, was also one of sixteenth-century England's foremost practical and theoretical scientists. He was a man of action as well as a

[1] Dee, *General and Rare Memorials*, p. 54. Dee's use of the phrase 'sayd he' should not mislead the reader for Dee is writing under a thin guise of anonymity.

[2] Gemistus Pletho brought Greek texts to Italy in the middle of the fifteenth century and, by inspiring Ficino's interest in Greek philosophy, was instrumental in the revival of neo-Platonism in Europe.

man of contemplation. Under his influence the mathematical sciences were disseminated among Elizabethan mechanicians, and Dee's publications and teaching promoted some of the most forward-looking scientific developments of the English Renaissance. Dee's theories about mathematics, architecture, navigation and technology – all part of a broader magically oriented philosophy – achieved results: they helped to pave the way for the momentous scientific advances of the seventeenth century.

John Dee as an Antiquarian

Antiquarianism, like so many other movements of the Renaissance, began in Italy. Flavio Biondo made his antiquarian journeys in the middle of the fifteenth century, but it was not until the next century that the movement spread throughout Europe.[1] The leaders in this new pursuit were Guillaume Budé in France, Conrad Celtis and Beatus Rhenanus in Germany, and John Leland, John Bale and John Dee in England. There were two different, though entirely complementary, emphases of early antiquarian research. On the one hand, antiquarians often accepted historical legends without verification; on the other hand, some men were using antiquities to determine the true facts about history.

In England, one type of antiquarian study focused on establishing the historicity of the British past as it was presented by Geoffrey of Monmouth in the *Historia Regum Britanniae*.[2] The bitter fight over Geoffrey's work, as is commonly known, centred around the authenticity of Brutus and Arthur, and the antiquarians who concerned themselves with this problem (as most of them did) frequently argued from an emotional nationalism and rather uncritically accepted ancient texts as

[1] Flavio Biondo was by no means the first figure of the Italian Renaissance to study antiquities. In the thirteenth century men like Lovato Lovati of Padua, and in the fourteenth century Petrarch and friends like Giovanni Dondi dell'Orologio and Lombardo della Setta, displayed an interest in antiquarianism. This tradition was carried on by Coluccio Salutati. But it was Biondo who introduced a methodical approach to the study of antiquities, and he is considered the father of Italian antiquarianism. See Roberto Weiss, *The Renaissance Discovery of Classical Antiquity* (Oxford, 1969).

[2] On English antiquarianism, see T. D. Kendrick, *British Antiquity* (London, 1950); Levy, *Tudor Historical Thought*.

authorities. The same men who engaged in this form of antiquarian activity (Leland, Bale and Dee among them) were often
also involved in what contemporaries called chorography. This
second type of antiquarian study centred around geographical
surveys of particular areas and tours on which local antiquities
were observed first-hand. This type of antiquarianism, which
was introduced in England by Leland, came into prominence
during the latter part of the sixteenth century and reached its
climax with the publication of William Camden's *Britannia* in
1586. Chorographical discoveries eventually led to the demoli-
tion of the Brutus and Arthur legends, and it is ironic that the
men who promoted this type of scientific antiquarian research
were also the men who supported the legends.

Both forms of antiquarianism were of paramount importance
to John Dee, who was extremely absorbed with the past and
treasured its remains. It has already been stressed that Dee
tried to transform medieval science and philosophy in the light
of the latest Renaissance theories and integrate them into
English Renaissance thought. It is hardly surprising, therefore,
that he also attempted to effect the same sort of transformation
for English history. He desperately wanted to salvage the
remnants of a rich heritage that was almost obliterated by the
social convulsions that racked the country during the English
Reformation. That anything was saved from the towering ruins
of the past is due primarily to the patriotism of a few farsighted
men like Leland, Bale and Dee.[1] With great collections like
Dee's of documents, manuscripts and other items of antiquarian
interest being formed and made readily available to scholars,
progress was rapidly made in antiquarian studies during
Elizabeth's reign.

The Brutus and Arthur legends, which were the overriding
concern of many Tudor antiquarians, were especially significant
for Dee because they were the principal basis of his claims for a
British Empire. The establishment of such an empire was an
idea that Dee passionately encouraged throughout his long life.
In the *General and Rare Memorials*, it is true, Dee appears to
ignore Arthur when he bases his plea for re-establishing a
peaceful British Empire largely on the Saxon King Edgar's
exemplary reign:

[1] See above, pp. 41 ff.

189

Peaceable (I say) even with the most parte of the self same Respects, that good KING EDGAR had, (being, but a SAXON:) And by sundry such means, as, he chiefly, in this Impire did put in proof and use, Triumphantly. Wherupon, his Surname, was *PACIFICUS*, most aptly and Justly. This Peaceable King EDGAR, had in his mynde (about 600. yeres past) the Representation of a great parte of the self same *Idea*, which (from above onely, and by no Mans advise,) hath gratiously streamed down into my Imagination: being (as it becommeth me, a Subject) Carefull for the Godly prosperity of this BRYTISH IMPIRE, under our most Peaceable QUEENE ELIZA-BETH.[1]

Dee accounts Edgar 'that SAXONICALL ALEXANDER'.[2] Like Elizabeth, however, Dee was Welsh and his great hero was Arthur. After all, Edgar was 'but a SAXON', and the name of Arthur 'was a Thorne in the Saxons eyes, of those Dayes: and his Name rehersed was Odible to their Eares: Whose Ancestors were by that Brytish Arthur, 12 times, overcome in Battaile'.[3] It was Arthur who was to be the main example for the re-establishment of a British Empire, and Dee makes this clear in the manuscript, 'Of Famous and Rich Discoveries'.

The bitter conflict over the British History has been studied extensively in recent years.[4] It has been shown that the two primary reasons that the issue was so hotly contested were national pride and the fact that the British History was exploited by the Tudors for political reasons. The argument was precipitated by the publication of Polydore Vergil's *Anglica Historia* in 1534.[5] In this work, Vergil critically examines the treasured

[1] Dee, *General and Rare Memorials*, p. 55.

[2] *Ibid.*, p. 57. It is curious that Dee compares Edgar to Alexander, for in 'A necessary Advertisement' (sig. *.iv) prefacing this work, he pointedly reminds Elizabeth that in his own lifetime Britain has seen no monarch worthy of comparison with Alexander. It is revealing that the queen should take such a rebuke, but she often received mild admonishment from Dee and accepted it graciously.

[3] *Ibid.*, p. 56.

[4] On this, see Kendrick, *Antiquity*, *passim*; Charles B. Millican, *Spenser and the Table Round* (Cambridge, Mass., 1932), *passim*; Josephine W. Bennett, *The Evolution of 'The Faerie Queene'* (Chicago, 1942), pp. 61–70.

[5] See Denys Hay, ed., *The Anglica Historia of Polydore Vergil, Camden Society Publications*, LXXIV (London, 1950), xxiii–xl.

legends of Brutus and Arthur, which were inextricably tied together.[1] Englishmen were not prepared to accept this sort of approach willingly, especially not with Tudors on the throne.

By the sixteenth century, cherished legends concerning the founding of Britain by Brutus and the heroic conquests of Arthur had grown to proportions that seem somewhat unreasonable today. Much of the distress over Vergil's analysis stemmed from the problem that, if the legend of Brutus were abandoned under critical examination, the even more important legend of Arthur would be easier to destroy as historical fact. Also, the abandoning of Brutus and his offspring (from whom Arthur himself was traditionally descended) would leave a long gap in the history of the British race; this would be an unbearable situation, especially in the face of the religious upheaval. It was extremely bothersome that a void existed in the period between the Flood and the conquest of Britain by Caesar. Since it was impossible to think that the island had remained unpopulated during the earliest days of history, many Tudor antiquarians expanded the story of Brutus. John Bale even claimed a Biblical descent for the Trojan,[2] while Arthur Kelton writes:

> Never none like, accompt the tyme
> Sens Brute, our first progenitoure
> Borne by dissent, of right noble lyne
> Beyng prince, kyng, and governonure [sic]
> Unto our parentes, chiefe protectoure
> Through whose manfull magnanimitie
> Thei wer delivered, from olde captivitie.

He continues by explaining:

> Holy *Eusebius*, doth testifie
> Also Sainct *Bede*, maketh mencion
> That noble Brute of the age, five and thirty
> Entered first into this region
> Whiche was before Christes incarnacion

---

[1] Kendrick, *Antiquity*, p. 38.
[2] Levy, *Historical Thought*, pp. 131-2.

A thousand. i. L. twenty and twayne
And after Troye, xliii. yeres playne.[1]

In the first edition of the *Chronicles*, Holinshed accepts the legend.[2] So does Humphrey Lhuyd in *The Breviary of Britayne*.[3] Henry Lyte records, '*Britannia Major*, (the countrie of the bright Britona called Britomartis) was first founde by *Brute* of Albania: the Conquerer of the Greekes: the mightie deliverer of the Troyans: & the first founder of the noble Britaynes.' In accord with the accepted legend, Lyte explains that, before the arrival of Brutus, 'there was neyther Towne, Cittie, Countrie, Ryver, region: or place of name in Britayne for Britannia (at *Brutes* arrivall) was no Britannia, but a rude and solitarie desart of wilderness without name'.[4]

John Dee accepted most of the stories surrounding Brutus, as is evident from the surviving fragments of his 'Of Famous and Rich Discoveries'. Dee invokes the authority of 'St Hierome his admiration of ETHICUS his assert[ion] that these Iles of ALBION and IRELANDE sho[ld] be called BRUTANICAE & not BRITAN-NICAE'. Like Leland, Lhuyd and other antiquarians, Dee believed that it was mistakes in orthography and pronunciation that had confused the spelling of the name and caused

> the [origin] all Di[s]coverer & Conqueror, and the very first absolute king of these Septentrionall BRYTISH Islands, to be forgotten: or some wrong person, in undue Chronography, with repugnant circumstances, to be nominated in our BRUTUS the ITALIEN TROIAN, his stede.[5]

Like the others who supported the legend, Dee believed that

---

[1] Arthur Kelton, *A Chronycle with a Genealogie Declaryng that the Brittons and Welshemen are Lineallye Dyscended from Brute* (London, 1547), sigs. c.iii^v, c.v^{r-v}.

[2] Raphael Holinshed, *The Firste Volume of the Chronicles of England, Scotlande and Irelande* (London, 1577), pp. 9 ff.

[3] Humphrey Lhuyd, *The Breviary of Britayne*, tr. Thomas Twyne (London, 1573), fol. 9.

[4] Henry Lyte, *The Light of Britayne* (London, 1588; reprinted, 1814), no pagination. See also Richard Harvey, *Philadelphus, or A Defence of Brutes, and Brutans History* (London, 1593).

[5] Dee's views on Brutus are found in British Museum, Cotton MS. Vitellius. C. VII, art. 3, fols. 201 ff. The quotation is found on fols. 202^{r-v}. The bracketed insertions are mine.

Brutus had discovered the island already populated, though the Trojan found the inhabitants 'unskillful in any Art', but 'both Industrous & very quick of wit to conceyve'.[1] Following Bale, Dee developed a genealogy for Brutus that connected him with Noah. He goes on to promise, '(Yf God will) at an other apter tyme & in more apt place merveilous agreement of the historyes of Antiquity & great unlooked for light & credit will be restored to the Originalls of BRUTUS his fir[st] conquest here in this Septentrionall yle.' (See Plate 15.)

As I have said, the Brutus legend had important ramifications since Arthur was thought to be a descendant of the Trojan, and any doubts about the authenticity of Brutus would lead to serious questioning of the claims for Arthur, who was supposedly reincarnated in the Tudor monarchs. Arthur Kelton outlines the accepted relationship:

> Noble Arthur the famous Brute
> Of the same line, and true succession
> Whiche by his conquest, and princely persute
> Vanquished full many a region
> Sonne of Uter, called Pendragon
> Chronicles, plainly doth it specify
> Yet ye Romaines, this prince will deny.

Toward the end of his poem, Kelton makes the political significance of the legends clear:

> Emong all princes, of excellence
> For length of tyme, bloud and progeny
> Let us preferre, the highe magnificence
> Of our moste royall, theight Kyng Henry
> Whiche at this houre, by grace of the deity
> Possesseth the same, Kyngdome and powre
> Like as did Brute, his first progenitoure.[2]

Dee tried to establish the relationship between Brutus and Arthur by a genealogical study of Arthur's coat of arms. He claims that Arthur's arms – three gold crowns in a field of

---

[1] *Ibid.*

[2] Kelton, *Chronycle*, sigs. c.vi[v], e.v.

azure – were appropriated to the 'enheritable Monarchy of LOEGRE' from the time of Brutus, and this coat Arthur 'quartered w^t the Troian coa[t of] his Auncestors: as in the Antiquityes of Aen[eas] you may see'.[1]

Arthur, so the legend went, had not really died but would return and lead England once more to imperial glory when a Welshman re-ascended the throne. With the enthronement of Henry VII, the Arthurian legends naturally acquired new importance, which the Tudor royalty encouraged and incipient British nationalism also promoted. Polydore Vergil's attack on Arthur aroused the wrath of British antiquarians; to them it seemed a slur on the British nation when, with the strained political and religious atmosphere, no doubts about its imperial heritage could be allowed to develop. Later, Elizabeth was metaphorically and commonly seen as the living Arthur, and John Dee consequently conceived it her sacred duty to build a British Empire like the early King's.

The first antiquarian to attack Polydore Vergil's *Anglica Historia* was John Leland, who admitted that there were some absurdities in the Arthur story and refused to defend them but tried instead to demonstrate the truths of the more tenable aspects of the legend. Leland generally accepted the major parts of the story and retained Brutus, King Arthur, the Welsh supremacy, the Tudor monarchy and Arthur's return as focal points.[2]

Leland was only the first of many antiquarians to take up the cudgels in defence of Arthur. Dee was well acquainted with the arguments and sources of contemporary antiquarians and undoubtedly had free access to Leland's papers, for they were in the possession of Dee's close friend John Stow.[3] In addition, Dee had the chronicles of Arnold, Hardyng, Grafton, Cooper, Stow and Holinshed, as well as the printed works of Bale and Leland himself.[4] His library boasted two copies of the work of Humphrey Lhuyd, which had been undertaken at the request

[1] British Museum, Cotton MS. Vitellius. C. VII, art. 3, fol. 262; Dee's views on Arthur cover fols. 249^v ff. The text is badly damaged by fire. The bracketed insertions are mine.　　　[2] Kendrick, *Antiquity*, p. 83.

[3] On Stow and Dee, see below, pp. 206 ff.

[4] British Museum, Harleian MS. 1879, art. 5; for Arnold, Hardyng, Grafton, Cooper, Stow, and Holinshed, see fols. 71–3; for Bale, various works, see fols. 33^v, 26^v, 71; for Leland, see fol. 35.

of Dee's friend Ortelius and was translated by Thomas Twyne and printed as *The Breviary of Britayne* in 1573.[1] Although he offers a highly emotional defence of the British History from Brutus onward, Lhuyd uses the latest and best scholarship and shows considerable knowledge of his topic. His work on British place-names, for instance, was basic to most subsequent research on the subject.[2] The best defence of King Arthur and the *Brut* is John Price's *Historiae Britannicae defensio*, which was published in the same year as Lhuyd's work. This book, which was also on Dee's shelves, presents favourable arguments for the British History in a well-organized and scholarly manner. Price's work was the major scholarly affirmation of the pro-Brutus–Arthur faction.[3]

Being a confirmed and vigorous imperialist, Dee was especially adamant about Arthur's role as a conqueror. It was on the Arthurian conquests that he based his claims for Elizabeth's titles to various foreign lands, and to bolster his case, he even extended Arthur's imperial dominions beyond those generally accepted by other contemporaries. In 'Of Famous and Rich Discoveries', Dee expresses annoyance with some antiquarians who refuse to admit 'that even there was any ARTHUR king [of this] BRYTISH MONARCHY', or if they do, they claim that 'the whole historie be utterly founded for the lighting of ydle heads'. Undoubtedly referring to Polydore Vergil, Dee contemptuously dismisses these antiquarians as 'Infants in o^r BRYTISH ANTIQUITIES'. He claims Arthur's empire 'to have byn of twenty Kingdomes', though he admits that 'very few kingdoms of those Dayes, were large'. Using the Abbot Trithemius as his authority, Dee explains that 'sundry forreyn provinces by the victorious prowes of o^r ARTHUR, And diverse Septentrionall Iles (besides Island & Groenland)' were 'brought under his subjection' and are therefore 'due to the Royall Government & allso the Enheritance, of his posterity, the awfull Kings & Quenes of this Brytish Monarchie'.[4] Dee claims as Arthurian

[1] British Museum, Harleian MS. 1879, art. 5; Dee's copies are listed on fols. 51, 80^v.

[2] Levy, *Historical Thought*, pp. 132–3.

[3] British Museum, Harleian MS. 1879, art. 5, fol. 36; on Price, see Kendrick, *Antiquity*, pp. 87 ff.

[4] British Museum, Cotton MS. Vitellius. C. VII, art. 3, fols. 254, 262^v. 263^v.

conquests 'All those Septentrionall Iles, as BRYTANNICAS, wch a[re] in MARI BRYTANNICO', which came to be called 'OCEANUS BRYTANICUS' and which flows 'about and between ALBION & Irela[nde] & u[p] NORTHERLY to Groenland & so between ATLA[ntis] & NORWAY'.[1]

Elizabeth was apparently concerned with her Welsh background and her title to foreign lands because Dee outlined her historical claims for her several times. An entry in his diary for 28 November 1577 mentions that he declared to the Queen her title to Greenland, Estetiland and Friseland. Another entry, made about two years later on 3 October 1580, shows that Elizabeth was still interested in her legal claims to foreign lands, and Dee was once again the authority on whom she depended for advice. He writes:

> On Munday, at 11 of the clok before none, I delivered my two rolls of the Quene's Majesties title unto herself in the garden at Richemond, who appointed after dynner to heare furder on the matter. Therfore betwene one and two afternone, I was sent for into her highnes Pryvy Chamber, where the Lord Threasurer allso was, who, having the matter slightly then in consultation, did seme to dowt much that I had or could make the argument probable for her highnes' title so as I pretended.

Though the Queen seems to have been enthusiastic over the documents prepared, it is not surprising that the cautious Burghley was doubtful about the validity of the spectacular claims Dee was making for British sovereignty. A few days after Dee's interview at court, however, the Queen rode out to Mortlake herself and informed him that the 'Lord Threasorer had gretly commended my doings for her title'.[2]

[1] British Museum, Cotton MS. Vitellius. C. VII, art. 3, fol. 264. For additional evidence that relates Dee's antiquarian activities to the Arthur legend and to his attempts to encourage Elizabethan imperialism, see Millican, *Spenser*, pp. 41–7.

[2] Dee, *Diary*, pp. 4, 9. Burghley's summary of 'Mr Dees book' opens with the statement, 'Arthur King of Britan was ye conquoror of these cuntryes'. From the subsequent list, which includes all of Scandinavia as well as parts of Russia and numerous other places, it appears that Dee was basing his claims for Arthur's extensive conquests on William Lambarde's *APXAIO-NOMIA, sive de priscis anglorum legibus libri* (1568), which was of course indebted to Geoffrey's *Historia*. See British Museum, Lansdowne MS. 94, art. 51, fol. 121.

One of the documents that Dee presented to Elizabeth was a map of America, on the back of which he outlined the Queen's 'Title Royall to . . . foreyn Regions'.[1] In this remarkably well-ordered document, Dee rests his claims almost entirely on past British conquests and explorations, though some of the voyages he cites are of doubtful validity. For example, he concluded that Elizabeth had the right to much of Atlantis, or America, because of the trip by 'the Lord Madoc, Sonne to Owen Gwynedd Prynce of Northwales', who, Dee believed, led 'a Colonie and inhabited in Terra Florida, or thereabowts'.[2] The greatest claims, as might be expected, are reserved for Arthur, who

> not only Conquered Iseland, Groenland, and all the Northern Iles cumpassing unto Russia, But even unto the North Pole (in manner) did extend his Jurisdiction: And sent Colonies thither, and into all the Isles betwene Scotland and Iseland, whereby yt is probable that the late named Friseland Iland is of the Brytish ancient Discovery and possession: And allso seeing Groeland beyond Groenland did receive their inhabitants by Arthur, yt is credible that the famous Iland Estotiland was by his folke possessed.

Dee makes his overall aim apparent at the end of this document: 'And generally, by the same Order that other Christian Princes do now adayes make Conquests uppon the heathen people, we allso have to procede herein: both to Recover the Premisses, and likewise by Conquest to enlarge the Bownds of the foresayd Title Royall.'[3] Dee's imperial ambitions are staggering, but it should be remembered that this document was composed about the time Drake returned from his successful voyage. Other British navigators had also been making exciting explorations, and there was the sprawling empire of Spain to dazzle Elizabethans. With the precedent of a Christian imperial Arthur – a monarch independent of Rome – behind her, Elizabeth could

---

[1] George Bruner Parks (*Richard Hakluyt and the English Voyages* (New York, 1928), p. 184) claims that this map marks the beginning of serious English cartography.

[2] British Museum, Cotton MS. Augustus I, i, iv.

[3] *Ibid.*

assume supreme control of church and state with complete equanimity; and in John Dee's eyes, she had a God-ordained duty to expand her empire in the Arthurian tradition.

The tremendous interest in Arthur during the middle of Elizabeth's reign clearly owed much to imperialist inspiration. Apparently, Dee discussed imperialism and Arthur with many people. He writes that on 30 June 1578, 'I told Mr. Daniel Rogers, Mr. Hackluyt of the Middle Temple being by, that Kyng Arthur and King Maty, both of them, did conquier Gelindia, lately called Friseland, which he so noted presently in his written copy of' Geoffrey of Monmouth.[1] Through conversations with Elizabeth and such ministers as Burghley, Walsingham, Leicester and Hatton, as well as with men like Rogers, the elder Hakluyt and Dyer, the expansionist ideas of Dee spread. One specific literary instance is Richard Hakluyt's reprinting of the whole of Dee's discourse on King Edgar from the *General and Rare Memorials*.[2]

The circle surrounding Philip Sidney must also have been well aware of Dee's views on Arthur. A spectacular recrudescence of interest in Arthur developed in the late 1570s and early 1580s, during the same time that Dee was adamantly pushing his imperialist schemes based on Arthur's conquests. We know that Sidney at one point planned to turn the *Arcadia* into an Arthuriad, and Spenser, whether he actually believed in the British History or not, certainly used it effectively in the *Faerie Queene*.[3] Although Mrs Bennett may be perfectly right in assuming that Arthur was a late accretion to the poem, his inclusion, as she explains, is probably a result of renewed interest in the Arthurian theme brought on by nascent imperialism.[4]

We look back upon Dee's faith in Geoffrey and the Arthurian legends with reservations, considering it a rather primitive attitude, and it is difficult to understand exactly why a more critical approach was not the rule of the day. Kendrick simply dismisses Dee's attempts to resuscitate the Arthurian legends

[1] Dee, *Diary*, p. 4.

[2] Richard Hakluyt, *The Principal Navigations, Voiages Traffiques and Discoveries of the English Nation* (London, 1598), I, 7–8; in Dee's *General and Rare Memorials*, the discourse covers pp. 56 ff.

[3] Millican, *Spenser*, p. 94.

[4] Bennett, *Evolution of 'The Faerie Queene'*, pp. 73–9.

and points out that Burghley and Elizabeth were wise enough not to follow his extravagant plans.[1] This is an inadequate explanation because there can be no doubt that Dee did help to revivify the image of Arthur, and it was primarily because of imperialist designs like John Dee's that Elizabethan expansion occurred.

Those who believed in the Arthur legends cannot simply be dismissed as backward antiquarians, for the same men who accepted the British History were often instrumental in the evolution of a forward-looking type of antiquarian research. Men like Leland and Price and Dee all thought that some definite historical proof of Arthur's existence was to be found in British records; Leland believed that, through his travels, he had encountered significant historical evidence about Arthur.[2] Like so many others, Leland never doubted that Arthur was buried in Glastonbury, the ruined abbey about which Dee writes poignantly:

O GLASTONBURY, GLASTONBURY: the Threasory of Carcasses of so famous, and so many rare Persons. . . . How Lamentable, is thy case, now? How hath Hypocrisie and Pride wrought thy Desolation? Though I omit (here) the names of very many other, both excellent holy Men, and Mighty Princes (whose Carcasses are committed to thy Custody,) yet, that Apostle-like Joseph, That Triumphant BRYTISH ARTHUR, And now, this Peacable, and Provident SAXON, KING EDGAR, do force me, with a certayn sorrowfull Reverence, here, to Celebrate thy Memory.[3]

Though they often accepted medieval texts too completely, men like Leland and Dee tried to use a factual and methodical approach in studying the antiquities of Britain, and there are traces in their work of the local antiquarianism that flowered in Camden and the *Britannia*.

Dee himself provides a viable definition of chorography – the antiquarian approach that informs Camden's work – in the 'Mathematicall Preface':

[1] Kendrick, *Antiquity*, p. 37.
[2] *Ibid.*, pp. 90–6.
[3] Dee, *General and Rare Memorials*, p. 56.

Chorographie seemeth to be an underling, and a twig, of
Geographie: and yet neverthelesse, is in practise manifolde,
and in use very ample. This teacheth Analogically to describe
a small portion or circuite of ground, with the contentes: not
regarding what commensuration it hath to the whole, or any
parcell, without it, contained. But in the territory or parcell
of ground which it taketh in hand to make description of, it
leaveth out (or undescribed) no notable, or odde thing,
above the ground visible. Yea and sometimes, of thinges
under ground, geveth some peculier marke: or warning: as of
Mettall mines, Cole pittes, Stone quarries, &c. Thus, a
Dukedome, a Shiere, a Lordship, or lesse, may be described
distinctly. But marveilous pleasant, and profitable it is, in
the exhibiting to our eye, and commensuration, the plat of a
Citie, Towne, Forte, or Pallace, in true Symmetry: not
approaching to any of them: and out of Gunne shot. &c.[1]

Although he does not specifically mention describing local
history, which is as much a part of chorography as topography
is, Dee would almost certainly include historical information
under the 'contentes' of an area. Since history is not a mathematical art, it is not particularly surprising that it is omitted
from this definition in the preface.

Throughout his life, Dee was engaged in collecting antiquarian information of various kinds. The earliest known evidence of
the type of local information that he was attempting to gather
is found in a letter addressed to him in 1573 by an unknown
antiquary with whom he apparently corresponded several
times. The writer mentions sending a previous missive 'con-
serninge the armes of the Towne of donwiche', but the letter
under consideration is an answer to Dee's inquiry concerning
'what compas or quantite the grownd of donwyche hathe bene
of in olde tyme paste'.[2] The text of the letter reveals that Dee's
conception of chorography was very much bound up with local
history. Of Dunwich, which was largely covered by the sea,
Dee's informant writes:

In that lytle parte of the towne that is there yet nowe
remayninge/: Whiche yf as before is sayd/Be but the forte

[1] Dee, 'Mathematicall Preface', sig. a.iiii.
[2] British Museum, Harleian MS. 532, art. 6, fols. 53v–60.

parte/ or the thyrde parte &c./then it is to be conjectuered & gathered/: that the other thre partes or two partes of yᵉ towne nowe drowned in the sea shoulde have placed in it parysshe churches and all other the lyke Byldyngs &c./as wele as that parte of yᵉ sayd towne was and is, that nowe remaynethe/&c. But to fortifie yowe howe manye & what they ware I can nott/therefore I put the judgement thereof to yower descression/who can judge thereof agrete dele better than I &c.

When Dee wonders about whether there had ever been a mint in the town, the writer answers that coins minted at Dunwich had been seen but that the mint was removed during the reign of Edward IV. Dee is also informed of curious archaeological discoveries such as were made when the church of St John's was pulled down. For example, a grave was found in which there was 'a greate hollowe stone hollowed after yᵉ faysshon of a man (for a man to lye in)'. The body inside was dressed in a strange manner and was 'thought to be one of the Bysshoppes of don-wiche but whan they towched & stered the same deade Bodie it felle & went all to powder'.[1] This letter makes it abundantly clear that Dee conceived of chorography as a combination of local geography and local history.

Another document recently identified as Dee's indicates that, as early as 1574, he was employing the method of first-hand observation. Dee's slim volume is entitled 'Certaine verie rare observations of Chester: & some parts of Wales: wᵗʰ divers Epitaphes Coatarmours & other monuments verie orderlie and labouriouslie gathered together'.[2] In brief, it is the record of a

[1] British Museum, Harleian MS. 532, art. 6, fols. 56–58ᵛ.

[2] British Museum, Harleian MS. 473. Dee wrote in a number of different hands: humanistic cursive, both calligraphic and informal; secretary hand; and a mixed hand. This manuscript contains secretary hand, a mixed hand and some words in informal humanistic cursive. Each of these varieties shows marked likeness to corresponding passages known to be in Dee's hand, and there is little doubt that this manuscript was written by him. Paleographic and some other information about this work has kindly been provided for me by Professor T. J. Brown of King's College, London. His judgment that the manuscript was written by Dee has recently been corroborated by Andrew G. Watson (*The Library of Sir Simonds D'Ewes*, British Museum Bicentenary Publications (London, 1966), p. 314, M⁶⁴). Kendrick (*Antiquity*, pp. 142–3) briefly discusses this work, though he wrongly refers to it as Harleian MS. 1046.

short antiquarian tour. The itinerary was as follows. Dee began at Chester on an unspecified date. Then he travelled from Westchester via Pulford to Gresford on 23 August, and on St Bartholomew's Day (24 August), he was at Wrexham. He later went to Bangor and Oswestry, and 30 August was spent at Presteigne. On Wednesday, 1 September, he arrived at Hereford at nine in the morning and met the mayor, a Mr Pryce. The next day, he went to Ledbury via the Malvern Hills and visited Mr Edward Threlkeld, Chancellor of Hereford, 'one of my old acqyantance syns K. Edward his tyme'. From there, Dee travelled to Gloucester and later to Cirencester. It is not possible to determine the exact amount of time spent on this tour, but the journal shows that Dee took a universal interest in all that he saw and heard, just as Leland had previously done.

Dee noted the condition and position of various edifices, copied down coats of arms, listed the pedigrees of local gentry, and recorded local history and topography. The most extensive notes in the volume (and perhaps the most revealing of his methods) concern the first great figure in the history of Chester – 'Gormundus a Roman Captayn, here in the Saxons tyme'. Dee transcribed some information about the Roman's activities 'fownd in *the Towre called of Julius Caesar in the Castell of Chester* in the minster ward, by William Stokes Aº 1551'. Among other things these showed that Gormundus had been responsible for cutting a new channel so the river Dee could pass through the middle of the town. Over the river was built a wooden bridge with an iron gate, which was taken up at night. By Dee's time, this 'iren bridg' was 'above two myle up the river' from whence the town had grown up. Having noted the various information found in the documents discovered in the tower, Dee concerned himself with a relevant and recent archaeological find:

> As concerning the foresaid Gormundus, besides the record in writing *had in the castell*, it is to be Noted that one John Robinson a dyer of Chester, in plowing the grownd betwene the now Chester, and the forsayd Iren bridg, brok his plow on a mayn stone. Which whan he had turned up: he perceyved therunder a whole man: which whan the ayre towched, fell all to dust, and on his thumb, was a ring of gold in the inside wherof was written Gormundus Romano*rum*.[1]

[1] British Museum, Harleian MS. 473, fols. 1ᵛ–2.

Though he admires this early antiquarian effort by Dee, Kendrick is quite right when he insists that the journal shows nothing of the zeal necessary to complete a work like the great *Britannia*.[1] The importance of just such a work on the early history of Britain was constantly in Dee's mind, however. He probably had no intention of producing it himself, but he did have a keen interest in seeing the task completed. In addition to his own short tour and his deep admiration of chorography, which would have stimulated his desire to see a survey of Roman Britain completed, he was involved with Ortelius and the various men whom that scholar requested to undertake such a project.[2]

The first of those who became engaged in the massive historical task was Humphrey Lhuyd, but he died long before the project was finished, and all that remained of his efforts were the fragments published as *The Breviary of Britayne*. Lhuyd sent Ortelius the manuscript of his '*Wales*, not beautifully set forth in all poinctes, yet truly depeinted, so be that certeyn notes be observed, which I gathered even when I was redy to die'.[3] When he visited Ortelius in Antwerp, Dee was most pleased to see the renowned cosmographer's library and be able to study Lhuyd's commentaries. After Lhuyd's death, Ortelius tried to persuade his nephew Daniel Rogers (whom Dee described as learned and industrious) to complete the job Lhuyd had started.[4] Rogers conferred with Dee about antiquarian matters concerning Arthur, but it seems that neither Ortelius nor Dee was able to interest Rogers in chorography. Rogers apparently did not wish to do much more than examine literary works, and it is quite possible that he would not have been capable of making the fullest use of the antiquarian material available had he bothered to travel throughout England to collect it.[5] For different reasons, therefore, Ortelius's attempts to inspire first Lhuyd and then Rogers to make a chorographical study of Roman Britain ended in failure. In the spring of 1577, he voyaged to England, where he visited John

[1] Kendrick, *Antiquity*, p. 143.
[2] On Ortelius and English antiquarianism, see Levy, *Historical Thought*, pp. 144–9.
[3] Lhuyd, 'Epistle of the aucthor', in *Breviary*, sigs. DVr–v.
[4] Taylor, *Tudor Geography*, p. 260.
[5] On Rogers, see F. J. Levy, 'Daniel Rogers as Antiquary', *Bibliothèque d'Humanisme et Renaissance*, XXVII (1965), 444–62.

Dee and at last made the acquaintance of the man who would complete a study of Roman Britain – William Camden.

Dee had known Camden for some time before Ortelius arrived in England. At least by 7 August 1574 (just before setting off on his own brief antiquarian tour), Dee was corresponding with him.[1] In a letter dated that day from Mortlake, Dee answered a number of questions that had apparently been put to him by Camden, ranging from the significance of the sign delta, which Dee used to refer to himself, to the proper spelling of the island as Brutanica. This letter suggests that John Stow was the intermediary through whom Camden was introduced to Dee. Camden and Dee long remained friends, for another letter written after Dee's extended trip to the Continent reveals that Camden became the teacher of his eldest son, Arthur, at Westminster School.[2]

Significant conclusions can be drawn from Dee's first letter to Camden. It is quite clear that Camden had some sort of antiquarian work in mind even at this early date, though its exact nature is impossible to determine. Also, it was apparently through John Dee that Camden met Ortelius; only after this introduction did his plans for the *Britannia* fully develop.[3] Obviously, Camden could freely use Leland's papers because they were in the possession of Stow, and he must have had access to Dee's library and his superb personal knowledge of the geography and antiquities of Britain.

Dee's magnificent library was a storehouse of antiquarian items. His manuscript collection, which was unsurpassed in England, contained large numbers of ancient documents. In describing the destruction wrought upon his library by the mob in 1583, Dee mentions many valuable antiquarian articles that had been carried off, including 'boxes, wherein some hundreds of very rare evidences of divers Irelandish territories, provinces, and lands were layd up'. As one would expect, 'There were also divers evidences antient of some Welsh princes and noblemen, their great giftes of lands to the foundations or enrichings of

---

[1] British Museum, Lansdowne MS. 19, art. 34.

[2] British Museum, Cotton MS. Julius. C. V, fol. 21; the letter is dated 22 May 1592.

[3] F. J. Levy, 'The Making of Camden's *Britannia*', *Bibliothèque d'Humanisme et Renaissance*, XXVI (1964), 82-3.

sundry houses of religious men.' Dee owned similar documents relating to the Normans and dating from the Conquest. Another box contained 'only ancient seales of arms'. All these treasures, he complained, were 'embeziled' from him. The rarity of his collection is demonstrated by the comment that there were 'divers of her majesties heralds, who saw them, and tooke some notes out of them: other of the Clerks of the Records in the Tower satt whole dayes at my house in Mortlake, in gathering rarities to their liking out of them: some antiquaries likewise had view of them'.[1] One person who certainly used Dee's splendid collection was Robert Glover, Somerset Herald; he was one of the most accomplished Elizabethan genealogists and helped Camden with the pedigrees for the *Britannia*.[2] And at least two antiquaries besides Glover and Camden availed themselves of Dee's library and extensive personal knowledge: Raphael Holinshed and John Stow.

Holinshed based his story of Richard II in the *Chronicles* on a pamphlet that belonged to Dee, for he notes in the margin next to Richard's history: 'Out of a French pamphlet that belongeth to master *John Dee*.' Similar references follow.[3] The pamphlet to which Holinshed refers is a copy of Créton's *Histoire*, which was widely circulated on the Continent but was not readily available in England because it was anti-Lancastrian in tone.[4] What Holinshed or any other antiquarian may have learned from Dee personally is, of course, unknowable, but Dee apparently had access to most government records and therefore had an extraordinary fund of historical information.[5] His

[1] Dee, *Rehearsal*, pp. 29–30. Dee also had an impressive collection of genealogies (British Museum, Harleian MS. 588, fols. 1–160v) covering the royalty and nobility of Britain and the Continent.

[2] British Museum, Lansdowne MS. 229, art. 76; Glover writes (fol. 98v), 'ex diversis cartis in custodia J. Dee. de Mortlake'.

[3] Raphael Holinshed, *The Third Volume of Chronicles* (London, 1587), pp. 497–500.

[4] The pamphlet with Dee's signature and the date 1575 is now in the library of Lambeth Palace.

[5] Just one example of many is British Museum, Harleian MS. 295, arts. 42–60. These are letters to Wolsey and Henry VIII concerning French and Spanish affairs, and they contain notations in Dee's hand such as (fol. 114), 'transcribe this', and (fol. 121v) 'this letter I have in cipher but not deciphered therefore to be interlined'. See Watson, *Library of Sir Simonds D'Ewes, passim*, for other examples.

great interest in geographical matters complemented his interest in historiography.

The antiquarian who apparently benefited most from John Dee's immense learning was John Stow. The relationship between Dee and the London annalist was well advanced in 1574, as Dee's letter to Camden of that year testifies, and the two men were in communication (see Plate 16) at least until 1592.[1] They shared books and manuscripts frequently; there are works that contain the handwriting of both.[2] Though no accurate dates can be assigned to the borrowing, it was done freely and continued from at least 1574 until 4 December 1592.[3]

These two antiquaries did more than share books, however. Dee gave freely of his knowledge and was consciously helping Stow to collect information. The missive he received about the town of Dunwich, for example, was passed on to Stow for examination.[4] And Dee's letter of 4 December 1592 provides Stow with a list of some former burgesses of the Cinque Ports. Dee not only encouraged Stow to press forward with his painstaking work, he even tried to promote the annalist's efforts among the courtiers. 'You shall understand', he informs Stow, 'that my frende Mr Dyer did deliver your bokes to the two erls: who toke them very thankfully: But (as he noted) there was no reward commanded of them. What shall hereafter, God knoweth.'[5] In 1592, when this letter was written, Dee was impoverished and he was fighting to get some assistance for himself from Queen Elizabeth, but his own difficult situation did not keep him from attempting to aid his 'loving frende' John Stow.

---

[1] British Museum, Harleian MS. 374, art. 11, is a letter to Stow from Dee dated 4 December 1592.

[2] British Museum, Harleian MS. 322: Dee's hand is on fol. 1*v; Stow's hand is on fol. 139.

[3] In a letter written on the latter date, Dee informs Stow, 'Your Asserius I think not to be of the best and perfectest copy', and he adds, 'If you have Floriacensis Wigorniensis, I would gladly see him a little.' See British Museum, Harleian MS. 374, art. 11, fol. 15.

[4] British Museum, Harleian MS. 532, art. 6, fol. 58v, contains the following note in Stow's hand (Watson, *Library of Sir Simonds D'Ewes*, p. 331, item X109), 'a mynt in dunwiche'.

[5] British Museum, Harleian MS. 374, art. 11, fol. 15.

Dee's role in the English antiquarian movement was a considerable and yet curious one. He was largely responsible for inspiring British imperial desires and, in the course of this, helped to reinvest the Arthur legends with their old appeal; this development, in turn, had important implications for men like Spenser, Sidney, Rogers and Hakluyt. In encouraging a rebirth of the idea of Arthur as the greatest of British imperialists, Dee may have accepted the British History too readily, but the end far surpassed the means. It may even be that Dee fully realized that the Arthurian conquests would afford him his most persuasive propaganda in promoting his dream of a peaceful and powerful and universally just British Empire.

Dee was a significant force in encouraging belief in the British History, but he was also completely capable of seeing the benefits of chorography, which Daniel Rogers, for example, did not see. Other subjects absorbed Dee's attention too deeply to allow him to produce a great chorographical work. However, his attempt to preserve ancient manuscripts, records and monuments; his encouragement of men like Stow, Holinshed and Camden; and his willingness to share his vast personal antiquarian knowledge are certainly achievements enough to give him a major place in the history of British antiquarianism.

Conclusion

At the beginning of this study I said that no doors would be closed. So much concerning John Dee and his philosophy remains obscure that, although I have tried to make a *fair* assessment of him and his role in Renaissance England, no *definitive* evaluation is yet possible. To understand fully his powerful personality, his abstruse philosophy, his genius and his lunacy will take more than one study; it will require the work of many scholars in different fields. After working on Dee for several years, I do not think a single individual is capable of examining adequately his importance in all areas of Renaissance thought. His role in the history of science – each branch of it – should be thoroughly evaluated by a historian of science. My own study of Dee's relationship with the Sidney circle presents that group in a rather different light, but it should be expanded. There are intriguing facets of Dee's role in Elizabethan England that I have barely mentioned; for instance, his curious association with the leading political figures of the time deserves careful scrutiny by a historian of politics. Finally, John Dee's considerable influence on the Continent certainly ought to be examined in detail. I have merely attempted to make a beginning, to present an overall picture of Dee that may induce others to study him and his thought.

Some conclusions can be drawn, however, about Dee and his diverse activities. His science and magic, his art and even his antiquarianism, all form part of a universal vision of the world as a continuous and harmonious unity. Dee did not gain his European reputation, as one of his nineteenth-century biographers claimed, for writing 'sheer nonsense'; rather, he

gained it because he was a brilliant representative of a philosophy that had inundated Renaissance Europe – Hermeticism.

John Dee was totally in the Hermetic tradition. By advocating that tradition in sixteenth-century England, Dee connected
the developments in Renaissance English thought with the
intellectual movements on the Continent and so served as a
link between the English Renaissance and the Renaissances of
other European countries. Because he espoused a philosophical
system that was different from the dominant humanism of
Renaissance England, Dee seems something of an aberration.
He was attempting, almost alone, to change the currents of
English thought during the period, and he clearly succeeded
to some extent. Until further investigations are made, however,
we cannot know exactly how great his influence was.

John Dee was a complex transitional figure who promoted the
developments of the future, who was conversant with the ideas
of his own time, and yet who remained rooted in the past. His
world view was formed by Hermetic seals, mathesis and mysticism, and attempts at direct contact with angels, but he also
promoted practical science and utilitarian education, toleration
and religious harmony. He advocated the Puritan ethic of
utility but without the intolerance that frequently went with
it.

The key to John Dee's philosophy and actions is his profound
faith in man's innate ability. He saw man as magus, the star-
demon who could achieve anything he desired: man could
become like God. The appalling intensity of Dee's faith led him
into exceedingly strange and often dangerous areas of thought;
but in groping for universal knowledge he was a complete
Renaissance man.

Bibliography

A complete John Dee bibliography is potentially enormous and would involve a good many technical problems. I have tried to gather as much pertinent material as possible here, but the list is by no means complete. Medieval manuscripts which Dee owned and annotated have not usually been included unless a marginal note has been of particular significance in this study; the manuscripts in Dee's collection should be dealt with in the catalogue of his library. On the other hand, I have listed all of Dee's own manuscripts that I have encountered as well as those written by others that relate to him. In the case of printed books with marginal annotations a problem arises: are they to be put in the manuscript or printed book section? I have classified them as they are catalogued in the libraries where they are deposited. Again, I have listed only the books which he owned that I actually examined and used in the body of my text. In such cases the existence of marginal notes is indicated. Among the printed books are most items that I have found that pertain directly to Dee; these are designated by an asterisk. In certain cases only a few lines are devoted to Dee himself, but they have been quoted in my text, or they are telling references. I have, of course, omitted many works that merely mention Dee in passing, or are of no scholarly value.

Manuscripts

Cambridge:

Trinity College MS. o. 4. 20. Dee's list of his library made on 6 September 1583.

London:

British Museum, Additional MS. 19065. Dee's signature and his motto. 'NIHIL UTILE' QUOD NON HONESTUM', appear on fol. 43.

Additional MS. 32092, arts. 9, 10. Concern Dee's calendar reform and its rejection by the bishops.

Additional MS. 35213, art. 1. Fragmentary catalogue of his library made by Dee sometime after 1589.

Appendix MS. XVLI, parts 1 and 2. Manuscript of Dee's 'Spiritual Diaries' published by Meric Casaubon.

Bibliography

Cotton MS. Augustus. I, 1, i. A map of part of the Northern hemisphere drawn by Dee in 1580 on the back of which is Dee's outline concerning Elizabeth's rights to foreign territories.

Cotton Charter XIII, art. 38. Pedigree by John Dee tracing his ancestry to the earliest Welsh princes and kings of Britain.

Cotton Charter XIII, art. 39. A chart drawn by Dee in 1570 outlining how to 'MAKE THIS KINGDOME FLOURISHING, TRIUMPHANT, FAMOUS, AND BLESSED'.

Cotton Charter XIV, art. 1. Traces the ancestry of Elizabeth and John Dee back to the earliest Welsh kings.

Cotton MS. Julius. C. III, arts. 11, 12. Letter to Sir Robert Cotton from Dee requesting him to spare his writer to copy an old record about the foundation of Manchester College; Letter to Sir Robert Cotton from Dee concerning the trustworthiness of a servant formerly employed by Cotton.

Cotton MS. Julius. C. V, art. 41. Letter to William Camden from Dee concerning Arthur Dee's temperament and his education at Westminster School.

Cotton MS. Otho. E. VIII, art. 16. Some directions for a voyage to the northern seas signed by John Dee and dated 15 May 1580.

Cotton MS. Vitellius. C. VII, arts. 1–7. Dee's account of his life (published as the *Compendious Rehearsal*) for Queen Elizabeth; 'Perspectiva, sive de arte mensurandi cum circino et regula'; 'Of Famous and Rich Discoveries'; 'De trigono circinoque analogico, opusculum mathematicum et mechanicum'; 'De speculis comburentibus: item de coni recti atque retanguli sectione illa quae parabola ab antiquis appellabatur, aliaque geometrica'; *Supplication* by Dee to Queen Mary to preserve ancient writings and monuments; letters and papers between Dee and Roger Edwardes on theological subjects. All of the treatises are by John Dee.

Cotton MS. Vitellius. C. IX, art. 1. 'Correctiones et supplemente in Sigberti chronicon' by Dee.

Harleian MS. 57. Manuscript of Albertus Magnus's *De mineralibus* acquired by Dee from the library of John Leland.

Harleian MS. 94, art. 3. A note dated 15 June 1573 to the Lord Treasurer proposing that the records of the exchequer be moved to the treasury of Westminster Abbey.

Harleian MS. 167. Items 6–8 are in Dee's handwriting, while notes by him appear on items 20, 28, 31–2, 34, 36, 38; his mark is also found on item 42. A collection of tracts and papers relating chiefly to sea affairs.

Harleian MS. 218. Miscellaneous historical, literary and chemical tracts which contain annotations by Dee.

Harleian MS. 249, art. 13. Tract on British sea limits written by John Dee for Edward Dyer to whom it is dedicated; also a letter from Dee to Dyer (104–5) dated 8 September 1597 concerning Manchester College.

Harleian MS. 251. Various papers of antiquarian and economic interest with Dee's handwriting on items 23, 24 and 25.

Harleian MS. 285. Items 4, 12–13, 64, 69–71, and 94 all bear notes by Dee. A series of papers dealing with political affairs in the Low Countries.

Harleian MS. 286. Items 19, 91–2 and 152 are in Dee's handwriting. A series of papers dealing with political affairs.

Harleian MS. 289. Items 25, 28–34, 37 and 42 are in Dee's handwriting. Items 1, 6, 20–1, 24, 27, 39–40, 45, 47, 50–5, 81, 103 and 106 contain notes by Dee. These deal mainly with Anglo-Scottish affairs.

Harleian MS. 290. Items 63–6, 88, 90–91 and 106 are in Dee's handwriting. Items 3, 8, 27, 37 and 114 contain notes by Dee. The papers relate mainly to Mary Stuart.

Harleian MS. 295. Items 42–60 contain notes by Dee. A series of letters to Cardinal Wolsey and Henry VIII concerning Spanish affairs.

Harleian MS. 322. Contents list similar to Dee's handwriting with the handwriting of John Stow on fol. 139.

Harleian MS. 359. Fols. 126–216 (*Itinerarium Cambriae*) contain a few notes by Dee.

Harleian MS. 374, art. 11. A letter from John Dee to 'my loving frende Mr. John Stow' dated 4 December 1592, concerning books of antiquarian interest and the former burgesses of the Cinque Ports.

Harleian MS. 473. Notes by Dee collected on an antiquarian tour through Chester and Wales previously assigned to Samuel Erdeswicke.

Harleian MS. 532, arts. 6, 14. Letter of an unknown antiquary to Dee concerning the town of Dunwich which had been largely covered by the sea; 'Epilogismus calculi diurnis planetarum, tum longitudinis, tum latitudinis, per D. Johannem Dee.'

Harleian MS. 588, arts. 1–108. An extensive series of pedigrees and genealogical material drawn up by Dee and covering much of the royalty and nobility of the Continent as well as of England.

Harleian MS. 601. 'A short account of the foundations & endowments of all the Colleges & Chantries in the City of London & County of Middlesex' with notes by Dee.

Harleian MS. 1879, arts. 1, 5, 6. 'Catalogus codd. MSS. numero plus minus 230, iam olim ut videtur, in Bibliotheca Joannis Dee M. D. conservatorum'; catalogue of Dee's printed books; catalogue of Dee's manuscripts. The last two items are dated 6 September 1583 and are in Dee's handwriting.

Harleian MS. 2407, art. 33. Dee's alchemical testament to John Gwynn.

Harleian MS. 5835, art. 2. Dee's own pedigree.

Harleian MS. 6485, art. 1. Though this treatise on the 'Rosie Crucian Secrets' is assigned to Dee, it is not in his handwriting and was probably not written by him.

Harleian MS. 6486. Hermetic treatise ascribed to Thomas Rudd that contains a likeness of Dee's monad.

Harleian MS. 6986, art. 26. Letter from Dee to Queen Elizabeth dated 10 November 1588 concerning his return from the Continent at her request.

Lansdowne MS. 19, arts. 34, 38. A letter from John Dee to William Camden dated 7 August 1574 concerning various matters of antiquarian and philosophical interest, and showing the early date of the friendship between these two men and John Stow; letter from Dee to Lord Burghley about treasure-seeking and the records Dee had discovered at Wigmore Castle on his recent antiquarian tour.

Lansdowne MS. 39, art. 14. Lord Burghley's memorandum of Dee's calendar reform.

Lansdowne MS. 61, art. 58. Letter from Dee to Lord Burghley concerning Parkins the Jesuit and the situation in the Low Countries.

Lansdowne MS. 94, art. 51. Dee's pedigree of English monarchs from the ancient kings of Britain with a summary of the Arthurian conquests as epitomized by Lord Burghley.

Lansdowne MS. 109, art. 27. Notes by Robert Cecil 'taken owt of Mr Dees discourse for the reformation of the Vulgar Kalendar'.

Lansdowne MS. 121, art. 13. William Bourne's treatise on optical glasses which suggests that Dee was particularly knowledgeable about that subject.

Lansdowne MS. 122, arts. 4, 5. Dee's summary of Sir Francis Drake's voyage; Dee's instructions to Charles Jackman and Arthur Pett concerning a proposed trip to the Orient.

Lansdowne MS. 158, art. 8. Letter from Dee to Dr Julius Caesar, Master of Requests, concerning litigation arising from the enclosure of Denton Moor by Robert Cecil about 1595.

Lansdowne MS. 229, art. 76. Antiquarian information gathered by Robert Glover from Dee's library.

Lansdowne MS. 983, art. 47. Bishop Kennett's notes on Dee.

Royal MS. 7. C. XVI, art. 35. A holograph copy of Dee's tract on British sea limits.

Sloane MS. 15. Dee's instructions and annotations for Euclid's *Elements*.

Sloane MS. 78, art. 11. An excerpt from Dee's 'Liber mysteriorum sextus et sanctus'.

Sloane MS. 885, art. 15. A manuscript *c.* 1700 which epitomizes Dee's 'Mathematicall Preface'.

Sloane MS. 1782, fol. 31. Horoscope notes for John Dee.

Sloane MS. 1902. Medical and astrological notes by Arthur Dee.

Sloane MS. 2599, art. 1. Transcript of a part of Dee's work on the angels.

Sloane MS. 3188. Dee's 'Spiritual Diaries' from 22 December 1581 to 30 May 1583.

Sloane MS. 3189. Dee's 'Liber mysteriorum sextus et sanctus' in Edward Kelley's handwriting.

Bibliography

Sloane MS. 3191, arts. 1–4. 'Claves Angelicae'; 'Liber scientia auxilii et victoria terrestris'; 'De heptarchia mystica'; 'Tabula bonorum angelorum invocationes'. All of these treatises are by Dee.

Sloane MS. 3677. Elias Ashmole's copy of Dee's 'Spiritual Diaries'.

Sloane MS. 3678, art. 1. Elias Ashmole's copy of Sloane MS. 3191.

Warburg Institute, Warburg MS. FBH 510. John Dee's 'Tuba Veneris'.

Oxford:

Bodleian, Additional MS. c. 194. Seventeenth-century copy of Dee's library catalogue.

Ashmole MS. 57. Copy made by Dee of Thomas Norton's *Ordinall of Alchemy*.

Ashmole MS. 174, arts. 74, 77. A table of longitude; 'De temporibus opportunis ad magicas artes operandas'.

Ashmole MS. 179, VII. Posthumous copy of Dee's work on the calendar.

Ashmole MS. 204, art. 18. List of drugs probably written by Dee.

Ashmole MS. 242, arts. 43, 44, 45. 'Arithmetical solution of the para-doxical compass'; 'Treatise on fractions'; 'On draining and embank-ing fens'.

Ashmole MS. 337, art. 3. Dee's accounts of household expenses and other memoranda from 22 January 1589 to October 1591.

Ashmole MS. 356, V. Philip Sidney's horoscope.

Ashmole MS. 421, fols. 178–222. Information about Dee gathered by William Lilly and later published in his autobiography.

Ashmole MS. 422, art. 2. Notes copied by Elias Ashmole from Dee's fifth 'Book of Mysteries'.

Ashmole MS. 423, art. 122. Transcript by Elias Ashmole of Dee's personal memoranda found in the margins of Stoffler's *Ephemerides*. The notes cover the period from 1543 to 1566.

Ashmole MS. 487–8. Two volumes in quarto, containing the *Ephemerides* of Stadius for 1554–1600 (Cologne, 1570), and of Maginus for 1581–1620 (Venice, 1582); on the margins of these, respectively, are written the short memoranda, or *The Private Diary* of Dee from January 1577 to December 1600, and from September 1586 to April 1601.

Ashmole MS. 580. Elias Ashmole's copy of Meric Casaubon's edition of *A True & Faithful Relation of what passed for many Years Between D*r *: John Dee . . . and Some Spirits* which contains copious notes by Ashmole.

Ashmole MS. 847, fols. 1ᵛ, 118ᵛ. Marginal notes made by Dee con-cerning some of his Welsh relatives.

Ashmole MS. 972, fols. 316–18. Notes on the nativities of John Dee, Edward Kelley and Katherine Dee; extract relating to Dee from a role of the wardens of Manchester College.

Ashmole MS. 1131, art. 188. Elias Ashmole's copy of his letter to Sir Thomas Browne concerning Arthur and John Dee.

Ashmole MS. 1142, II. Elias Ashmole's copy of Dee's library list.

Ashmole MS. 1394, III. Three stories in Dee's handwriting of how transmutation was achieved by certain individuals.

Ashmole MS. 1440, art. 15. Explanatory notes by Thomas Tymme meant to be added to his intended translation of Dee's *Monas Hieroglyphica*.

Ashmole MS. 1442, art. 1, fols. 31–2. Copy of Dee's alchemical letter to John Gwynn.

Ashmole MS. 1446, IX. Mr Townesend's annotations on *Theatrum Chemicum* and miscellaneous notes about Dee.

Ashmole MS. 1459, III. Thomas Tymme's introduction to his intended translation of the *Monas Hieroglyphica*.

Ashmole MS. 1486, V, arts. 1–2. Dee's journal concerning a chemical experiment lasting from 4 December 1607 until 21 January 1608; Dee's transcription of George Ripley's 'vade mecum'.

Ashmole MS. 1488, II, fol. 21^v. A note that Dr Richard Napier dined with Dee on 2 July 1604.

Ashmole MS. 1788, arts. 1–18. A copy of Dee's *Compendious Rehearsal*; John Dee's 'Praefatio Latina in actionem in Latinam primum ex 7 (habitam 10 die Aprilis Pragae) etiam in Latinam conversam semonem, an^o 1586'; letter from Dr N. Bernard to Meric Casaubon concerning his book of Dee's actions with spirits and Archbishop Usher's opinion of it, as well as Sir Robert Cotton's note concerning that statement of opinion, and a letter by Casaubon concerning his book about Dee's angelic conferences; copy of Dee's letter of 7 August 1574 to William Camden; list of the contents of 'Of Famous and Rich Discoveries'; Dee's supplication to Queen Mary to save the libraries; notes of some 'pieces of Dr. Dee's bound up in the book entitled Vitell. C. 7'; copy of a letter from William Aubrey to John Dee; 'Medicina ad cancrum curandum' written by Dee; two horoscopes for John Dee; Dee's horoscope for Edward Kelley; Elias Ashmole's speculum concerning the aspects of the planets in Dee's horoscope; information about Dee from Hollinsworth's book of antiquities; John Aubrey's account of Dee gathered from Goodwife Faldo; the effect of the discourse between Goodwife Faldo and Elias Ashmole on the latter; Sir Thomas Browne's reminiscences about Arthur Dee; letter from Sir Thomas Browne to Ashmole concerning Arthur Dee. Much of the above is transcribed by Ashmole.

Ashmole MS. 1789, I–V. Four couplets by Dee to Lord Burghley and Dee's discourse on the reformation of the calendar; original letter from William Aubrey to John Dee; prologue to the reformed calendar and Dee's calendar; Dee's manuscript of *General and Rare Memorials*; a copy in Dee's hand of the letter sent to him by William Aubrey concerning the *General and Rare Memorials*.

Ashmole MS. 1790, I–IV. 'Praefatio Latina in actionem'; papers relating to Dee's actions with the spirits; Elias Ashmole's observations and collections concerning Dee's religious magic; Elias Ashmole's correspondence relating to Dee.

Bibliography

Ashmole MS. 1819, art. 15. First part of Thomas Tymme's 'Epistle Dedicatory' to the *Monas Hieroglyphica* in cipher, and 'natulo de Joannis Dee'.

Corpus Christi MS. 191. Notes of books borrowed, read and bought by Dee in 1556.

Corpus Christi MS. 243. Medieval manuscript containing works by Albertus Magnus, Plato and others which belonged to Humphrey, Duke of Gloucester, and was purchased by John Dee in 1557.

Corpus Christi MS. 254, arts. 3–9. Brief treatise by Dee on 'Pythagoras his wheele' of fortune; holograph copy of Dee's calendar treatise and Burghley's report on it; two copies of the reformed calendar; three letters from Walsingham to Dee concerning his work on the reformed calendar; short mathematical treatise by Dee; transcripts by Dee of works by Roger Bacon and Alkindi.

Dugdale MS. 24. At one time used by Dee as a Commonplace Book.

Museum MS. e. 63, fols. 147^{r-v}. Copy of a letter from John Gwynn to Dee which refers to the *Monas Hieroglyphica*.

Rawlinson MS. 241. Diary by Dee (partly in another hand) concerning some chemical experiments from 22 June to 6 October 1581.

Rawlinson MS. 923, arts. A. 12; B. 10. An account of John Dee's family taken from Rowland Dee; various notes on Meric Casaubon's edition of the 'Spiritual Diaries'.

Selden Supra MS. 79, fols. 171–87^{v}. Notes copied by Brian Twyne from various manuscripts written by John Dee.

Smith MS. 35. Transcript of Dee's Calendar treatise.

Smith MS. 86, fols. 97–108. Notes on Dee gathered by his early biographer Thomas Smith.

Smith MS. 95, fols. 131–46. Notes on Dee gathered by his early biographer Thomas Smith.

Smith MS. 96, fols. 66–133. Copy of Dee's *Supplication* to Queen Mary; copy of the *Compendious Rehearsal*; information transcribed by Thomas Smith from Dee's manuscript 'Of Famous and Rich Discoveries'.

Editions of Dee's Works

Dee, John. *Autobiographical Tracts of Dr. John Dee, Warden of the College of Manchester*, ed. James Crossley. *Chetham Society Publications*, Vol. XXIV. Manchester, 1851.

Compendious Rehearsal, in *Johannis confratris & monachi Glastoniensis, chronica, sive historia rebus Glastoniensis*, ed. Thomas Hearne. 2 vols. Oxford, 1726.

and Commandinus, Frederic, eds. *De superficierum divisionibus liber*. Pesaro, 1570.

and Commandinus, Frederic, eds. *Book of the Divisions of the Superficies*, tr. John Leeke and George Serle. London, 1661.

Diary for the years 1595–1601, ed. John E. Bailey. Privately printed, 1880.

'Mathematicall Preface' to *The Elements of Geometrie of the most auncient Philosopher Euclide of Megara*, tr. Sir Henry Billingsley, ed. John Dee. London, 1570.

Bibliography

'Mathematical Preface' to the *Elements of Geometry*, ed. Thomas Rudd. London, 1651.

'Mathematical Preface' to *Euclid's Elements of Geometry*, ed. John Leeke and George Serle. London, 1661.

General and Rare Memorials pertayning to the Perfect Arte of Navigation. London, 1577.

ed. and augmenter. *Grounde of Artes* by Robert Recorde. London, 1561.

and John Mellis, eds. *Grounde of Artes* by Robert Recorde. London, 1582.

A Letter, Containing a Most Briefe Discourse Apologeticall, with a Plaine Demonstration, and Fervent Protestation, for the Lawfull, Sincere, Very Faithfull and Christian Course, of the Philosophicall Studies and Exercises, of a Certaine Studious Gentleman. London, 1599.

Letter of Dr. John Dee to Sir William Cecyl, ed. R. W. Grey. *Bibliographical and Historical Miscellanies*, Vol. I. London, 1854.

Monas Hieroglyphica. Antwerp, 1564; reprinted Frankfurt, 1591.

Monas Hieroglyphica, in *Theatrum Chemicum*, ed. L. Zetzner. Ober-Ursel, Germany, 1602.

La Monade Hiéroglyphique, tr. Grillot de Givrey. Paris, 1925.

The Hieroglyphic Monad, tr. J. W. Hamilton-Jones. London, 1947.

Monas Hieroglyphica, tr. C. H. Josten, *AMBIX*, XII (1964), 84–221.

Parallaticae commentationis praxeosque. London, 1573.

'Preface' to *Ephemeris Anni 1557* by John Feild. London, 1556.

'Prefatory Verses' to *The Compound of Alchymy* by George Ripley, set forth by Ralph Rabbards. London, 1591.

'Prefatory Verses' to *Egluryn Phraethineb* by Henri Perri. London, 1595; reprinted, Caerdydd, 1930.

The Private Diary, ed James O. Halliwell. *Camden Society Publications*, Vol. XIX. London, 1842.

Propaedeumata Aphoristica. London, 1558; reprinted London, 1568.

A Supplication to Queen Mary for the Recovery and Preservation of Ancient Writers and Monuments, in *Johannis confratris & monachi Glastoniensis, chronica, sive historia rebus Glastoniensis*, ed. Thomas Hearne. 2 vols. Oxford, 1726.

Testamentum Johannis Dee Philosophi Summi ad Johannem Gwynn, transmissum 1568, in *Theatrum Chemicum Britannicum*, ed. Elias Ashmole. London, 1652.

To THE HONORABLE Assemblie of the COMMONS in the present Parlament. London, 1604.

To the King's most excellent Majestie. London, 1604.

A True & Faithful Relation of what passed for many Yeers Between Dr: John Dee . . . and Some Spirits, ed. Meric Casaubon. London, 1659. Casaubon's own copy with his handwritten corrections is in the Bodleian Library, shelf mark D. 8. 14 art. A Copy in the British Museum contains revealing marginal notes by contemporaries of Casaubon's, shelf mark 719. m. 12.

'An Unknown Chapter in the Life of John Dee', ed. C. H. Josten, *JWCI*, XVIII (1965), 223–57.

*Acta Eruditorum. Leipzig, 1707.

*Acts of the Privy Council.

Agrippa, Henry Cornelius. *Three Books of Occult Philosophy*, tr. J[ames] F[rench]. London, 1651.

    Of the Vanitie and Uncertaintie of Artes and Sciences, tr. Ja[mes] San[ford]. London, 1569.

*Ainsworth, William Harrison. *Guy Fawkes, or The Gunpowder Treason.* London, n.d.

*Allen, Don C. *The Star-Crossed Renaissance.* Durham, North Carolina, 1941.

*Ames, Joseph. *Typographical Antiquities.* 3 vols. London, 1785–90.

Ammann, Peter J. 'The Musical Theory and Philosophy of Robert Fludd', *JWCI*, XXX (1967), 198–227.

Anderson, James. *Constitutions of the Free-masons.* London, 1723.

*Anonymous. *The Copie of a Leter, Wryten by a Master of Arte of Cambridge to his friend in London, concerning some talke past of late betwen two worshipful and grave men, about the present state, and some procedings of the Erle of Leycester and his friendes in England.* N. p., 1584.

*   'Crepundiae Literaris', *Gentleman's Magazine*, LXXXIV (1814), 207–8.

*   'Dr. Dee', *Blackwood's Edinburgh Magazine*, LI (1842), 626–9.

*   *The Earthquake in London, in the year 1842: The Life of Dr. John Dee . . . His various Prophecies among which may be noticed an Earthquake to Destroy London, in the Year 1842.* London, 1842.

*Archibald, Raymond Clare. *Euclid's Book on Divisions of Figures.* Cambridge, 1915.

Armstrong, Arthur H., ed. *The Cambridge History of Later Greek and Early Medieval Philosophy.* London, 1967.

Ascham, Roger. *The Whole Works*, ed. John A. Giles. 3 vols. London, 1864.

*Ashmole, Elias. *Theatrum Chemicum Britannicum.* London, 1652.

*   ed. *His Autobiographical and Historical Notes, his Correspondence, and other Contemporary Sources Relating to his Life and Work*, ed. C. H. Josten. 5 vols. Oxford, 1966.

*Aubrey, John. *The Natural History and Antiquities of the County of Surrey.* 5 vols. London, 1718–19.

*   *Brief Lives*, ed. Oliver Lawson Dick. London, 1958.

Bacon, Francis. *The Philosophical Works*, ed. John M. Robertson, based on Ellis and Spedding. London, 1905.

Bacon, Roger. *De mirabili potestate artis et naturae, or Friar Bacon his Discovery of the Miracles of Art, Nature, and Magick.* London, 1659.

*Bailey, John E. 'Dee and Trithemius's "Steganography"', *N&Q*, 5th ser., XI (1879), 401–2, 422–3.

*   'Dr. John Dee's copy of Arrian's "Periplus"', *The Bibliographer*, I (1882), 72–4.

Bainton, Roland H. *Erasmus of Christendom.* New York, 1969.

*Ballard, George. *Memoirs of Several Ladies of Great Britain, who have been celebrated for their writings or skill in the learned language arts and sciences.* Oxford, 1752.

Bibliography

*Beloe, William. *Anecdotes of Literature and Scarse Books*. 6 vols. London, 1807–12.

*Bennett, Josephine. *The Evolution of 'The Faerie Queene'*. Chicago, 1942.

*Besterman, Theodore. *Crystalgazing: A Study in the History, Distribution, Theory and Practice of Skrying*. London, 1924.

Blau, Joseph L. *The Christian Interpretation of the Cabala in the Renaissance*. New York, 1944.

Boas, Marie. *The Scientific Renaissance 1450–1630*. London, 1962.

*Bongus, Petrus. *Mysticae numerorum significationis liber*. Bergamo, 1585.

*Bosanquet, Eustace F. *English Printed Almanacks and Prognostications: A Bibliographical History to the Year 1600*. London, 1917.

*Bourne, William. *A Booke called the Treasure for Traveilers*. London, 1578.

* *A Regiment for the Sea*. London, 1592. The British Museumcopy contains marginal notes by Gabriel Harvey.

Bradbrook, Muriel C. *The School of Night: A Study in the Literary Relationships of Sir Walter Ralegh*. Cambridge, 1936.

Bradwardine, Thomas. *Tractatus de proportionibus*, ed. H. Lamar Crosby, Jr. Madison, Wisconsin, 1955.

*Brooks, Eric St John. *Sir Christopher Hatton*. London, 1956.

*Browne, Sir Thomas. *Works*, ed. Geoffrey Keynes. 4 vols. Chicago, 1964.

Bush, Douglas. *Science and English Poetry: A Historical Sketch, 1590–1950*. New York, 1950.

*Butler, E. M. *The Myth of the Magus*. Cambridge, 1948.

* *Ritual Magic*. Cambridge, 1949.

* *The Fortunes of Faust*. Cambridge, 1952.

*Butler, Samuel. *Hudibras*, ed. Alfred R. Waller. Cambridge, 1905.

*Buxton, John. *Sir Philip Sidney and the English Renaissance*. London, 1954.

*Calder, I. R. F. 'John Dee Studied as an English Neo-Platonist'. Unpublished University of London Dissertation. 1952.

Calendar of Patent Rolls, Edward VI.

Calendar of State Papers, Domestic Series.

Calendar of State Papers, Foreign Series.

*Camden, Carroll, Jr. 'Astrology in Shakespeare's Day', *Isis*, XIX (1933), 26–73.

*Camden, William. *Annales*. London, 1615.

Britannia. London, 1695.

Campana, Augusto. 'The Origin of the Word "Humanist"', *JWCI*, IX (1946), 60–73.

*Campbell, Lily B. *Scenes and Machines on the English Stage during the Renaissance*. Cambridge, 1923.

*Carré, Meyrick H. *Phases of Thought in England*. Oxford, 1949.

* 'Visitors to Mortlake: The Life and Misfortunes of John Dee', *History Today*, XII (1962), 640–7.

Cassirer, Ernst. *The Individual and the Cosmos in Renaissance Philosophy*, tr. Mario Domandi. New York, 1963.

Chamber, John. *The Praise of Astronomie*. London, 1601.

A Treatise Against Judicial Astrologie. London, 1601.

*Chambers, Edmund K. *The Elizabethan Stage*. 4 vols. Oxford, 1923.

Bibliography

Clark, Eleanor Grace. *Ralegh and Marlowe: A Study in Elizabethan Fustian.* New York, 1941.

Coffin, Charles M. *John Donne and the New Philosophy.* New York, 1946.

Colet, John. *Two Treatises on the Hierarchies of Dionysius*, tr. J. H. Lupton. Ridgewood, New Jersey, 1966.

Collingwood, Robin G. *The Idea of Nature.* New York and Oxford, 1945.

*Cooper, Charles Henry, and Cooper, Thompson. *Athenae Cantabrigiensis.* 3 vols. Cambridge, 1858–1913.

Copernicus, Nicolaus. *On the Revolutions of the Heavenly Spheres,* tr. C. G. Wallis, in *Great Books of the Western World*, ed. R. M. Hutchins, Vol. XVI. London, 1952.

Corpus Hermeticum, tr. A. J. Festugière with text established by A. D. Nock. 4 vols. Paris, 1945–54.

Coxe, Francis. *A Short Treatise declaringe the detestable wickednesses of Magical Sciences.* London, 1561.

Craig, Hardin. *The Enchanted Glass: The Elizabethan Mind in Literature.* Oxford, 1950.

Craven, J. B. *Doctor Robert Fludd.* Kirkwall, 1902.

Crombie, A. C., *et al.* 'Thomas Harriot (1560–1621): an Original Practitioner in the Scientific Art', reprint from *TLS*, 23 October 1969.

*Cunningham, George Godfrey. *Lives of Eminent and Illustrious Englishmen from Alfred the Great to the Latest Times.* 8 vols. Glasgow, 1834–7.

*Curtis, Mark. *Oxford and Cambridge in Transition, 1558–1642.* Oxford, 1959.

Curtius, Ernst Robert. *European Literature and the Latin Middle Ages*, tr. Willard R. Trask. New York, 1953.

Cusae, Nicolai, Cardinalis. *Opera.* 3 vols. Paris, 1514; reprinted, Frankfurt, 1962.

*Dalton, Ormonde M. 'Notes on Wax Discs used by Dr. Dee', *Proceedings of the Society of Antiquaries of London*, XXI (1906–7), 380–3.

*Davis, John. *The Seamans Secrets.* London, 1595.

*Deacon, Richard. *John Dee: Scientist, Geographer, Astrologer and Secret Agent to Elizabeth I.* London, 1968.

Debus, Allen G. *The English Paracelsians.* New York, 1966.

 The Chemical Dream of the Renaissance. Cambridge, 1968.

* 'Mathematics and Nature in the Chemical Texts of the Renaissance', *AMBIX*, XV (1968), 1–28.

Dee, Arthur. *Fasiculus Chemicus*, tr. James Hasolle, pseud. for Elias Ashmole. London, 1650.

*De Jong, H. M. E. *'Atalanta Fugiens': Sources of an Alchemical Book of Emblems.* Leyden, 1969.

*Denison, Edward. 'Queen Elizabeth's Astrologer', *The Month*, CLVIII (1931), 302–8.

*Dennistoun, James. *Memoirs of the Dukes of Urbino*, ed. Edward Hutton. 3 vols. London, 1909.

*Dickens, Charles. 'Modern Magic', *All the Year Round*, III (1860), 370–4.

*Digges, Thomas. *Alae seu scalae mathematicae.* London, 1573.

 A Perfit Description of the Caelestiall Orbes. London, 1576.

* *Stratioticos.* London, 1579.

Bibliography

Dijksterhuis, Edward J. *The Mechanization of the World Picture*, tr. C. Dikshoorn. Oxford, 1961.

*D'Israeli, Isaac. *The Amenities of Literature*, ed. Earl of Beaconsfield. London, n.d.

Ellrodt, Robert. *Neoplatonism in the Poetry of Spenser*. Geneva, 1960.

*Espejo, Antonio de. *El viaje hizo A. de E. en el anno de ochenta y tres*. Madrid and Paris, 1586. The British Museum copy has an inscription by Dee.

Fale, Thomas. *Horologiographia*. London, 1593.

Festugière, A. J. *La Révélation d'Hermès Trismégiste*. 4 vols. Paris, 1950–4. *Hermétisme et Mystique Païenne*. Paris, 1967.

*Ffarington, William. *The Derby Household Books*, ed. Francis R. Raines. *Chetham Society Publications*, Vol. XXXI. Manchester, 1853.

*Firpo, Luigi. 'John Dee, scienziato, negromante e avventuriero', *Rinascimento*, III (1952), 25–84.

*Fletcher, Harris F. *The Intellectual Development of John Milton*. 2 vols. Urbana, Illinois, 1956–61.

Fludd, Robert. *Utriusque cosmi maioris scilicet et minoris, metaphysica, physica atque technica historia*. 2 tomes. Oppenheim and Frankfurt, 1617–21.

*Forster, Richard. *Ephemerides Meteorographicae*. London, 1575.

*Fowler, Alastair. *Spenser and the Numbers of Time*. London, 1964.

*Foxe, John. *Actes and Monuments*. London, 1563.
Actes and Monuments. London, 1576.

Fraunce, Abraham. *The Lawiers Logike*. London, 1588.

*Fuller, Thomas. *The History of the Worthies of England*, ed. P. Austin Nuttall. 3 vols. London, 1840; reprinted, New York, 1965.

*Fulton, Thomas W. *The Sovereignty of the Sea*. Edinburgh, 1911.

Galilei, Galileo. *Dialogue of the Great World Systems*, tr. Salusbury, revised and annotated by Giorgio de Santillana. Chicago, 1953.

Garin, Eugenio *et al.*, eds. *Testi umanistici su l'ermetismo*. Rome, 1955.

*Gibson, Strickland. 'Brian Twyne', *Oxoniensa*, V (1940), 94–114.

*Gilbert, Humphrey. *A Discourse of Discoverie for a new passage to Cataia*, ed. George Gascoigne. London, 1576.

* *The Voyages and Colonising Enterprises of Sir Humphrey Gilbert*, ed. D. B. Quinn. *Hakluyt Society Publications*, Vols. LXXXIII–LXXXIV. London, 1938–9.

Giorgi, Francesco. *L'Harmonie du Monde*, tr. Guy Le Fèvre de la Boderie. Paris, 1579.

*Godwin, William. *Lives of the Necromancers*. London, 1834.

*Gosling, William Gilbert. *The Life of Sir Humphrey Gilbert*. London, 1911.

*Greaves, John. *Miscellaneous Works*, ed. T. Birch. 2 vols. London, 1737.

Greene, Robert. *The Honourable Historie of Frier Bacon and Frier Bungay*. London, 1594.

Greville, Fulke. *The Life of the Renowned Sʳ Philip Sidney*. London, 1652.

Gunther, Robert T. *Early Science in Oxford*. 2 vols. Oxford, 1923.

Guthrie, William K. C. *A History of Greek Philosophy*. 2 vols. Cambridge, 1962–5.

Hakewill, George. *An Apologie of the Power and Providence of God in the Government of the World*. Oxford, 1627.

Bibliography

*Hakluyt, Richard. *The Principal Navigations, Voiages Traffiques and Discoveries of the English Nation.* 3 vols. London, 1598–1600.

*Halsted, George B. 'Note on the First English Euclid', *American Journal of Mathematics*, II (1879), 46–8.

*Harvey, Gabriel. *Pierces Supererogation.* London, 1593.

   Letter Book. A.D. 1573–1580, ed. E. J. L. Scott. *Camden Society Publications*, Vol. XXXIII. London, 1884.

*   *Marginalia*, ed. G. C. Moore-Smith. Stratford-upon-Avon, 1913.

*Harvey, Richard. *An Astrological Discourse.* London, 1583.

   Philadelphus, or *A Defence of Brutes, and Brutans History.* London, 1593.

*Haydn, Hiram. *The Counter-Renaissance.* New York, 1950.

Heydon, Christopher. *A Defence of Judiciall Astrologie.* Cambridge, 1603.

Hieatt, A. Kent. *Short Time's Endless Monument: The Symbolism of the Numbers in Edmund Spenser's 'Epithalamion'.* New York, 1960.

*Hill, Christopher. *Intellectual Origins of the English Revolution.* London, 1966.

*Hillyer, Anthony. *Elizabeth's Merlin.* Los Angeles, 1947.

Hippocrates Junior, pseud., ed. *The Predicted Plague.* London, 1889. The 'Astrology of her Most Sacred and Illustrious Majestie Queene Elizabeth of Armada Renowne' assigned to Dee is spurious.

Hirst, Désirée. *Hidden Riches: Traditional Symbolism from the Renaissance to Blake.* London, 1964.

Holinshed, Raphael. *The Firste Volume of the Chronicles of England, Scotlande and Irelande.* London, 1577.

*   *The Third Volume of Chronicles.* London, 1587.

Hollander, John. *The Untuning of the Sky: Ideas of Music in English Poetry, 1500–1700.* Princeton, 1961.

*Hood, Thomas. *The Use of both the Globes, Celestiall, and Terrestriall.* London, 1592.

*Hooke, Robert. *The Posthumous Works.* London, 1705.

*Hookyaas, R. *Humanisme, Science et Réforme: Pierre de la Ramée (1515–1572).* Leyden, 1958.

*Hopper, Vincent F. 'Spenser's "House of Temperance"', *PMLA*, LV (1940), 958–67.

*Hort, Gertrude M. *Dr. John Dee: Elizabethan Mystic and Astrologer.* London, 1922.

*Howell, Roger. *Sir Philip Sidney: The Shepherd Knight.* London, 1968.

Howell, Wilbur S. *Logic and Rhetoric in England: 1500–1700.* Princeton, 1956.

*Hylles, Thomas. *The Arte of Vulgar Arithmetic.* London, 1600.

*Irwin, Raymond. *The Origins of the English Library.* London, 1958.

*Jacquot, Jean. 'Humanisme et science dans l'Angleterre élisabéthaine: L'oeuvre de Thomas Blundeville', *Revue d'Histoire des Sciences et de leurs Applications*, III (1953), 190–202.

*James, Montague R. *A descriptive Catalogue of the MSS at Trinity College.* 3 vols. Cambridge, 1900–2.

*   *A descriptive Catalogue of the MSS in the Library of Corpus Christi College.* 2 vols. Cambridge, 1912.

*   *Manuscripts formerly owned by Dr. John Dee, with Preface and Identifications*, Supplement to the Bibliographical Society's Transactions. London, 1921.

Bibliography

*Jantz, Harold. *Goethe's Faust as a Renaissaance Man: Parallels and Prototypes.* Princeton, 1951.

Jayne, Sears. *Library Catalogues of the English Renaissance.* Berkeley and Los Angeles, 1956.

John Colet and Marsilio Ficino. Oxford, 1963.

and Johnson, Francis R. *The Lumley Library: The Catalogue of 1609.* British Museum Bicentenary Publications. London, 1956.

*Johnson, Francis R. *Astronomical Thought in Renaissance England.* Baltimore, 1937.

* 'Gresham College: Precursor of the Royal Society', *JHI*, I (1940), 413–38.

and Larkey, Sanford V. 'Thomas Digges, the Copernican System and the Idea of the Infinity of the Universe in 1576', *HLB*, V (1934), 69–117.

'Robert Recorde's Mathematical Teaching and the Anti-Aristotelian Movement', *HLB*, VII (1935), 59–87.

Jonson, Ben. *The Alchemist.* London, 1612.

Josten, C. H. *see* Editions of Dee's Works.

Jung, Carl. *Psychology and Alchemy*, tr. R. F. C. Hull. London, 1953.

*Kargon, Robert H. *Atomism in England from Hariot to Newton.* Oxford, 1966.

Kelton, Arthur. *A Chronycle with a Genealogie Declaryng that the Brittons and Welshemen are Lineallye Dyscended from Brute.* London, 1547.

*Kendrick, Thomas D. *British Antiquity.* London, 1950.

*Kippis, Andrew. *Biographia Britannica.* 5 vols. London, 1778–93.

Klibansky, Raymond. *The Continuity of the Platonic Tradition during the Middle Ages.* London, 1939.

*Kocher, Paul H. *Science and Religion in Elizabethan England.* San Marino, California, 1953.

Kristeller, Paul O. *Supplementum Ficinianum.* 2 vols. Florence, 1937.

Studies in Renaissance Thought and Letters. Rome, 1956.

Renaissance Thought. New York, 1961.

Eight Philosophers of the Italian Renaissance. Stanford, 1965.

**Lancashire Funeral Certificates*, ed. Thomas William King. *Chetham Society Publications*, Vol. LXXV. Manchester, 1869.

*Leigh, Edward. *A Treatise of Religion & Learning and of Religious and Learned Men.* London, 1656.

**Letters Illustrative of the Progress of Science in England*, ed. James O. Halliwell. London, 1841.

**Letters written by Eminent Persons in the Seventeenth and Eighteenth Centuries*, ed. John Aubrey. 2 vols. London, 1823.

*Levy, Fred. J. 'The Making of Camden's *Britannia*', *Bibliothèque d'Humanisme et Renaissance*, XXVI (1964), 70–98.

* 'Daniel Rogers as Antiquary', *Bibliothèque d'Humanisme et Renaissance*, XXVII (1965), 444–62.

* *Tudor Historical Thought.* San Marino, California, 1967.

Lhuyd, Humphrey. *The Breviary of Britayne*, tr. Thomas Twyne. London, 1573.

Bibliography

*Lilly, William. *The History of His Life and Times*. London, 1774.

Lullus, Raymundus. *Opera*. 10 vols. Mainz, 1721–42; reprinted, Frankfurt, 1965.

*Lynam, Edward. *British Maps and Map Makers*. London, 1944.

*Lysons, Daniel. *The Environs of London*. 4 vols. London, 1792–6.

Lyte, Henry. *The Light of Britayne*. London, 1588.

*McCulloch, S. C. 'John Dee: Elizabethan Doctor of Science and Magic', *South Atlantic Quarterly*, L (1951), 72–85.

*Mackay, Charles. *Extraordinary Popular Delusions and the Madness of Crowds*. London, 1841; reprinted, Boston, 1932.

*Marcus, Geoffrey J. *A Naval History of England: The Formative Centuries*. London, 1961.

Marlowe, Christopher. *The Tragical History of Doctor Faustus*, ed. Frederick Boas. London, 1949.

*Maynard, K. 'Science in Early English Literature 1550 to 1650', *Isis*, XVII (1932), 94–126.

Maziarz, Edward A., and Greenwood, Thomas. *Greek Mathematical Philosophy*. New York, 1968.

*Meadows, Denis. *Elizabethan Quintet*. London, 1956.

Melton, John. *Astrologaster, or, the Figure-Caster*. London, 1620.

*Millican, Charles B. *Spenser and the Table Round*. Cambridge, Mass., 1932.

*Milton, John. *The Complete Works*, gen. ed. Frank Allen Patterson. 20 vols. New York, 1931–40.

Poetical Works, ed. Helen Darbishire. 2 vols. Oxford, 1955.

*Moffett, Thomas. *Nobilis, or A View of the Life and Death of a Sidney*, tr. and ed. Virgil B. Heltzel and Hoyt H. Hudson. San Marino, California, 1940.

Mulcaster, Richard. *Positions*. London, 1581.

*Nash, Treadway Russell. *Collection for the History and Antiquities of Worcestershire*. 2 vols. London, 1781–2.

*Nashe, Thomas. *Works*, ed. Ronald B. McKerrow. 5 vols. London, 1904–40.

*Naudé, Gabriel. *The History of Magick by way of Apology for all the Wise Men who have unjustly been reputed Magicians from the Creation to the present Age*, tr. J. Davies. London, 1657.

Nauert, Charles G., Jr. *Agrippa and the Crisis of Renaissance Thought*. Urbana, Illinois, 1965.

Neale, John E. *Queen Elizabeth I*. London, 1967.

*Nicéron, Jean Pierre. *Mémoires pour servir à l'histoire des Hommes Illustres*. 43 vols. Paris, 1729–45.

*Nichols, John. *Literary Anecdotes of the Eighteenth Century*. 9 vols. London, 1812–15.

The Progress and Public Processions of Queen Elizabeth. 3 vols. London, 1823.

*Nicolas, Harris. *Memoires of the Life and Times of Sir Christopher Hatton*. London, 1847.

Nicolson, Marjorie Hope. *Science and Imagination*. Ithaca, New York, 1956.

The Breaking of the Circle. New York, 1960.

*Norman, Robert. *The Newe Attractive*. London, 1581.

Ong, Walter J. *Ramus, Method, and the Decay of Dialogue.* Cambridge, Mass., 1958.

**Original Letters of Eminent Literary Men of the 16th, 17th, and 18th Centuries,* ed. Henry Ellis. *Camden Society Publications,* Vol. XXIII. London, 1843.

*Osborn, James. '*Mica, mica, parva stella*: Sidney's Horoscope', *TLS* (1 January 1971), pp. 17–18.

Pagel, Walter. *Paracelsus.* Basel and New York, 1958.

William Harvey's Biological Ideas. Basel and New York, 1967.

Palingenius, Marcellus. *The Zodiake of Life,* tr. Barnabe Googe. London, 1565.

*Parks, George Bruner. *Richard Hakluyt and the English Voyages.* New York, 1928.

*Parr, Richard. *Life of James Usher.* London, 1686.

Peers, Edgar A. *Ramon Lull: A Biography.* London, 1929.

*Penrose, Boies. *Travel and Discovery in the Renaissance, 1420–1620.* Cambridge, Mass., 1952.

*Phillips, James E. 'Daniel Rogers: A Neo-Latin Link Between the Pléiade and Sidney's "Areopagus"', in *Neo-Latin Poetry of the Sixteenth and Seventeenth Centuries,* William Andrews Clark Memorial Library. Los Angeles, 1965.

*Philpot, John. *The Examinations and Writings,* ed. Robert Eden. Cambridge, 1892.

Pico della Mirandola, Giovanni. *Opera Omnia.* 2 vols. Basel, 1572.

Oration on the Dignity of Man, tr. Elizabeth Livermore Forbes, in *The Renaissance Philosophy of Man,* ed. Ernst Cassirer *et al.* Chicago and London, 1967.

Plato. *The Dialogues,* tr. Benjamin Jowett. 4th ed. 4 vols. Oxford, 1953.

Porta, John Baptista della. *Natural Magick.* London, 1658.

Price, John. *Historiae Britannicae Defensio.* London, 1573.

*Prideaux, W. R. B. 'Books from John Dee's Library', *N&Q,* 9th ser., VIII (1901), 137–8.

* 'Books from John Dee's Library', *N&Q,* VIII (1904), 241.

Proclus. *Philosophical and Mathematical Commentaries,* tr. Thomas Taylor. 2 vols. London, 1788–9.

*Purchas, Samuel. *Purchas his Pilgrimes.* 5 vols. London, 1625–6.

Raine, Kathleen. *Blake and Tradition.* 2 vols. London, 1969.

*Raines, Francis R. *The Rectors of Manchester, and the Wardens of the Collegiate Church of that Town. Chetham Society Publications,* Vols. V–VI. Manchester, 1885.

Ralegh, Walter. *History of the World.* London, 1687.

*Rami, P., and Telei, A. *Collectaneae.* Paris, 1577.

Ramus, Peter. *The Logike,* tr. M. R. Makylmenaeum Scotum. London, 1574.

Elementes of Geometrie, tr. Thomas Hood. London, 1590.

Art of Arithmeticke in whole Numbers and Fractions, tr. William Kempe. London, 1592.

**Rara Mathematica,* ed. James O. Halliwell. London, 1841.

*Rattansi, P. M. 'Paracelsus and the Puritan Revolution', *AMBIX*, XI (1963), 24–32.

*Read, Conyers. *Mr. Secretary Walsingham and the Policy of Queen Elizabeth*. Oxford, 1925.

Read, John. *Through Alchemy to Chemistry*. London, 1961.

Recorde, Robert. *Grounde of Artes*. London, 1543.

Pathway to Knowledge. London, 1551.

Whetstone of Witte. London, 1557.

Rogers, John. *The Displaying of an horrible secte of grosse and wicked Heretiques, naming themselves the Familie of Love*. London, 1578.

Rosen, Edward. 'The Ramus–Rheticus Correspondence', *JHI*, I (1940), 363–8.

Rosenberg, Eleanor. *Leicester, Patron of Letters*. New York, 1955.

Rossi, Paolo. *Francis Bacon: From Magic to Science*, tr. Sacha Rabinovitch. London, 1968.

*Rowse, A. L. *The Elizabethans and America*. London, 1959.

* *The England of Elizabeth*. London, 1961.

Ryan, Lawrence. *Roger Ascham*. Stanford, 1963.

*Salerno, Luigi. 'Seventeenth-Century English Literature on Painting', *JWCI*, XIV (1951), 234–58.

Sambursky, Samuel. *The Physical World of the Greeks*, tr. Merton Dagut. London, 1956.

*Sargent, Ralph M. *At the Court of Queen Elizabeth: The Life and Lyrics of Sir Edward Dyer*. London and New York, 1935.

Scholem, G. G. *Major Trends in Jewish Mysticism*. Jerusalem, 1941.

Scot, Reginald. *The Discoverie of Witchcraft*. London, 1584.

Secret, F. 'L'Humanisme florentin du Quattrocento vu par un kabbalist français, Guy Le Fèvre de la Boderie', *Rinascimento*, V (1954), 105–12.

* *Les Kabbalistes Chrétiens de la Renaissance*. Paris, 1964.

*Seecombe, Thomas. *Lives of Twelve Bad Men: Original Studies of Eminent Scoundrels*. London, 1894.

Seigel, Jerrold E. *Rhetoric and Philosophy in Renaissance Humanism*. Princeton, 1968.

*Selden, John. *Of the Dominion, or, Ownership of the Sea*, tr. Marchemont Nedham. London, 1652.

Shakespeare, William. *Works*, ed. C. J. Sisson. London, 1954.

**Shakespeare's England: An account of the life & manners of his age*. 2 vols. Oxford, 1916.

*Shenton, W. R. 'The First English Euclid', *American Mathematical Monthly*, XXV (1928), 505–11.

Sidney, Sir Philip. *The Complete Works*, ed. Albert Feuillerat. 4 vols. Cambridge, 1912–26.

An Apology for Poetry, ed. Geoffrey Shepherd. London, 1965.

The Poems, ed. William A. Ringler, Jr. Oxford, 1962.

*Singer, Dorothea Waley, and Annie Anderson. *Catalogue of Latin and Vernacular Alchemical Manuscripts in Great Britain and Ireland*. 3 vols. Brussels, 1928–31.

*Sitwell, Edith. *The Queens and the Hive*. London, 1963.

*Smith, Charlotte Fell. *John Dee: 1527–1608*. London, 1909.
*Smith, Thomas. *Vita Joannis Dee*, in *Vitae quorundam eruditissimorum et illustrium virorum*. London, 1707.
* *The Life of John Dee*, tr. William A. Ayton. London, 1908.
*Sondheim, Moriz. 'Shakespeare and the Astrology of his Time', *JWCI*, II (1938–9), 243–59.
Spenser, Edmund. *Poetical Works*, ed. James C. Smith, and Ernest De Selincourt. London, 1966.
*Steele, Robert R. 'Meeting of Cardan and Dr. Dee', *N&Q*, I (1892), 126.
Stevens, Henry. *Thomas Hariot: The Mathematician, the Philosopher and the Scholar*. London, 1900.
*Strathmann, Ernest A. 'Sir Walter Ralegh on Natural Philosophy', *MLQ*, I (1940), 49–61.
* 'John Dee as Ralegh's "Conjurer"', *HLQ*, X (1947), 365–72.
*Strong, F. W. *Procedures and Metaphysics*. Berkeley, 1936.
*Strype, John. *Annals of the Reformation*. 4 vols. Oxford, 1824.
Stubbes, Philip. *The Anatomie of Abuses*. London, 1583.
*Tait, Hugh. '"The Devil's Looking-Glass": The Magical Speculum of Dr. John Dee', *Horace Walpole: Writer, Politician, and Connoisseur*, ed. Warren Hunting Smith. New Haven and London, 1967.
*Taylor, E. G. R. 'John Dee, Drake and the Straits of Annian', *Mariner's Mirror*, XV (1929), 125–30.
* 'More Light on Drake, 1577–1588', *Mariner's Mirror*, XVI (1930), 134–51.
* *Tudor Geography: 1485–1583*. London, 1930.
* 'Sir William Monson Consults the Stars', *Mariner's Mirror*, XIX (1933), 22–6.
* *Late Tudor and Early Stuart Geography: 1583–1650*. London, 1934.
* ed. *The Original Writings & Correspondence of the Two Richard Hakluyts. Hakluyt Society Publications*, Vols. LXXVI–LXXVII. London, 1935.
'Camden's England', in *An Historical Geography of England before A.D. 1800*, ed. H. C. Darby. Cambridge, 1951.
* *The Haven-Finding Art*. London, 1956.
* 'John Dee and the Map of North-East Asia', *Imago Mundi*, XII (1955), 103–6.
* tr. 'A Letter Dated 1577 from Mercator to John Dee', *Imago Mundi*, XIII (1956), 56–68.
* *The Mathematical Practitioners of Tudor and Stuart England*. Cambridge, 1967.
*Taylor, René. 'Architecture and Magic: Considerations on the *Idea* of the Escorial', in *Essays presented to Rudolf Wittkower on his sixty-fifth birthday, Pt. 1. Essays in the History of Architecture*, ed. Douglas Faber *et al*. London, 1967.
*Taylor, William Cooke. *Romantic Biography in the Age of Elizabeth*. 2 vols. London, 1842.
*Thomas-Stanford, Charles. *Early Editions of Euclid's Elements*. London, 1926.
*Thompson, Edward. *Sir Walter Ralegh: The Last of the Elizabethans*. London, 1935.

Bibliography

*Thorndike, Lynn. *A History of Magic and Experimental Science*. 6 vols. New York, 1923–41.

Tillyard, E. M. W. *The Elizabethan World Picture*. New York, 1944.

Traherne, Thomas. *Christian ETHICKS*. London, 1675.

Centuries, Poems and Thanksgivings, ed. H. M. Margoliouth. Oxford, 1958.

*Trattner, Walter I. 'God and Expansion in Elizabethan England: John Dee, 1527–1583', *JHI*, XXV (1964), 17–34.

Trithemius, Johannes. *Steganographia*. Frankfurt, 1606.

Tuve, Rosemond. *Elizabethan and Metaphysical Imagery*. Chicago, 1947.

*Tymme, Thomas. *A Dialogue Philosophicall*. London, 1672.

Van Dorsten, J. A. *Poets, Patrons, and Professors*. London, 1962.

* *The Radical Arts: First Decade of an Elizabethan Renaissance*. Leyden, 1970.

Vergil, Polydore. *Anglica Historia*, ed. Denys Hay. *Camden Society Publications*, Vol. LXXIV. London, 1950.

Walker, D. P. 'The *Prisca Theologia* in France', *JWCI*, XVII (1954), 204–59.

'Ways of Dealing with Atheists: A Background to Pamela's Refutation of Cecropia', *Bibliothèque d'Humanisme et Renaissance*, XVII (Geneva, 1955), 252–77.

Spiritual and Demonic Magic from Ficino to Campanella. London, 1958.

'Kepler's Celestial Music', *JWCI*, XXX (1967), 228–50.

*Ward, B. M. 'Martin Frobisher and Dr. John Dee', *Mariner's Mirror*, XII (1926), 453–5.

*Ward, Seth. *Vindiciae Academiarum*. Oxford, 1654.

*Ware, Samuel Hibbert. *History of the Foundation in Manchester of Christ's College, Chetham Hospital, and the Free Grammar School*. 3 vols. Edinburgh and Manchester, 1831–4.

*Waters, David W. *The Art of Navigation in England in Elizabethan and Early Stuart Times*. London, 1958.

*Watson, Andrew. 'Christopher and William Carye, Collectors of Monastic Manuscripts, and "John Carye"', *The Library*, XX (1965), 135–42.

* *The Library of Sir Simonds D'Ewes*. British Museum Bicentenary Publications. London, 1966.

*Webb, John. 'A Translation of a French Metrical History of the Deposition of King Richard the Second, Written by a Contemporary', *Archaeologia*, XX (1824), 1–423.

*Webster, John. *Academiarum Examen*. London, 1654.

* *The Displaying of Supposed Witchcraft*. London, 1677.

Weiss, Roberto. *The Renaissance Discovery of Classical Antiquity*. Oxford, 1969.

*West, Robert H. *The Invisible World: A Study of Pneumatology in Elizabethan Dramas*. Athens, Georgia, 1939.

Wightman, W. P. D. *Science and the Renaissance: An Introduction to the Study of the Emergence of the Sciences in the Sixteenth Century*. 2 vols. London, 1962.

*Wilkins, John. *Mathematicall Magick; or, the wonders that may be performed by mechanical geometry*. London, 1648.

Bibliography

*Wilkinson, Ronald Sterne. 'The Alchemical Library of John Winthrop, Jr. (1606–1676)', *AMBIX*, XI (1963), 33–51.

*Wilson, Harry Bristow. *The History of Merchant-Taylors' School from its Foundation to the Present Time*. 2 vols. London, 1812–14.

Wittkower, Rudolf. *Architectural Principles in the Age of Humanism*. London, 1949.

*Wood, Anthony. *The History and Antiquities of the Colleges and Halls in the University of Oxford*, ed. John Gutch. 3 vols. Oxford, 1786–90.

* *Athenae Oxonienses*, ed. Philip Bliss. 4 vols. London, 1813–20.

*Wormald, Francis, and Wright, C. E. *The English Library before 1700*. London, 1958.

*Worsop, Edward. *A Discoverie of sundrie errours and faults daily committed by Landemeaters*. London, 1582.

*Worthington, John. *The Diary and Correspondence*, ed. James Crossley. *Chetham Society Publications*, Vol. XIII. Manchester, 1847.

*Yates, Frances A. 'Giordano Bruno's Conflict with Oxford', *JWCI*, II (1938–9), 227–42.

* 'Queen Elizabeth as Astraea', *JWCI*, IX (1946), 27–82.

French Academies of the Sixteenth Century. London, 1947.

* 'The Art of Ramon Lull: An Approach to it through Lull's Theory of Elements', *JWCI*, XVII (1954), 115–173.

'Ramon Lull and John Scotus Erigena', *JWCI*, XXIII (1960), 1–44.

* *Giordano Bruno and the Hermetic Tradition*. London and Chicago, 1964.

* *The Art of Memory*. London and Chicago, 1966.

* 'The Hermetic Tradition in Renaissance Science', in *Art, Science, and History in the Renaissance*, ed. Charles S. Singleton. Baltimore, 1968.

* *Theatre of the World*. London and Chicago, 1969.

*Yeandle, W. H. *The Quadricentennial of the Birth of Dr. John Dee*. London, 1927.

*Zouch, Thomas. *Memoirs of the Life and Writings of Sir Philip Sidney*. York, 1808.

Index

Abraham, 110 n. 4

Academies, Continental, 8, 50, 60, 132, 134–6, 138–9, 141–2, 154–6, 159; of Pythagoras, 82

Adelard of Bath, 166

Aeneas, 194

Aeschylus, 57

Agrippa, Henry Cornelius, 1, 19, 22, 31, 60, 76, 84, 87, 103, 109 n. 4, 119, 140 n. 3; *De occulta philosophia*, 28, 30, 52–3, 78 n. 2, 82, 89–91, 108–9, 113–17 n. 1; *De vanitate*, 52–3, 144

Ainsworth, W. H., *Guy Fawkes*, 16 n. 1

Aion, 82

Alasco, Albertus, 13 n. 3, 154 n. 1, 177

Albania, 192

Alberti, Leone Battista, 57–8

Albertus Magnus, 50, 109

Albion, 192, 196

Alchemy, 2, 28, 49, 52, 77–8 n. 2, 80 n.1, 94, 113 n. 2, 127–8, 159, 161 n. 3

Alexander, 64, 190

Algebra, 169 n. 4

Algorist mathematics, 164

All Souls, Oxford, 163 n. 4

Allen, Thomas, 113 n. 2, 129, 171

America, 179, 197.

Amphion, 138–9

Anderson, James, *Constitutions of the Free-masons*, 161 n. 3

Andromache, 34

Andronicus, Livius, 139

Angelic hierarchies, 10, 88, 100–1, 112, 117, 120

Anglican Church, 11 n. 3, 12

Anglo-Saxon language, 163, n. 4

Anthropographie, 140 n. 3

Antiquarianism, English, 56, 163 n. 4; and Dee, 6, 188–208; French, 188; Italian, 188; German, 188

Antwerp, 29, 37–8, 40, 177, 203

Aquinas, St Thomas, 50, 100

Arabic mathematics in England, 26, 164

Archemastrie, 163

Archimedes, 125

Architecture, 2, 57–8, 150–3, 167, 176, 187

Archites, 108

Areopagus, 132–8, 141–2, 154–5, 159

Aries, 80

Aristophanes, *Pax*, Dee's production of, 24

Aristotelianism, 23, 26, 161–2, 168, 171, 176

Aristotle, 46–7, 51, 61, 69, 171

Aristoxenus, 58

Arithmetic, 65, 108, 163–6, 169

Arnold, *Chronicle*, 194

Arthur, King, 188–91, 193–5, 196 n. 1, 197–9, 207

Ascham, Roger, 33–4, 132, 137

Asclepius, 85–6, 109, 110

Ashmole, Elias, 13, 43, 62, 116; and *Theatrum Chemicum Britannicum*, 14

Asia, 181

Astrology, 1–2, 6, 37, 61, 70–1, 76, 79–80, 82–3, 87, 185; Dee's attitude toward, 6, 91–7, 129 n. 4, 130–1, 185

Astromonia inferior, 130

Astronomy, 1, 27, 66, 89, 96, 98 n. 3, 108, 137, 146; at medieval Oxford, 23 n. 4, 27

Athens, 100

'Atlantes of English mathematics', 171

Atlantis, 179, 197

Atticus, 21

Aubrey, John, 4, 129

Augustine, St, 54–5, 86, 105

Augustinianism, 26, 47

Bacchus, 12

Bacon, Sir Francis, 19, 163; experimental method, 162–3; in magical tradition, 162; *Advancement*, 176; *De augmentis*, 17

Bacon, Sir Nicolas, 63

Bacon, Roger, 26–7, 50, 163 n. 1, 181

Bagdedine, Machomet, 37 n. 4

Baïf, Antoine de, 126, 134–7, 141, 156

Bale, John, 42, 188–9, 191, 193

Barbo, Ermolao, 33

Barn Elms, 62, 127

Basel, 139, 166

Bathori, Stephen, King of Poland, 124

Bede, 191

Behmen, Jacob, 80 n. 3

Benger, Thomas, 34

Bennett, Josephine, 198

Bernardines, 120

Bible, 10, 54, 86, 112, 156, 158, 182

Billingsley, Sir Henry, 165–6

Biondo, Flavio, 188

Bissham, 154 n. 1

Boethius, 50, 58, 104–5, 108, 137

Bohemia, 4, 113 n. 2, 126, 155

Bond, James, 16 n. 3

Bongus, Petrus, 80 n. 3

Bonner, Edmund, Bishop of London, 35

Borough, Stephen, 178

Borough, William, 178

Boswell, Sir William, 175

Bourne, William, 172 n. 3; *Treasure for Traveilers*, 173

Bower of Bliss, the, 150

Boyle, Robert, 161 n. 3

Bradwardine, Thomas, *Tractatus de proportionibus*, 26 n. 3

Brahe, Tycho, 1, 5 n. 4, 89

Britain, 64, 183–4, 186, 191–2, 199, 203–5 n. 1; source of name, 192–3

British Empire, 56, 180, 183, 189–90, 194, 207

British History, the, 190, 195, 198–9, 207

Browne, Sir Thomas, 14 n. 2

Brown, T. J., 201 n. 2

Bruno, Giordano, 1, 19, 69, 83, 87, 143 n. 4, 149 n. 2, 153 n. 2, 154 n. 1, 155, 158; religion of, 119–20, 159; *De gli eroici furori*, 147

Brussels, 4, 29

Brut, 195

Brutus, 188–9, 191–3, 195

Bry, Johann Theodore de, 76 n. 1

Budé, Guillaume, 188

Burton, Richard, 44

Butler, Samuel, *Hudibras*, 13 n. 3

Buxton, John, 137, 143

Cabala, the, 28, 32, 49–50, 53, 66, 78 n. 2, 87, 111, 118, 124, 129, 135, 140, 156, 179; Dee's angel-magic, 5, 9, 10–16, 19, 36–7, 49, 52–3, 86–8, 110–23, 125, 131, 135, 179–80, 209; secrecy of, 82; three worlds of, 30–1, 49, 87, 91, 115, 131

Cabot, Sebastian, 178

Caesar, Julius, 191, 202

Calculus, 50

Calvin, John, *Adversus astrologiam* and *Institutes*, 54

Cambridge, 22–8, 44, 163 n. 4, 171–2, 175

Camden, William, 206–7; *Britannia*, 189, 199, 203–5

Camillo, Giulio, 148; *L'Idea del Theatro,* 149
Campanella, Tommaso, 1, 104; *Magia et Grazia,* 109
Campanus of Novara, 166
Canada, 179
Canterbury, 12
Capella, Martianus, *The Nuptials of Philology and Mercury,* 23 n. 1
Capuchins, 120–1
Cardanus, 51, 89
Casaubon, Isaac, 11 n. 2, 68–9
Casaubon, Meric, 11–13, 15, 17, 68 n. 4, 80
Cassiodorus, 50; *Arts and Disciplines of Liberal Letters,* 23 n. 2
Cathay, 178
Catoptrics, 95
Cecil, William, Lord Burghley, 6, 10, 32, 36–7, 196, 198–9
Celtis, Conrad, 188
Chalcidius, 46
Chaldean wisdom, 54; *see* Ptolemaic universe
Chancellor, Richard, 81, 178
Charles V, Emperor, 4–5, 29, 177, 185
Charms, magical, 83, 118
Cheke, Sir John, 23–4, 26, 32
Chelmsford, 22–3
Chemistry, 2, 127–31
Chester, 201–2
China, 181
Chorography, 189, 199–200, 203, 207
Christ, 120, 122, 191
Christianity, 54, 56, 68, 99–100, 183, 185, 197; attempts to re-unite, 118–25, 135–6, 155–7
Christ's College, Cambridge, 175
Christ's College, Manchester, 7, 9, 10 n. 3
Cicero, 6, 21, 33; *De officiis,* 186
Ciceronianism at Oxford and Cambridge, 23, 27, 46
Cinque Ports, 206
Cirencester, 202
Civil Wars in England, 11 n. 3

Clement, 54
Coimbra, University of, 177
Colet, John, 20–1, 28, 60; *Celestial Hierarchy,* 100–1
Collège de France, 31, 177
Commandinus, Frederic, *De superficierum divisionibus,* 37
Commonwealth period, 11 n. 3, 13
Concordia mundi, 181
Constable, Henry, 155.
Constantine, Emperor, 185
Convocation, 9
Cooper, Thomas, 194
Copernicus, Nicolaus, 6; heliocentricity, 18, 35, 99, 102–3, 135; *De revolutionibus,* 97, 102–3
Corabiel, 118
Corpus Christi College, Oxford, 45–6
Cosmopolites, 186
Counter-Reformation, 59
Cracow, 120, 121 n. 3
Cratippus, 6
Créton, *Histoire,* 205
Cromwell, Oliver, 11 n. 3
Cromwell, Thomas, 42
Cryptography, 15 n. 1, 16 n. 3, 36–7, 52
Ctesibus, 109
Cusa, Nicolaus of, 105; *De docta ignorantia,* 103–4
Cyprian, 54–5

Danesius, 31 n. 3
Daniel, 110 n. 4
Dante, *Inferno,* 153
David, 97, 134, 138–9
Davis, John, 179
Day, John, 165.
Deacon, Richard, *John Dee,* 16 n. 3
Dead Sea scrolls, 68
De Banos, Théophile, 143 n. 4
Decans, 70
Dee, river, 202
Dee, Arthur, 14 n. 2; 114–15, 128, 204

Dee, John: ancestry and birth, 20; calendar reform, 7; at Cambridge, 22–6; Copernicanism of, 18–19, 35, 97–103; doctor, 28 n. 1, 52; and economy of England, 180; educational reformer, 167–71; and experimental method, 162–3; foreign travel, 9, 24–5, 28–32, 36–9, 110–11, 120–5, 181; lectures at Paris, 5, 29–31, 143; and medieval traditions, 27, 41–2, 47, 60, 89, 118, 142, 189; nationalism of, 56, 183–6, 189–99, 207; persecution of, 8–10, 34–5, 44, 121–3; plea to James I, 10; religion of, 54–6, 99, 103, 109–25, 155, 158–9, 209; reputation of, 4–19, 29–31, 121–2, 173–4; secrecy of, 8, 81–2, 103, 163; and the Sidney circle, 126–59, 198; *Brytish Monarchie*, 183–6; *Ephemerides*, 178; English *Euclide*, 2, 90, 162, 169–70, 177; first translation in English, 165–6; preface to, 17, 19, 30, 32, 51, 76 n. 3, 163, 167–71, 180, 199–200; influence of, 172–7; 'Of Famous and Rich Discoveries', 181–3, 190, 192, 195; 'On Fractions', 165; *General and Rare Memorials*, 9 n. 2, 81, 182–6, 189–90, 198; *Grounde of Artes*, additions to, 81, 163–5; 'De heptarchia mystica', 118–19; *Monas Hieroglyphica*, 36, 38–9, 76–81, 90, 96–7, 102, 167, 174 n. 3; symbol of, 65–6, 78–81, 84, 94, 100, 150; 'Mercurius coelestis', 28; 'My loving friend to science bent', 165; 'The Philosophicall and Poeticall Originall Occasions of the Configurations, and Names of the Heavenly Asterismes', 32; *Propaedeumata Aphoristica*, 93–6; 'Treatise of the Rosie Crucian Secrets', 142 n. 2; 'Tuba Veneris', 84; 'The True Cause, and Account (not vulgar) of Floods and Ebbs', 32–3; *True & Faithfull*

Relation (and 'Spiritual Diaries'), 11–12, 15, 110–12, 114, 121–4; *see also* Antiquarianism, Aristophanes, Astrology, Cabala, Geography, Hermeticism, Imperialism, Libraries, Louvain, Magicians, Manchester, Mechanicians, Mortlake, Science
Dee, Katherine, 10 n. 3
Dee, Rowland, 20 n. 1
Delight, the, 179
Democritus, 77
Demosthenes, *Orations*, 46
Denmark, 4
Diacetto, Francesco da, 97
Dickson, Alexander, 149 n. 2
Digges, Leonard, 99
Digges, Thomas, 98–9
Diogenes Laertius, 46
Diomedes, 108
Dionysius Alexandrinus, 181
Dionysius the Areopagite, 88, 99, 112, 120, 134, 156; *Celestial Hierarchy*, 100–1; *De mystica*, 55
Donne, John, 44, 171
Drake, Sir Francis, 62, 179, 197
Drama, 2, 57; production of *Pax*, 24
'Dranting' of verse, 134
Du Bartas, Guillaume, *History of the World*, 152
Du Bellay, Joachim, 136
Dudley, Ambrose, Earl of Warwick, 63 n. 3
Dudley, John, Earl of Warwick, 32
Dudley, Robert, Earl of Leicester, 6, 10, 32 n. 2, 33–4, 62, 126, 130, 154–5, 157 n. 5, 179, 198
Duns Scotus, 50
Du Plessis-Mornay, Phillipe, 69; and *A Woorke concerning the Trewnesse of the Christian Religion*, 157–8
Dunwich, 200–1, 206; St John's church, 201
Dürer, Albrecht, 58, 140 n. 3
Durkan, John, 149 n. 2
Dutch, 155, 184

Dyer, Sir Edward, 9, 62, 127–9, 131–2, 133–4, 136, 154–5, 159, 179, 198, 206

East, the, 180–1
Eden, Richard, 178
Edgar, King, 189–90, 198–9
Education, in England, 22–7, 143, 164, 209; reform of, 59, 167–8, 170–1, 175–6; reform of in France, 60, 167–70
Edward IV, King, 201
Edward VI, King, 21, 32, 126, 202; reforms under, 27, 42, 142
Egypt, ancient, 54, 67; religion, 66, 70, 84–6, 102, 110, 119, 135
Eirenicism, 120, 135, 154–6, 159; *see also* Christianity
Elizabeth I, Queen, 5 n. 1, 6–9, 20 n. 1, 32 n. 2, 33–4, 45, 62–3, 126, 143, 154 n. 1, 168, 180, 183, 185–6, 189–90, 194, 196–9, 206; Age of, 1–2, 9–10, 18, 33, 40, 58, 60, 61, 63, 160, 163 n. 4, 183, 187, 199
Elyot, Sir Thomas, 23
Englefelde, Sir Francis, 34
Ennius, 139
Enoch, 110 n. 4
Ephemerides, 98
Erasmus, Desiderius, 20–1, 23, 26, 144
Erastus, Thomas, 61
Escorial, 69
Esdras, 110 n. 4
Eskimo brought back by Frobisher, 178
Estetiland, 196
Estotiland, 197
Ethicus, 192
Euclid, 5, 30, 33, 37 n. 4, 58 n. 3, 141, 161 n. 3, 165; *Elements*, 29, 162, 166; first English translation, *see also* Dee, John
Euripides, 57
Eusebius, 54, 191
Experimental method, 162–3

Faldo, Goodwife, 62
Family of Love, 124 n. 2
Faustus, 19
Feild, John, *Ephemeris Anni 1557*, 97–8
Fernelius, 31
Ferrys, George, 34
Festugière, A. J., 69, 161
Ficino, Marsilio, 1, 19, 22, 31, 50–1, 54, 59–60, 64, 67, 70, 72, 83, 87, 89, 99–102, 115, 135–6, 140 n. 3, 146, 156; musical magic, 97, 138; translation of *Pimander*, 55, 66, 68–9; *Epistolae*, 50; *De religione Christiana*, 50; *Theologica Platonica*, 50; *De triplici vita*, 50
Finé, Oronce, 33, 177
Fletcher, Harris F., 176 n. 2
Flood, the, 191
Florence, 27, 31, 60, 66, 142, 156
Florida, 197
Fludd, Robert, 1, 69, 76, 80 n. 3, 89, 140, 161 n. 3; and *Utriusque cosmi . . . historia,* 76 n. 1, 108
Flushing, 158
Foix de Candale, François de, Bishop of Aire, 157
Forster, Richard, 5–6
Four elements, 87, 94–5
Foxe, John, *Actes and Monuments*, 8–9, 185
France, 8, 31–2, 126, 136, 143 n. 4, 156–7, 188, 167–70, 205
Friseland, 196, 198
Frisius, Gemma, 25, 177
Frobisher, Martin, 128, 178
Fromond (Dee), Jane, 10 n. 3
Fuller, Thomas, 162 n. 1
Fulton, Thomas, 183, n. 1

Galen, 52
Galilei, Galileo, 30 n. 2, 172
Gascoigne, George, 6, 173
Gauricus, Pomponius, 58
Gelindia, 198
Gematria, 112
Genealogy, 193, 205
Genesis, 71–4

Geoffrey of Monmouth, *Historia*, 188, 196 n. 2, 198

Geography, 2, 17, 32, 177–83, 200–1, 204, 206

Geometry, 23 n. 4, 27, 66, 87, 108, 141, 161–2, 165–76; *see also* Euclid

Gesner, Conrad, 37

Giambullari, Pier Francesco, 153

Gideon, 110 n. 4

Gilbert, Adrian, 62, 129, 172, 179–80

Gilbert, Sir Humphrey, 62, 129, 172, 179; *A Discourse*, 173

Giorgi, Francesco, *De harmonia mundi*, 58, 139–40, 142

Glareanus, 58; *Dodecachordon*, 139

Glastonbury abbey, 199

Gloucester, 202

Glover, Robert, 205

Gnosticism, 2–3, 69, 71, 74–81, 94, 107, 115, 127, 146, 150

God, 48–9, 56, 70, 76, 99, 111, 120, 123–4, 128, 134, 157–8, 184–6, 204; Lullism, 48; mathematics, 105–7; *Pimander*, 71–4; the sun, 101–3

Gods, the making of, 85–6

Godwin, William, 16 n. 1

Gohory, Jacques, 136

Golding, Arthur, 157 n. 5

Gormundus, 202

Goupylus, Jacobus, 31 n. 3

Governors, seven, 70, 72–3

Grafton, Richard, 194

Greece, 54, 186; philosophy, 54, 69; science, 161; people, 145–6, 161, 165, 192

Greek language, 23–4, 163 n. 4

Greenland, 195–7

Greenwich, 38

Grene, Barthlet, 35

Gresford, 202

Gresham College, 172

Gresham, Sir Thomas, 180 n. 2

Greville, Fulke, Lord Brooke, 143; *Life of Sidney*, 132, 158

Groeland, 197

Grolier, Jean, 44

Grosseteste, Robert, Bishop of Lincoln, 26–7

Grynaeus, Simon, 166

Guise, Charles de, Cardinal of Lorraine, 155

Guyon, Sir, 150

Gwynedd, Owen, Prince, 197

Hague, The, 175 n. 1

Hakewill, George, 145 n. 2

Hakluyt, Richard, the elder, 198

Hakluyt, Richard, the younger, 198, 207

Haller, John, 181

Hamelius, Paschasius, 31 n. 3

Hampton Court, 34, 62

Hardyng, John, 194

Hariot, Thomas, 171–2

Hartlib, Samuel, 175

Harvey, Gabriel, 133, 136, 154–5

Harvey, Richard, 6

Harvey, William, 19, 161 n. 3

Hatton, Sir Christopher, 6, 179, 198

Hawkins, Sir John, 62, 179

Hayden, Hiram, 17 n. 5, 163 n. 1

Hebrew, cabalist, 124; language, 23, 49, 66, 111, 118; prophets, 157; Tetragrammaton, 185

Heliocentricity, 97–9, 102–3, 135

Hellenism, 22, 134–5

Hellenist period, 66 n. 5

Henry VII, King, 20 n. 1, 194

Henry VIII, King, 20–1, 24, 32 n. 2, 42, 193, 205 n. 5

Herbert family, 32 n. 2

Herbert, Mary Sidney, Countess of Pembroke, 129

Herbert, William, Earl of Pembroke, 33

Herbert, William, 131

Hereford, 202

Hermes (Mercurius) Trismegistus, 3, 54, 81, 83–6, 96, 102, 112, 156, 161 n. 3; *Asclepius*, 55, 68, 85–6, 89, 101, 106, 108, 110, 119; *Corpus Hermeticum*, 55, 66–70, 78, 86–7, 89, 158; dating, 68; *NOUS*

Hermes—*contd.*
to *Hermes*, 74–6; *Pimander*, 68,
71–4, 78, 106, 120, 140, 148;
Smaragdine Table, 178 n. 2
Hermeticism, 49, 52, 64–5, 76, 99,
110, 112, 115, 139–40, 142–3
n. 4, 145–6, 148, 174 n. 3, 184,
209; religious, 54–6, 102–3, 119–
21, 135, 156–9; and science, 87,
161–3; secrecy, 81–2; and Dee, 2,
7, 19, 28, 32, 61, 66, 108, 127–9,
132, 154, 209
Herodotus, 56
Heron, 109, 128 n. 3
Hervagius, John, 166
Hesiod, 57
Hickman, Bartholomew, 114–15
History, 21, 56, 100–3, 105–6,
163 n. 4, 189
Holinshed, Richard, 194, 207;
Chronicles, 192, 205
Holy Ghost, 85
Homer, 57
Hooke, Robert, 15 n. 1
Hookyaas, R., 170
Hopper, Vincent, 142
Horace, *Ars poetica*, 57
Horoscopes, 1, 34; Philip Sidney's,
129–30, 132
Hotman, Jean, 155
Humanism, 7, 21–3, 47, 59, 135,
137, 154, 209
Humphrey, Duke, 43
Hungary, 38
Hydraulics, 109, 128 n. 3
Hydrography, 177
Hylles, Thomas, *Vulgar Arithmetic*,
174

Iamblichus, 55, 83, 99
Iceland, 197
Ida, 107
Imagination, 94, 139, 147, 149–53
Imperialism, 183–6, 194–9; *see also*
British Empire
Ireland, 170, 192, 196, 204
Isaac, 110 n. 4
Isocrates, 46

Italy, 8, 21, 37, 50, 137, 188, 192

Jacob, 110 n. 4
James I, King, 10
James, M. R., 45, 53
Jayne, Sears, 44
Jerome, St, 192
Jesuits, 123
Jesus College, Cambridge, 175
Jews, 124; cabala, 112; philosophy,
68
John, King, 185
Johnson, F. R., 17, 45, 60, 162, 168
Joseph of Arimathea, 199
Josephus, 54
Joshua, 110 n. 4
Josten, C. H., 13, 77 n. 2, 121
Julian, 99
Julian Calendar, 7
Jung, Carl, *Psychology and Alchemy*,
77 n. 2
Jungius, 175
Jupiter, 24
Justin Martyr, 54

Kelley, Edward, 9, 11, 13 n. 3, 16,
113–17, 120–2, 177, 180
Kelton, Arthur, *Chronycle*, 191–3
Kendrick, T. D., 198, 201 n. 2, 203
Kennet, Bishop, 15
Kepler, Johann, 2, 30 n. 2, 80 n. 3
Kircher, Athanasius, 80 n. 3
Koran, 54

Lactantius, 54–5, 68
Lambarde, William, *APXAIO-
NOMIA*, 196 n. 2
Lancaster, 113 n. 2
Lancastrian, 205
Languet, Hubert, 155
Larkey, Sanford, 168
Latin style, 21, 26, 47
Lavaniel, 118
Lazzarelli, Ludovico, 55
Ledbury, 202
Le Fèvre de la Boderie, Guy, 135,
139, 140 n. 2, 156–7
Le Fèvre de la Boderie, Nicolas,
142 n. 2

Leibniz, Gottfried Wilhelm von, Baron, and symbolic logic, 50

Leipzig, 121

Leland, John, 188–9, 192, 194, 199, 202, 204; *Laboryouse Journey*, 42

Lhuyd, Humphrey, 194; *Breviary of Britayne*, 192, 195, 203

Libraries, English, 41–7; Dee's, 40–1, 43–61, 98, 104, 139, 152–3, 194–5; French, 44

Lipsius, Justus, 155

Livy, 56

Logre, 194

London, 20, 22, 62–3, 98, 124 n. 2, 163 n. 4, 178, 201 n. 2, 206; Gresham college, 172; mechanicians, 4, 173–4

Long Leadenham, 32 n. 1

Louvain, Dee at, 4–5, 28–9

Lovati, Lovato, 188 n. 1

Low Countries, 25, 32

Lucan, 57

Lucilius, 64

Lucretius, *De rerum natura*, 46

Lull, Ramon, 47, 60; philosophy of, 48–50, 61, 87, 112–13, 145 n. 2; *Ars brevis*, 48; Agrippa calls Lull's art useless, 52

Lumley, Lord, 44

Luther, Martin, 20; *Catechism* and *Chronica*, 54

Lycium philosophal San Marcellin, 136

Lyte, Henry, *Light of Britayne*, 192

Mademiel, 118

Madoc, Lord, 197

Magic, medieval, 4, 82–4, 142; Renaissance, 2, 7, 14, 22, 28, 31, 51, 58–60, 61, 76–80, 82–8, 89–97, 101, 124, 128, 130, 135–6, 142–6, 150–4, 159, 176, 187, 208–9; angelic, *see* Cabala; mathematical, *see* Mathesis; and music, 134, 137–9; and poetry, 149–54; and science, 108–9, 161–2

Magicians (magi), medieval, 83;

Renaissance, 8, 10, 12, 30–1, 35, 39, 49, 52, 55, 63–4, 68, 76–7, 81–2, 85, 86–90, 96–7, 101, 108, 110, 113 n. 2, 118, 126, 132, 145–7, 159–62, 166, 186, 209; advocate experimentation, 162; Dee's definition, 64–5; Pico's definition, 63–4; religious, Agrippa's definition, 115–16; and heliocentricity, 97–103

Magnionus, J., 31 n. 3

Maier, Michael, 80 n. 3

Majorca, Mount Randa, 47

Manchester, Dee's presence in, 7, 9, 10 n. 3

Manticism, 119

Manuel, Emperor, 186

Malvern Hills, 202

Marco Polo, 181

Marian martyrs, 155

Marlowe, Christopher, 171

Martyn, Thomas, 34

Mary, Queen, 6, 34–5, 41–2

Mary, Queen of Scots, 155

Masons, 161 n. 3

Mathematics, 2, 5–6, 26, 28, 33, 59, 98, 104, 108–9, 131–2, 135, 142–3, 145 n. 2, 146, 160, 162–4, 168–9, 173–6, 187, 200; measured verse, 141

Mathesis, 2, 28–31, 36–7, 103–10, 125, 131, 143, 160, 166, 209

Maty, King, 198

Mauduit, Jacques, 141

Maximilian II, Emperor, 38, 39 n. 1, 64–5, 128

Mechanicians, 19, 30, 59, 60, 90, 104, 151–2, 160–1, 164, 171–4, 177, 187; and Dee, 4–6, 160–87

Mechanics, 2, 8, 24, 32, 108–9, 128 n. 3, 132, 141, 160, 162–3

Medici, Cosimo de, 66

Medicine, 2, 66 n. 5; *see also* Dee, John

Megethologia, 169

Melancthon, Philip, 155

Melissus, Paul, 155

Mellis, John, 165

Memory, 50, 151, 153 n. 2; art of, 147–9; art of called useless by Agrippa, 52

Mens, 30 n. 2, 67, 71–2, 77, 84, 89, 146–7, 150, 153

Mercator, Gerard, 5, 25, 35 n. 2, 177, 181

'Mercurie', images of, 109

Merton College, Oxford, 26–7

Michael, archangel, 185

Michelangelo, 153, 155

Microcosm-macrocosm, 87, 139–40

Middle Ages, 18, 42, 47, 68, 82–3, 89, 103, 118, 139, 141

Middle Temple, 198

Milton, John, *Of Education*, 176

Mirror for Magistrates, 153

Mizauldus, 31 n. 3

Moffett, Thomas, 127, 130–2, 141

'Mohamet', 12

Mongolian, 178

Montaigne, Michel de, 48

Montaureus, Petrus, 31 n. 3

More, Sir Thomas, 20–1, 26, 60

Morisiel, 36

Mortlake and Dee, 8, 10 n. 3, 27, 40, 44–5, 60, 62–3, 113 n. 2, 126–7, 129, 196, 204

Moses, 84–5, 110 n. 4, 111; revelations to, 54, 67, 82

Muscovy Company, 178

Muscovy voyage, 181

Music, 2, 49, 58, 66, 87, 108, 146, 152; and poetry, 137–41; *see also* magic

Musidorus, 159

Napier, Dr, 10 n. 3

Navigation, 5, 33, 160, 187, 197; *see also* Geography

Neoplatonism, 46–7, 100

Netherlands, 184

Newfoundland, 179

New Testament, 20

Newton, Sir Isaac, 161 n. 3

New World, 180

Nicéron, Jean, 15 n. 4

Niobe, 34

Noah, 193

Nogabel, 118

Nonesuch, 62

Normans, and the Conquest of England, 205

Northampton, Marchioness of, 38, 40

North-eastern passage, 178

North Pole, 197

Northumberland, Duchess of, 32; Duke of, 33, 63 n. 3, 126–7, 178

North Wales, 197

North-western passage, 178

Norway, 196

Norwich, 14 n. 2

Notarikon, 112

Nous (God), 72–6

Nuñez, Pedro, 35, 177

'Occasio', 184

Ophirian voyages, 182

Opticians, 66, 160

Optics, 66, 108, 172

Orfiel, 36

Orient, 178, 180; wisdom of the, 181

Orologio, Giovanni Dondi dell', 188 n. 1

Orpheus, 54, 83, 97, 134, 138–9

Ortelius, Abraham, 5, 62, 124 n. 2, 177, 181, 195, 203–4

Osborn, James, 129 n. 4

Osiander, Andreas, 98

Oswestry, 202

Ovid, 144; *Metamorphoses* and *Ars amatoria*, 57

Oxford, 23 n. 4, 25–7, 43–5, 113 n. 2, 130–1, 121 n. 2, 154 n. 1, 163 n. 4, 171–2

Paciolus, Lucas, *De divina proportione*, 58

Padua, 188 n. 1

Painters, 160; and painting, 2, 150–3

Pamela, 159

Paracelsus, 1, 37, 52, 60, 76; philosophy of, 61, 78 n. 2, 127–8, 136

Paris, 29, 32, 55, 134; University of, 5, 26, 31, 48, 143
Patrizi, Francesco, 51
Paul, St, 100
Pena, Johannes à, 31 n. 3
Pendragon, Uter, 193
Percy, Henry, Earl of Northumberland, 62; his circle, 171–2
Persia, 178; philosophy, 68; people, 83
Petrarch, 21–2, 26, 188 n. 1
Philip II, King, 34, 48, 69, 185
Phillips, James, 132–3
Philo, 54
Philolaus, 54
Pickering, Sir William, 29, 81
Pico della Mirandola, Giovanni, 1, 19, 22, 30–1, 33–4, 49, 59, 69, 76, 89; *Conclusiones*, 51; *Oration*, 63–4, 87, 145, 150 n. 1, 156
Pindar, 57
Plano Carpini, Cornelius de, 181
Plato, 51, 54–5, 61, 66–7, 83, 99, 156; *Timaeus*, 46; *Ion*, 149
Platonism, 22, 26–7, 30–1, 49–51, 66, 68, 100, 102–5, 107, 135–6, 142, 159, 171
Plautus, 57
Pléiade, 132–4, 137, 141, 156
Pletho, 186
Pliny, 46
Plotinus, 47
Plutarch, *Lives*, 56
Pneumatithmie, 167, 176
Poetry, 21, 57, 133–9, 141, 146, 148; *see* Magic
Poets, 145–153
Poland, 124
Pole, Cardinal, 155
Pomponazzi, Pietro, *De incantationibus*, 51
Poniel, 36
Porta, John Baptista della, 104; *Magia naturalis*, 91
Portugal, 177
Postel, Guillaume, 31, 155, 157, 181
Post-Romantics, 150

Prague, 110, 121–2; University of, 28 n. 1
Pressburg, 38
Presteigne, 202
Price, John, 199; *Historiae Britannicae defensio*, 195
Prideaux, Mr, 34
Prisca theologia, 55–6, 84, 100, 102, 156–7
Prisci magi, 83, 96
Prisci theologi, 54–6, 83, 84, 100, 102, 124, 158
Proclus, 47, 100
Prospero, 19
Protectorate, 175
Protestantism, 20, 54, 119, 121 n. 3, 136, 154, 156
Prudentius, 57
Pryce, Mr, 202
Ptolemaic universe, 89, 95, 97
Pucci, Francesco, 121 n. 3
Pulford, 202
Purchas, Samuel, *Purchas his Pilgrimes*, 182
Puritans, 56, 142, 153–4, 159, 175–6, 209
Pyrocles, 159
Pythagoras, 30, 54, 82, 99, 106, 138
Pythagoreanism, 30, 87, 102–8, 143

Quadrivium, 23, 167
Quintilian, *Orations*, 46

Raines, F. R., 16 n. 1
Ralegh, Sir Walter, 62, 129, 171–2; and *History of the World*, 69
Ramism, 59, 142–5, 148–9, 153–4, 159, 167–71
Ramus, Peter, 31, 98 n. 3, 141–3, 148–9, 167–71; *Arithmetica*, 59, 167; *Dialecticae*, 59; *Geometria*, 59, 167; *De religione* and *Scholae in liberales artes*, 59
Ranconetus, 31
Recorde, Robert, 17, 167–71; *Castle of Knowledge*, 164; *Grounde of Artes*, 81, 163–4, 174, 176; *Whetstone of Wit*, 174

Index

Red Sea, 182

Reformation in England, 7, 20–2, 59–60, 142, 189

Religion, universal, 31, 56, 81, 84–6, 89, 96–7, 118–19, 123–5, 135, 154–9, 163, 181, 209

Reuchlin, Johann, 113; *De arte Cabalistica*, 28 n. 1, 53; *De verbo mirifico*, 53

Rheinholdt, Erasmus, 6, 98

Rhemes College, Paris, 29

Rhenanus, Beatus, 188

Rheticus, Georg, 98

Richard II, King, 205

Richmond, 62, 196

Ripley, George, *Compound of Alchymy*, 82

Robinson, John, 202

Roderick the Great, 20 n. 1

Rogers, Daniel, 62, 132, 134, 155, 178, 198, 203, 207

Rogers, John, *The Displaying of an horrible secte of grosse and wicked Heretiques*, 124 n. 2

Rogers, Thomas, *The Second Coming of Christ*, 54

Roman Catholic church, 20–1, 41, 48, 54, 84, 100, 109, 118–19, 121–4, 136, 155–7, 185

Romance of the Rose, 152

Roman Britain, 203–4

Roman civilization, 21

Roman numerals, 164

Romans, 139, 193, 202

Rome, 38, 121, 185, 197

Ronsard, Pierre de, 137

Rosenberg, Count of Bohemia, 122

Rosenberg, Eleanor, 33

Rosicrucians, 14

Rosseli, Hannibal, 120–1

Rossi, Paolo, 162

Royal Society, 60, 142

Rudd, Thomas, 174

Rudolph II, Emperor, 110–11, 113 n. 2, 121–2, 124

Russell, Lord, 154 n. 1

Russia, 14 n. 1, 196 n. 2, 197; Emperor of, 5

Sadael, 36

Sadoleto, Jacopo, 155

St Bartholomew's Day, 202

St Cross's, Hampshire, 63

St John's College, Cambridge, 23–4

Salamian, 113

Salutati, Coluccio, 188 n. 1

Sambursky, S., 161

Sansovino, Jacopo, *Chronology of the World*, 152

Saturn, 36

Saul, Barnabus, 114–15

Savile, Sir Henry, 23 n. 4

Savile, Sir Thomas, 5 n. 4

Saxons, 189, 190, 199, 202

Scandinavia, 196 n. 2

Scarabeus, 24, 29

Scholasticism, 47, 156

School divinity, 27

Schoolmen, 26

Science; and Dee, 1–2, 4–5, 17, 59–61, 63, 89, 96, 108–9, 126, 128 n. 3, 132, 141–3, 159–68, 171–3, 176–7, 186–7, 208–9, Aristotelian, 69, 87, 161; tradition of in England, 20, 25–7, 50, 142, 154 n. 1, 171, 181; in French academies, 135, 141; *see* Dee, *Euclide*; Hermeticism; Magic

Scotland, 197

Scripture, 20

Sculptors, 150

Sculpture, 152

Seals, 95, 100, 112–13, 116, 118, 209

Selden, John, 11

Semeliel, 118

Seneca, 57

Setta, Lombardo della, 188 n. 1

Sibylline prophecies, 137

Sidney, Sir Henry, 178; Lady Sidney, 126–7

Sidney, Sir Philip, 27, 62, 126, 128, 130–4, 136–42, 148–51, 153, 157–9, 198, 207; his circle, 59, 126, 129, 132–3, 142, 147, 154–5, 159, 198, 208; *Apology*, 137, 141,

Index

Sidney, Sir Philip—*contd.*
 143–5, 147, 153–4; *Arcadia*, 137,
 198; *Astrophel and Stella*, 130
Sidney, Robert, 132
Sidrophel, 13 n. 3
Siena cathedral, 67
Sigillum Emeth, 116–19
Silvius, William, 36
Simonides, 148
Sixtus V, Pope, 121
Smart, Peter, 14 n. 2
Smith, Charlotte Fell, 16–17
Smith, Thomas, *Vita Joannis Dee*, 15
Socrates, 99
Solomon, 182
Somerset Herald, 205
Sophocles, 57
Soul of the world, 49, 83, 92
Spain, 34, 205 n. 5; empire of, 197
Spenser, Edmund, 133–4, 136, 207;
 Faerie Queene, 142, 150, 192
Squirrel, the, 179
Stadius, John, *Ephemerides*, 99
Star Chamber, 35
Star-demon, 73, 76, 78, 111
Statics, 176
Statius, 57
Stella, 130
Stoicism, 68
Stokes, William, 202
Stow, John, 194, 204–7
Straselius, 31 n. 3
Stratarithmetrie, 176
Surveyors, 160
Swineshead, Richard, *Calculationes*,
 26 n. 3
Sylvius, Jacobus, 31 n. 3
Synesius, 47, 83
Syon House, 62, 171

Talbot, Edward, 113 n. 2
Talismans, 2, 83, 92, 97 n. 2, 100,
 152
Tat, 109
Taylor, E. G. R., *Tudor Geography*,
 17, 35, 45, 60
Telepathic communication, 37
Telescope, 172

Temurah, 112
Terpander, 138
Tertullian, 68
Tetragrammaton, 185
'Thaumaturgike', 109
Thebes, 139
Theocritus, 57
Theodore, 186
Theophrastus, 57
Theurgy, 2, 10
Thorndike, Lynn, 18
Thou, Jacques de, 44
Threlkeld, Edward, 202
Thucydides, 56
Timaeus, 109
Timotheus, 138
Tobias, 110 n. 4
Topography, 200, 202
Torporly, Nathaniel, 171
Toth, 66 n. 5
Townesend, Mr, 14
Trebona, 122
Trent, Council of, 155
Trinity College, Cambridge, 24–5,
 29
Trithemius, Abbot of Sponheim, 1,
 60, 82, 84, 113, 195; *Polygraphia*
 and *De septem secundadeis*, 52;
 Steganographia, 36–7, 52, 111
Trivium, 23
Trojan, Brutus, 191–4
Troy, 192
Tudors, 91, 190–1, 193–4
Tully, *see* Cicero
Turk, 124 n. 2
Turnebus, 31, 55, 155, 157
Tuve, Rosemond, 143 n. 4
Tyard, Pontus de, 156
Tymme, Thomas, 84–5, 128, 195

Upton-upon-Severn, 32 n. 1
Urbino, 38; Duke of, 37
Uriel, 113, 116–17
Ut pictura poesis, 149, 153

Valla, Giorgio, 51
Valla, Laurentius, 26, 51, 185
Vatican library, 41

242

Venice, 58, 166; St Mark's library,
41
Vergerius, 157
Vergil, 57
Vergil, Polydore, 195; *Anglica Historia*, 190, 194
Vesalius, Andreas, *Anatomy*, 52
Vicomercatus, 31 n. 3
Vienna, 31, 39 n. 1
Vinci, Leonardo da, 58, 153
Vis imaginativa, 96
Vitruvianism, 18, 32
Vitruvius, 140 n. 3; *De architectura*, 57, 167 n. 3
Vives, Juan Luis, 23

Wales, 201, 203
Walker, D. P., 36, 53, 62, 96, 158
Walsingham, Frances, 127
Walsingham, Sir Francis, 6, 10, 62, 127, 129, 179, 198
Warner, Walter, 171
Warwick, Countess of, 63
Waters, D. W., 17 n. 3, 177
Watson, Andrew G., 201 n. 2
Webster, John, 12–13, 175–6
Welsh, 20 n. 1, 190, 194, 196, 204
Westchester, 202

Westminster School, 204
Wild, Johanna, 20 n. 1
Wilton Abbey, 32 n. 2, 129
Winthrop, John, 80 n. 3
Winthrop, John, II, 80 n. 3
Winthrop, Wait Still, 80 n. 3
Wolsey, Cardinal, 205 n. 5
Wood, Anthony, 15 n. 3, 27, 33, 129, 171
Woodstock, 34
Worcester, 113 n. 2
Worsop, Edward, 6, 173–4
Worthington, John, 175
Wrexham, 202

Yates, Frances A., 18, 40, 58, 60, 66, 114, 153 n. 2

Zabathiel, 118
Zarlino, Gioseffo, 58; *Institutioni Harmoniche*, 139
Zedekiel, 118
Zeiglerus, Philip, 14
Zodiac, 70, 148
Zographie, 151–3
Zoroaster, 54–5, 83
Zurich, 37